Shakespe

Oxford Wells Shak

CU00739091

In distracted times like the present, Shakespeare too has been driven to distraction. *Shakespeare | Cut* considers contemporary practices of cutting up Shakespeare in stage productions, video games, book sculptures, and YouTube postings, but it also takes the long view of how Shakespeare's texts have been cut apart in creative ways beginning in Shakespeare's own time. The book's five chapters consider cuts, cutting, and cutwork from a variety of angles: (1) as bodily experiences, (2) as essential parts of the process whereby Shakespeare and his contemporaries crafted scripts, (3) as units in perception, (4) as technologies situated at the interface between "figure" and "life," and (5) as a fetish in western culture since 1900. Printed here for the first time are examples of the cut-ups that William S. Burroughs and Brion Guysin carried out with Shakespeare texts in the 1950s. Bruce R. Smith's original analysis is accompanied by twenty-four illustrations, which suggest the multiple media in which cutwork with Shakespeare has been carried out.

Shakespeare | Cut

Rethinking Cutwork
in an Age of Distraction

BRUCE R. SMITH

OXFORD
UNIVERSITY PRESS

OXFORD
UNIVERSITY PRESS

Great Clarendon Street, Oxford, OX2 6DP,
United Kingdom

Oxford University Press is a department of the University of Oxford.
It furthers the University's objective of excellence in research, scholarship,
and education by publishing worldwide. Oxford is a registered trade mark of
Oxford University Press in the UK and in certain other countries

First published 2016
First published in paperback 2019

Impression: 1

Published in the United States of America by Oxford University Press
198 Madison Avenue, New York, NY 10016, United States of America

British Library Cataloguing in Publication Data
Data available

Library of Congress Cataloging in Publication Data
Data available

ISBN 978–0–19–873552–6 (Hbk.)
ISBN 978–0–19–883117–4 (Pbk.)

Printed and bound in Great Britain by
Clays Ltd, Elcograf S.p.A.

Table of Contents

Acknowledgments

The thought that "cut" might be a phenomenon worth investigating first occurred to me in 2012 while writing a chapter on "Making the Scene" for *The Cambridge Guide to the Worlds of Shakespeare*. Cuts and cutting, I realized, were involved in all the varieties of "scene" that I was investigating: marked units in printed texts, engraved illustrations, extracts in anthologies of "beauties of Shakespeare," outrageous behavior onstage and off. I am grateful to the Bogliasco Foundation for a two-month fellowship at the Ligurian Study Center that not only facilitated the writing of the chapter but put me into conversation with fellow residents whose work involves cutwork, including Yotam Haber, a composer who incorporates archived sounds and visual images in his work; Mary Ellen Strom, a video producer; and Stacy Woolf, an historian of American musical theater. I extend thanks to all of my fellow fellows at Bogliasco, but to these three in particular. My move from a chapter on scene-making to a projected book on cutwork was encouraged at just the right moment by Katherine Rowe.

For the invitation to deliver the 2014 Oxford Wells Shakespeare Lectures, for endorsement of my proposed topic, and for hospitality during my time at Oxford, I want to thank the Faculty of English, particularly Laurie Maguire, Emma Smith, Tiffany Stern, Bart Van Es, and Seamus Perry, Chair of the Faculty Board at the time of my visit.

Broader thanks are due to the students and colleagues who answered my questions and calls for advice at various times and pointed me toward instances of cutwork that I would otherwise have missed: Emily Anderson, Gina Bloom, Anston Bosman, Susan Bennett, David Carnegie, Sharon Carnicke, Christie Carson, Thomas Cartelli, Karin Chien, Christy Desmet, Michael Dobson, Richard Edinger, Gray Fisher, Brett Hirsch, Peter Holland, Farah Karim-Cooper, Jeffrey Knight, Kevin Laam, Douglas Lanier, Jeffrey Masten, Jean-Christophe Mayer, Jennifer Richards, Jessica Rosenberg, Amanda Ruud, Rebecca Schneider, Stuart Sillars, Steven Urkowitz, Paul Werstine, and Richard Wistreich. Many people offered passing suggestions along the way. If I have overlooked any of them, I do apologize.

Regarding Shakespeare-inspired videogames, I take to heart Espen Aarseth's admonition that no one should analyze them without playing them: "If we comment on games or use games in our cultural and aesthetic analysis," Aarseth insists, "we should play those games" (Aarseth 2012: 190). I have not, I confess, been able to take Aarseth's advice in every case, but I have instead framed my comments by drawing on the expertise of some of my students at the University of Southern California, several of whom are Game Design minors in the School of Cinematic Arts. I want to thank in particular Esteban Farjado, Jordan Klein, Patrick Tam, Kelsi Yu, and Yingbao Zhu. Another student, Jade Matias-Bell, introduced me to James P. Carse's very useful distinction between "finite" and "infinite" games. For directing me to particular YouTube videos I am grateful to two other students: Omar Zineldine at USC and Carla Jenness in Middlebury College's Bread Loaf School of English graduate program.

At Oxford University Press I have met with unfailing encouragement, sound advice, and sustaining patience from Jacqueline Norton, Senior Commissioning Editor for Literature, and Eleanor Collins, Senior Assistant Commissioning Editor for Literature. I thank both of them for their consummate professionalism. For editorial assistance I am grateful to my husband Gordon Davis. Helen B. Cooper's copyediting was meticulous and tactful. Subvention funds for illustrations were generously made available by Dornsife College of Letters, Arts and Sciences at the University of Southern California, through the good graces of Peter Mancall, Vice Dean for the Humanities and Social Sciences. In connection with illustrations and quotations, I want to extend special thanks to Isaac Gewirtz, Curator of the Henry W. and Albert A. Berg Collection in the New York Public Library, for giving me access to the unpublished papers of William S. Burroughs; to Percy Stubbs of the Wylie Agency for granting permission to publish excerpts from the papers; and to the Tim Tadder Studio, Encinitas, California, for use of the photograph "Once more unto the breach" from the suite "Diving into Character."

—B.R.S.

Los Angeles,
February 2016

Illustrations

Tables

Citations

Unless otherwise indicated, all quotations from Shakespeare's plays and poems are taken from *The Complete Works*, 2nd edition, ed. Stanley Wells and Gary Taylor (Oxford: Clarendon Press, 2005).

In quotations from early modern sources, spelling has been modernized but original punctuation has in general been retained.

Oxford University Press has no responsibility for the persistence or accuracy of URLs for external or third-party Internet Web sites referred to in this publication and does not guarantee that any content on such Web sites is, or will remain, accurate or appropriate.

1

Cuts In, To, By, From, and With Shakespeare

Forms and Effects Across Four Centuries

> Once more unto the breach.
> Dear friends, once more.
>
> —King Henry to his troops, *Henry V* 3.1.1,
> in *Mr William Shakespeare's Comedies,*
> *Histories, and Tragedies* (1623), sig. h5

Tim Tadder's image of Matthew Bellows as Henry V comes from a suite of photographs in which Tadder, an artist working in southern California, asked actors in the MFA acting program at the University of San Diego to reprise certain moments from Shakespearean roles they had played—but this time in a different medium. (See Figure 1.) "Immersion: Diving into Character" removed the actors from their usual medium—air—and plunged them into water. Actually, most of the images in the series show the actors at the verge between the two media, just where water meets air. In that space between media, words that were once invisible in air have assumed visible, palpable presence as bubbles in water. In that intermedial space words that have assumed visible, palpable presence as bubbles in water are becoming, once again, *in*visible and *im*palpable as words in air.

The most arresting detail in Tadder's photograph may be the sword that Bellows brandishes. Tadder's image puts new meaning into Hamlet's line "to take arms against a sea of troubles" (3.1.61). The thin, straight line of light along the blade suggests that the sword is cutting not only the water, but also the interface between the two media. Henry V's character is emerging from the dark water below

Figure 1. Tim Tadder, "Once more unto the breach," from "Immersion: Diving into Character." By permission of Tim Tadder Photography.

into the light-filled air above. We speak of "cutting the air" with our hands and arms (*Oxford English Dictionary*, "cut, *v.*," IV.18.a), and boats and ships can cut a course through water (IV.21), but air and water—unlike paper—resist such acts of cutting. Air and water resume their fluidity, their wholeness, when the gesture has been completed, when the boat or ship has passed. Unlike air, however, water lets us see the cut. *Shakespeare | Cut* seizes on that fleeting perception and attends closely to its effects. Flow versus cut will be a continuing concern in this book. In terms of recording technology, we might regard the distinction as one between analogue and digitalization.

Another word for "cut" in Shakespeare's time was "breach." George Puttenham in *The Art of English Poesy* (1589) invokes this now obsolete sense of "breach" as "a break in continuity, an interruption, interval" (*OED*, "cut, *n.*," 2.†10) when he describes an historical narrative that he himself has written:

a little brief romance or historical ditty in the English tongue of the Isle of Great Britain in short and long metres, and by breaches or divisions to be more commodiously sung to the harp in places of assembly, where the company shall be desirous to hear of old adventures and valiances of noble knights in times past, as are those of King Arthur and his knights of the round table, Sir Bevis of Southampton, Guy of Warwick, and others like (131).

Shakespeare's *Henry V*, first acted ten years or so after Puttenham's treatise was published, seems designed to satisfy the same desires "in places of assembly." The "breaches" that Puttenham catalogues have their counterparts in Shakespeare's play: not just "divisions" to facilitate performance (speeches and scenes), but also "metres" (divisions of language into shorter or longer "feet"). Shakespeare's words may seem to "run" or "flow"—he was renowned as "honey-tongued" in his own time—but, paradoxically, it is cuts that create that sense of flow.

=

In their fluidity, air and water are like unmediated human experience, before the mind disposes the sensations into cuts. Ferdinand de Saussure realized as much when he included in his lectures on *General Linguistics* (first published 1916) a diagram showing in wavy lines "the indefinite plane of jumbled ideas" on plane A and "the equally vague plane of sounds" on plane B (Saussure 1916, 122), as indicated in Table 1.

Vertical lines in Saussure's diagram indicate cuts made by language in the flow of thought and sound. The vertical lines, let us note, are

Table 1. Ferdinand de Saussure, Cuts from *Course in General Linguistics* (1916). Public domain.

themselves cut into segments. Saussure's cuts emerged in the twentieth century as the fundamental principles first of structuralism and later of "*de*-structuralism," or deconstruction. Whether cuts be regarded as constitutive of or subversive of meaning seems, at our own moment in time, a critic's choice. In this book I choose constructive.

In the very act of choosing, we acknowledge that we live in an age in which cuts and cutting are fetishized. It has been a long time since anyone expected a stage production of a Shakespeare play—much less a film—to include all the lines of the earliest printed text. If Lukas Erne is right in *Shakespeare as Literary Dramatist* (2013), there never was such a time. In Shakespeare postings on YouTube the two hours' traffic of the stage has been cut, on average, to three to five minutes. Uploading and downloading speeds, not to mention most users' patience, dictate an upper limit of about fifteen minutes (McKernan 2016).

Cutting of a more sophisticated kind informs some widely noticed twenty-first-century productions of Shakespeare: the Wooster Group's *Hamlet* (premiered 2005), Ivo van Hove's *Roman Tragedies* (2007–10, revived 2012, 2014) and *Kings of War* (2015–continuing at the time of this writing) with the Toneelgroep Amsterdam, Punchdrunk's *Sleep No More* (2009–continuing), and Annie Dorsen's *Hamlet* production entitled *A Piece of Work* (2009–13). In distinctive ways, these productions express the current passion for cutting up Shakespeare.

In the Wooster Group's *Hamlet* constant intercutting between live performance and film projections of John Gilgeud's 1964 stage production with Richard Burton energized, if it did not inaugurate, a fad for intermedial performances of Shakespeare. That fad continues still, notably in the company's own *Troilus and Cressida*, co-produced with the Royal Shakespeare Company for the 2012 World Shakespeare Season in Britain, and in Van Hove's six-hour *Roman Tragedies*, played amid constant electronic distractions, including opportunities for the audience to check their email and post their responses on Twitter. In Van Hove's hands, the crowd scenes and battle scenes in *Coriolanus*, *Julius Caesar*, and *Antony and Cleopatra* had been cut entirely, leaving audience members to play the role of the public and to follow the battles as distant media events (Ball 2013). Except for its title, the 2011–15 version of *Sleep No More*, co-produced in New York by Punchdrunk and Emursive, dispensed entirely with the text of *Macbeth* and enacted the story through incessant movement—that of the spectators as well as of the actors. Co-produced by theater organizations in Europe and the United States, Dorsen's seventy-minute *A Piece of Work* was different at each performance thanks to changing computer algorithms that generated entirely new combinations of words, visuals, lighting, and music. *A Piece of Work* is in fact part of a trilogy of "algorithmic theater" pieces that also includes *Hello Hi There* (premiered 2010, with words from Shakespeare intercut with words from Michel Foucault and Noam Chomsky) and *Yesterday Tomorrow* (premiered 2015) (Dorsen 2016).

To celebrate the four hundredth anniversary of Shakespeare's death in April 2016, Shakespeare's Globe in London streamed short films of Shakespeare's plays on thirty-seven screens along the South Bank walk from Westminster Bridge to Tower Bridge. Each film was a collage, combining on-location shoots (the rocks of Elsinore, the Pyramids, the Jewish Ghetto in Venice) with clips from Globe productions, silent films archived by the British Film Institute, and newly commissioned animations. Placement of the screens along a stretch of the Thames more than two miles long meant that the Shakespeare videos were cut into the very fabric of the city as well as into the spatial and temporal experiences of walkers. Clearly, the time is ripe for rethinking "cut" as concept and practice. Once more unto the breach—this time with hindsight about where cutting has landed us.

=

Despite instances such as Van Hove's *Roman Tragedies*—or perhaps because of them—cutting Shakespeare's plays in stage performance, film, and digital media remains a contentious practice. Reviewers often note how "deeply cut," "heavily cut," or "severely cut" a given production or film script or video is, as if the "cuts" were bodily wounds. Habitually, many scholars, actors, and directors regard such cuts as acts of vandalism. Peter Hall's diary during his 1975 Royal National Theatre production of *Hamlet*, for example, worries over the financial and logistical necessity to cut a script that would run to five hours if played in its entirety: "I don't want to *interpret* the play by cutting it," he writes (Hall 1984: 177). The next day's entry is positively anguished:

> It seems to me that we have come some distance in the last twenty-five years in understanding the rhythm of a Shakespeare play, how it

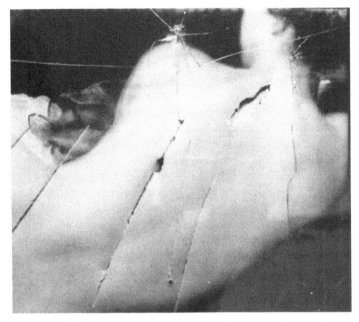

Figure 2. Diego Velázquez, "The Toilet of Venus" (1647–51), National Gallery London, detail of photograph (c. 1914) showing damage inflicted by Mary Richardson. Public domain.

operates, how one segment reacts on another. We have also come some way in understanding how to speak the verse. But we still cut like barbarians. Do we know *what* we cut? (177).

Passages like Hall's conjure up images of vandalized paintings: Velázquez's "Rokeby Venus" in the National Gallery London, for example, slashed with a chopper by suffragette Mary Richardson in 1914 (see Figure 2), or Rembrandt's "The Night Watch" in the Rijksmuseum Amsterdam, attacked three times: first by a man with a shoemaker's knife in 1911; then by an unemployed school teacher with a bread knife in 1975; and, most recently, by a man with a pump bottle of acid in 1990 ("Ten Famous Works," 2011).

Controversy over cuts is not limited to contemporary stage performances, films, and videos. In the second edition of *Shakespeare as Literary Dramatist* (2013), Erne has to rebut vigorous attacks on the argument he made in the first edition (2003) that almost all the original printings of Shakespeare's scripts restore speeches, parts of speeches, and even entire scenes that had been left out in stage performances during Shakespeare's lifetime. Erne occasionally uses the word "cut" to refer to these left-out bits, but his most frequent term is "abridgement," a text-based idea, as in the abridged edition of a book. The term "abridgement" (ultimately derived from late Latin *abbreviare* [*OED*, "abridge, v.," etymology]) tends to erase traces of cutting and to preserve a sense of continuity. "Cuts," by contrast, are apt to leave a mark. Many Shakespeare scholars—perhaps most— would like to believe that the earliest printed texts of Shakespeare's plays, long as they may be in comparison with other scripts of the period, were not cut or abridged but represent performance texts.

=

Controversy over cuts flares today but, strictly speaking, "cuts" were never made to Shakespeare's plays in his own time—or for many years afterward. More was printed "than hath been publicly spoken or acted" (Jonson, *Everyman Out of his Humour*, title page to 1600 quarto), "diverse things" were "left out of the presentation" (Webster, *The Duchess of Malfi*, title page to 1623 quarto), "the actors omitted some scenes and passages (with the authors' consent) as occasion led them" (Humphrey Moseley, "The Stationer to the Readers" in the 1647 Beaumont and Fletcher folio), but "omissions" became "cuts" only in the 1670s, more than two generations after Shakespeare's death. Evidence of printed texts restoring passages that had been omitted in performance is studied in Erne (2013: 168–73) and Rasmussen (1997: 441–60).

The second edition of the *OED* leaves the impression that "to cut" in the sense of "to shorten (a play, etc.) by omitting portions" ("cut, *v.*," V.21.a) was a current word in Shakespeare's time, but close inspection of the cited examples reveals this not to have been the case. In the *OED*'s quotation from Lydgate's *The Pilgrimage of the Soul* (1413, printed by Caxton 1483) the terms "glosynge, cuttynge, kouerynge, and cloutynge" do refer to manipulations of texts, but all four terms derive from working with cloth: figuratively at least, *to glose* is "to veil with specious comments" (*OED*, "glose, *v.*," 2. *trans.*) or "to clothe (words, etc.) with specious adornment" (3.†c. *trans.*), and a *clout* is a patch ("clout, *n.¹*," I.1). "Cutting" in the quotation from Lydgate has more to do with refashioning a text than with excising pieces and tossing them aside. The *OED*'s other pre-1865 citation for "cutting" as "shortening" is actually a technical term for a category of verse. James VI and I's *The Essays of an Apprentice in the Divine Art of Poesy* (1585) catalogues at the end of the treatise "maist kyndis of versis quhilks are not cuttit or brokin, but alyke many feit in euerie lyne of the verse"—that is to say, James includes only verse forms in which all lines contain the same number of feet (James I and VI 1585: 55). "Cut verse" in James's *Essays* has nothing to do with excising passages or shortening an extant text. "To cut" as "to shorten by omitting" did not become established until the 1670s.

The earliest references to cuts as textual excisions preserve the literal, physical sense of cutting as action with a knife. John Lacy in the epistle prefaced to his comedy *The Dumb Lady, or The Farrier Made Physician* (printed 1672) jokes,

> I have observed, how much more precious to a poet the issue of his brain is than that of his loins: for I have known them bury children without grief or trouble; but the issue of their brain is so dear and tender to them, that if you go about to persuade them but to cut a play or poem shorter, they are so concerned, that every line you cut is valued at a joint, and every speech a limb lopped off (sig. A3).

Lacy's jest depends on a strong association of cuts with bodies. The same sense of "cut" as violence against a human body informs George Granville's complaint in the preface to his play *Heroic Love A Tragedy* (printed 1698) that, in the play's first performance, "the last scene may be more properly said to have been murdered than cut, for the conveniency of acting" (sig. A2).

For many eighteenth-century theater practitioners, "alter" and "alterations" remained the preferred, perhaps politer terms for excisions. The whole business is played out for comic effect in material Henry Fielding added to the third iteration of *The Author's Farce* (1750), when Mr. Marplay Junior, a theatrical impresario, explains his craft to the would-be playwright Luckless and his shocked friend Witmore. This time the metaphor has shifted from bodies to clothes:

> *Luck*[*less*]… I have a tragedy for your house, Mr Marplay.
> *Mar*[*wit*] *Jun*[*ior*]. Ha! If you will send it to me, I will give you my opinion of it, and if I can make any alterations in it that will be for its advantage, I will do it freely

Wit[*more*].   Alterations, sir?

Mar[*wit*] *Jun*[*ior*].   Yes, sir, alterations—I will maintain, let a play be never so good, without alteration, it will be nothing...Why, sir, would you guess that I had altered Shakespeare?

Wit[*more*].   Yes faith, no one sooner.

Mar[*wit*] *Jun*[*ior*].   Alack-a-day! Was you to see the plays when they are brought to us, a parcel of crude, undigested stuff. We are the persons, sir, who lick them into form, that mold them into shape—The poet make the play indeed! The colour-man might be as well said to make the picture, or the weaver the coat: my father and I, sir, are a couple of poetical tailors; when a play is brought us, we consider it as a tailor does a coat, we cut it, sir, we cut it: and let me tell you, we have the exact measure of the town, we know how to fit their taste. The poets between you and me, are a pack of ignorant—(Fielding 1750: sig. B1).

And then Witmore cuts back in.

Call it what you might, cutting was what "alterations" by the likes of Marwit mostly came down to. In Fielding's *Pasquin. A Dramatic Satire of the Times* (1736) a rehearsal of Fustian's tragedy has to be postponed because the actor playing the Ghost is still in bed with a "church-yard cough." "I wish you could cut the Ghost out, sir," says one of the players to the Prompter. "Cut him out, sir?" Fustian exclaims. "He is one of the most considerable persons in the play" (Fielding 1736a: 2). Fielding's farce *Tumble-down Dick: or, Phaeton in the Suds*, published the same year, begins with a stand-off between high art and low that anticipates Richard Strauss and Hugo von Hofmannsthal's opera *Ariadne auf Naxos*. The high art in Fielding's case is *Othello*; the low art, a pantomime:

Mach[*ine*]...   Mr Prompter, I must insist that you cut out a great deal of *Othello*, if my pantomime is performed with it, or the audience will be palled before the entertainment begins.

Promp[*ter*].   We'll cut out the fifth act, sir, if you please.

Mach[*ine*].   Sir, that's not enough, I'll have the first cut out too. (Fielding 1736b: sig. B1v).

If cuts to Shakespeare in eighteenth-century theater carried a certain opprobrium, the reason may well have been the publication of the Shakespeare editions edited by Samuel Johnson (1765), George Steevens (1773), and Edmund Malone (1790). Thanks to these rigorously edited texts, the late eighteenth century witnessed a revolution in ideas about "authenticity," to use Margreta de Grazia's term (de Grazia 1991a). Any deviation in the theater from the "authentic" text could, for perhaps the first time, be regarded as dubious. Among the first theater professionals to express guilt about making changes to Shakespeare's texts was David Garrick. In December 1773 Garrick wrote to a French friend, "I have played the devil this winter, I have dared to alter *Hamlet*, I have thrown away the gravediggers, and all the fifth act, and notwithstanding the galleries were so fond of them" (qtd. in Stone 1934: 893). In fact, Garrick had been acting in altered texts of *Hamlet* since he made his debut in the role in 1742. His sudden pang of conscience in 1773 may well have been, therefore, a response to the newly published authoritative texts. Garrick actually consulted Johnson's edition for readings of individual words and phrases (Stone 1934: 900), but Steevens is said by a contemporary to have encouraged Garrick in his remodeling of Shakespeare's text (Stone 1934: 893).

In the course of the nineteenth century "alterations" increasingly gave way to "cuts," as the *OED* recognizes in the increasing number of citations, but without the edge of violence that attended cuts in the eighteenth century. There was a very good reason for that uptick in cuts. Aristotle in the *Poetics* may have ranked *opsis* as the least important of the six elements of tragedy, but nineteenth-century producers of Shakespeare's plays, particularly the history plays and tragedies, cleared away text to make room for spectacular set pieces such as the siege of Harfleur in Charles Kean's production of *Henry V* at the Princess's Theatre in 1859 (Sillars 2013, Schoch 1998, Foulkes 2002). (See Figure 3.) *The Saturday Review* on April 2, 1859 proclaimed the scene "the first genuine battle ever seen on theatrical boards—a noisy, blazing, crowding, smoking reality that appeals to all the senses at once" (qtd. in Gurr 2016: 2:1572). The reviewer goes on to commend Kean's decision to cut the fourth Chorus's lines about disgracing the name of Agincourt by bringing onstage "four or five most vile and ragged foils,/ Right ill-disposed in brawl ridiculous" (*H5* 4.0.50–1). In effect, the reviewer is commending Kean for substituting a visual cut for a verbal cut.

With the advent of motion-picture cameras the substitution of visual cuts for verbal cuts became even more prominent. Indeed, the

Figure 3. Thomas Grieve, preliminary design in watercolor for the Siege of Harfleur in Charles Kean's production of *Henry V* (1859). © Victoria and Albert Museum.

earliest films of Shakespeare, such as those archived on the British Film Institute's online website (http://www.screenonline.org.uk) and collected on the DVD "Silent Shakespeare," dispense with the verbal text almost entirely. With the development of editing machines such as the Moviola later in the twentieth century, violence returned to the cut once more. Walter Murch, whose work on Francis Coppola's film *The Conversation* won a double British Academy Award in 1974 for best editing and for best sound mixing, offers a graphic description of this violence:

> I recall once coming back to the editing room after a few weeks in the mixing theater (where all movements are smooth and incremental) and being appalled at the brutality of the process of cutting. The "patient" is pinned to the slab and: Whack! Either/Or! This not That! In or Out! We chop up the poor film in a miniature guillotine and then stick the dismembered pieces together like Dr. Frankenstein's monster (Murch 2001: 57).

The pain registered in many twentieth- and twenty-first-century complaints about performance cuts to Shakespeare's texts probably has
more to do with editing machines than with sword-fights or surgery.
The heuristic power of "cut" as a way of thinking about alterations has
been hyped even more by the quick and easy cut-and-paste capacities of
digital media. Witness Dorsen's *A Piece of Work*—a *piece* of work, indeed.

=

Ironically, it was not scripts for performance that Shakespeare and his
contemporaries cut, but printed texts designed for reading—the very
documents revered by some Shakespeareans for being uncut. To read
the quarto of *The Chronicle History of Henry the Fifth As it Hath Been Sundry
Times Played by the Right Honorable the Lord Chamberlain His Servants* (1600),
a purchaser would first have had to slit the folds created when a sheet
of folio paper was doubled over and creased, then doubled over again
and creased to create the eight pages of a quarto gathering. The
generic woodcut of "The Study" (Latin *Muséum*) in Johannes Amos
Comenius's pictorial Latin textbook *Orbis Sensualium Pictus* (1658, first
English edition 1659) includes a pair of scissors among the student's
tools. (See Figure 4.) Most scholarly libraries contain books where
such cutting never happened or else never got beyond the first few
gatherings—testimony to the books' unread status. Uncut, a codex
remains an object; cut, it becomes an event.

In early modern practice, the event was developed through further
cuts. Comenius describes how the student (numbered 2 in the woodcut), shown in the woodcut with one of his books (3) open before him,
"picketh all the best things out of them into his own manual (5), or
marketh them…with a dash (6) or a little star (7) in the margent" (sigs.
O5v–O6). "Commonplacing," the activity is called by modern
scholars (Moss 1996; Sherman 2008). The marked text becomes a
"passage" (another aspect of the water in Figure 1). When the student
returns to the book, the marks direct cuts in his attention. To mark a
passage with a dash or an asterisk is to cut the passage from its context.
If the mark is a pointing finger (or "manicule," as William Sherman
calls it), the effect of psychologically cuing a cut in the reader's
attention is added to the physical cut-mark on the page.

The pen that makes these marks, as we shall see in Chapter 4, has
itself been made with a knife, probably by the student himself. The

Figure 4. Johannes Amos Comenius, "The Study" (detail), from *Orbis Sensualium Pictus... Visible World, or, A Picture and Nomenclature of all the Chief Things that are in the World, and of Men's Employments Therein* (London, 1685). By permission of the Folger Shakespeare Library.

desktop in Figure 4 includes, just to the right of the scissors, a small pen-knife. To write *out* the passage in one's own manual or "tables" is to cut the text in question, to excise a set of words from *there* and insert it *here*. The specific "place" in the printed text is being *re*-placed, its "commonness" reaffirmed. The cut text becomes, ironically, a "passage," a term that implies flow. *Studying* in Comenius's woodcut is *cutting*. The student represented in Comenius's illustration—along with the desk, the book, the knife, indeed the whole ensemble—are embedded in a network of cuts made with a woodcutter's knife. It was through the cuts of studying that passages from Shakespeare's plays and poems found their way into manuscript tables such as Edmund Pudsey's (1609–12) and into printed anthologies such as *Bel-vedére* and *England's Parnassus* (both 1600), all three of which we shall consider in Chapter 4. This very book, *Shakespeare | Cut*, with its selective quotations and decontextualized illustrations, is itself an instance of study-as-cutting.

When a copy of a printed book was handed over to a binder, scissors and knife were needed to cut the text down to size. Copy 63 of the First Folio in the Folger Shakespeare Library's collection is not the only example of an early modern book in which the rusted shadow of a binder's scissors has been preserved (Blayney 33.) (See Figure 5.) Further cutwork happened when copies of a printed text were bound together with copies of other printed texts to create a purpose-made anthology or *Sammelband,* as with some surviving copies of the Pavier

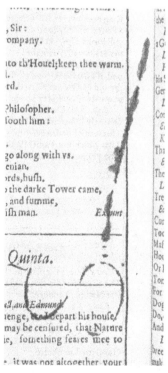

Figure 5. William Shakespeare, *Comedies, Histories, and Tragedies* (1623), rust shadow of scissors left in Folger Library First Folio copy 63, sig. rr3v. By permission of the Folger Shakespeare Library.

quartos of Shakespeare's plays printed in 1619 (Knight 2013: 69–70; 2016: 2:1684–8). The binder would trim the edges of the variously sized editions to create smooth fore-edges on three sides. The Folger's copy 63 happens to be a *Sammelband* of a sort, since it is made up of fragments from multiple copies of the First Folio. Even if a single book were being bound or re-bound, the pages' edges might be cut down. Due to cuts during rebinding in the eighteenth, nineteenth, and early twentieth centuries, many quartos in collections such as the Folger and the Huntington Library are as much as an inch smaller all around than the original quarto would have been. The copy of *The True Chronicle History of Henry V* at the Huntington (call number 69321) is an example.

=

If Shakespeare and his contemporaries did not cut physical scripts, what *did* they cut in their writings? Touchstone's turn on courtly quarreling in *As You Like It* insinuates four of the main things that could be cut in sixteenth- and early-seventeenth-century plays: beards, speeches, intentions, and bodies. Touchstone explains the quarrel thus to Jaques and Duke Senior:

> I did dislike the cut of a certain courtier's beard. He sent me word if I said his beard was not cut well, he was in the mind it was. This is called the Retort Courteous. If I sent him word again it was not well cut, he would send me word he cut it to please himself. This is called the Quip Modest.

[A "quip," let us note, was and is "a sharp, sarcastic, or *cutting* remark" (*OED*, "quip, *n*.," 1.a, emphasis added).]

> If again it was not well cut, he disabled my judgment. This is called the Reply Churlish. If again it was not well cut, he would answer I spake not true. This is called the Reproof Valiant. If again it was not well cut, he would say I lie. This is called the Countercheck Quarrelsome. And so the Lie Circumstantial, and the Lie Direct (*AYL* 5.4.68–80).

Each successive repost in Touchstone's story is an attempt to cut off the other speaker's aggressive intentions. And through it all runs the threat of cuts to the speakers' bodies. A sword fight is successfully avoided by knowing when to stop: "I durst go no further than the Lie Circumstantial, nor he durst not give me the Lie Direct; and so we measured swords, and parted" (5.4.83–5).

You won't find a single reference to "cut" as an alteration to a play script in any of Shakespeare's works; what you *will* find are roughly 180 references to cuts and cutting as stabbings (*OED*, "cut, *v.*," I.1), severings (II.7), slashings (IV.15), carvings (VI.21), sarcastic remarks ("cut, *n.²*," I.4), tribulations (I.4), passages of boats or ships through water (IV.21), beard fashions (III.17), garment styles (IV.20), and insults derived from vaginas and castrated testicles ("cut, *v.*," VII.26. a, "cut, *n.²*," †VI.30). ("Send for money, knight," Sir Toby encourages Sir Andrew in *Twelfth Night*. "If thou hast her not i'th'end, call me cut" [2.3.180–1]). As for the things that get stabbed, severed, slashed, carved, and trimmed in Shakespeare, they are primarily six, in this order of frequency: (1) miscellaneous body parts (including tongues, hands, ears, legs, hearts, brains, phalluses, and Shylock's pound of flesh); (2) actions and speeches in progress; (3) throats; (4) heads; (5) garments; and (6) beards. Violence—often violence of the most visceral, flesh-tingling sort—attends all but the last two. Take, for example, the Fool's jibe to the female audience members who are laughing at him at the end of Act 1, Scene 5 of *The Tragedy of King Lear*: "She that's a maid now, and laughs at my departure, Shall not be a maid long, unless things be cut shorter" (1.5.48–9). And by "things" he does not mean just his exit speech or the play's performance. As usual, "cut" entails bodily violence. Touchstone's shtick suggests even the cut of a beard could become provocation for drawing a sword. Let us note that in the Revels Office accounts for 1604–5, eight plays now known as Shakespeare's are recorded as having been performed by the King's Men. The author's name for three of those eight is specified in the margin: "Shaxberd" (Salgādo 1975: 24). Add the phallic suggestiveness of the "spear" in the usual spelling of Shakespeare's name, and the interchangeability of upper and lower "bodily strata" is hard to miss (Johnston 2011: 164). Fleshly violence reaches its apogee in what is probably the most famous "cut" in Shakespeare's works: "This was the most/ unkindest cut of all" (*Julius Caesar* 3.2.181), a stabbing that is also an insult

For us, the surprise in the list of cut objects in Shakespeare is likely to be the second: the "cutting off" of an intended action, a life, or a speech in progress, often accompanied by cuts to a body or by severed heads. Two of the three kinds of cutting off figure in Mark Antony's speech to the conspirators moments after they have stabbed Caesar:

> Live a thousand years,
> I shall not find myself so apt to die.
> No place will please me so, no mean of death,
> As here by Caesar, and by you cut off,
> The choice and master spirits of this age (3.1.160–4).

Present in this and other images of death as a cutting off are the three Fates, who spin, draw out, and cut the thread of a human life. The sense of cutting off as thwarting an intended action is likewise exemplified in *Julius Caesar* when Brutus strategizes the battle of Philippi. Between Philippi and their present position, Brutus tells Cassius, Titinius, and Messala, the inhabitants will give only grudging support in the confrontation with Antony:

> From which advantage shall we cut him off,
> If at Philippi we do face him there,
> These people at our back (4.2.262–4).

The death of Hotspur in *Henry IV, Part One*, cuts off not only intended action, but also intended speech. The cut or cuts that Prince Harry has inflicted on Hotspur's body cut short Hotspur's heretofore irrepressible way with words:

HOTSPUR

O, Harry, thou hast robbed me of my youth.

…

            O, I could prophesy
But that the earthy and cold hand of death
Lies on my tongue. No, Percy, thou art dust,
And food for—   *He dies*

PRINCE HARRY

For worms, brave Percy. Fare thee well, great heart (5.4.76, 82–6).

What is cut off here is Hotspur's very life—or at least his part in this play. Cuts in still another sense figure in the immediate context, as scenes from the Battle of Shrewsbury move from one camp to another and one encounter to another, albeit not so rapidly as in other history plays or in *Macbeth*. Cleopatra is another Shakespeare character who dies mid-sentence:

What should I stay—   *She dies* (5.2.308).

Aposiopesis is the technical name for the figure of speech that stops mid-sentence. Peacham calls it "the figure of silence, or of interruption" (250). Stand back far enough, and *all* tropes and schemes, with their alterations to syntactic order and conventional logic, might be regarded as varieties of cutting. (In the previous sentence, with my cut between "stand back" and the implied subject of the sentence, "you," I have performed *anacoluthon*. And with my *parenthesis*—Puttenham calls it "the inserter" [252]—I have just cut this passage from its context and *re*-placed it *here*.)

Speeches in Shakespeare's theater could be cut off in less dire circumstances: by self-imposed interruption, by *occupatio*, by other characters interrupting the speaker. A particularly striking example of self-imposed interruption occurs in *Henry VI, Part Two*, when Gloucester, shocked at the terms of peace being offered by the French king, stops reading the document in the middle of a word:

> GLOUCESTER *(reads)*…
>> Item: it is further agreed…that the duchy of Anjou and the county of Maine shall be released and delivered to the King her fa—
>> [*Gloucester lets the paper fall*]
> KING HENRY
>> Uncle, how now?
> GLOUCESTER   Pardon me, gracious lord.
>> Some sudden qualm hath struck me at the heart
>> And dimmed mine eyes that I can read no further (*2H6* 1.1.48–53).

Cuts can also operate at the level of syntax, in shifts in linguistic registers, even in shifts between languages. King Harry provides several such moments in his wooing of Catherine in *Henry V*. The cuts in this case are to be found not only in King Harry's paratactic syntax—"take me, take a soldier; take a soldier; take a king. And what sayst thou then to my love? Speak, my fair—and fairly, I pray thee" (*H5* 5.2.166–8)—but also in his cuts from English to French and back again:

> *Je quand suis le possesseur de France, et quand vous avez le possession de moi*—let me see, what then? Saint Denis be my speed!—*donc vôtre est France, et vous êtes mienne.* It is as easy for me, Kate, to conquer the kingdom as to speak so much more French (5.2.181–5).

In all these instances, let us note, speeches and planned actions are cut *off* but not *out*. Shakespeare himself, then, was a cutter-off of speeches, a cutter-off of intended actions, and a cutter-off of scenes.

In Shakespeare's theater cuts to speeches or to intended actions were not altogether under the author's control. Sudden rain might cut off a performance, just as it often did during outdoor entertainments for Queen Elizabeth on her summer progresses. So might an audience's reactions. Middleton in *Father Hubbard's Tales, or The Ant and the Nightingale* (1604) has the ant tell the reader about his encounters with lawyers, specifically "gallants of the Inns of Court." After dinner, a would-be gallant

> must venture beyond sea, that is, in a choice pair of noblemen's oars to the Bankside where he must sit out the breaking up of a comedy or the first cut of a tragedy; or rather (if his humour so serve him), to call in at the Blackfriars where he should see a nest of boys able to ravish a man (Middleton 2007: 173).

Sit *out*, break *up*, call *in*: the prepositions in Middleton's account of theater-going are eloquent. To "sit out" a play at one of the Bankside theaters implies a certain social and aesthetic distance on the gallant's part, a readiness to ridicule; to "call in" at the Blackfriars, a willingness to be ravished. Based on the history of the word *cut* that I have outlined here, I hope it will be apparent that "the first cut of a tragedy" is likely not, as the *OED* and the Middleton editors state in connection with this passage, "an excision or omission of a part" (*OED*, "cut, *n.*^{2}," I.5), but the jeering *down* or cutting *off* of a tragedy by verbal cuts from the audience. There is abundant testimony that play-goers in Shakespeare's time—gallants in particular—were not shy about noising their approval or their displeasure in the very midst of a performance (Gurr 2009: 279–83). "Cutting" a tragedy was the same thing as "breaking up" a comedy.

Excisions to Shakespeare's scripts across the past four hundred years need to be seen in the context of cuts already cued in the original scripts, as well as cuts occasioned by exigencies like interruptions by Middleton's gallant young man. In Chapter 2 we will survey not only the kinds of cuts made to Shakespeare's scripts across the past four centuries, but also the cuts built into the scripts themselves: speeches by chorus figures, sound effects in stage directions like "*flourish*" and "*alarum*," words spoken "aside," soliloquies, the provision of multiple focal points within a single scene, and revelations cued by the stage direction "*discovers*." Cuts are, and always have been, part and parcel of performance.

=

Throughout this book I shall be paying particular attention to a curiosity that sets cuts apart from other manipulations of flesh, paper, words, cloth, vinyl, celluloid film, and video: a "cut" can be the space opened up between the things being cut apart, or it can be either of the resulting pieces, or it can be what is left when one of the resulting pieces has been discarded. Take, for example, the prompt book for *Hamlet* as produced at the Smock Alley Theatre, Dublin, in the 1660s, '70s, and '80s. (See Figure 6.) In this and other surviving Smock Alley prompt books, leaves from the 1664 third folio have been extensively marked up. G. Blackmore Evans detects two rounds of cutting in the *Hamlet* text: an initial pass-through, in which certain lines and parts of lines were circled as possible cuts, and a second round, in which final decisions were taken about just which lines and parts of lines would be left out in performance, signaled this time by cancelling or lining-out the chosen lines (Evans 1960–96: vol. 4).

Circled for possible deletion is almost half of Horatio's forty-line speech to Marcellus and Bernardo after the Ghost's first appearance in 1.1 and during the Ghost's second appearance two thirds of the way through Marcellus's speech. In the second round of cutting, six of those nineteen possible line cuts were retained, the others cancelled by being lined-through. As for Marcellus's concluding speech, all but one line were both circled and cancelled. Claudius's opening speech in 1.2 shows the same pattern: almost half of the speech's thirty-nine lines have been circled for possible cutting; in the final round three of those lines were retained.

In these markings we can see the cut being deployed in two different—indeed, contradictory—ways: (1) to call attention to certain passages by circling them in the first mark-up and (2) to discard certain passages by lining them out in the second mark-up. The marked-out

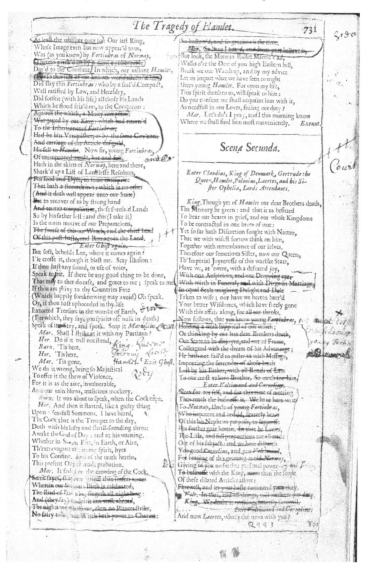

Figure 6. Fragment of promptbook for *Hamlet*, Smock Alley Theatre, Dublin (1660s–1680s). By permission of the Research Collection, University of Edinburgh Library.

material might be regarded as less interesting or important than the rest of the text, as it is in the second round of Smock Alley cuts; on the other hand, it might be regarded as *more* interesting or important, for the time being at least, as in the first round of Smock Alley cuts. Davenant's acting version of *Hamlet*, printed in 1676, illustrates the same ambivalence about which of the two cut pieces is the more important and how that piece should be marked. (See Figure 7A.) The text of *Hamlet* that Davenant uses is the 1604 quarto, the longest of the three early printings of the play.

An address to the reader advises:

> This play being too long to be conveniently acted, such places as might be least prejudicial to the plot or sense, are left out upon the stage: but that we may no way wrong the incomparable author, are here inserted according to the original copy with this mark " (Shakespeare 1676: sig. A2).

It is the cuts, we might say, that are quoted. This mark /"/ in North American English is referred to as a "quotation mark," heightening the sense of the marked passage as being quotable. In modern British English this mark /"/ is called "inverted commas," which comes closer to what Davenant has in mind. In classical rhetoric a *comma* is a short clause or phrase, a *colon* a longer one (*OED*, "comma, *n.*," 1.a). Quotability is not in question. Instead, Davenant's inverted commas mark a series of *commae*.

However, as Margreta de Grazia has pointed out, inverted commas down the left margin of printed texts were also used in the eighteenth century to indicate passages especially worthy of note (de Grazia 1991b). Zachary Lesser and Peter Stallybrass have argued that one leaf (sigs. C2- C2v) of the first quarto of *Hamlet* (1603) uses inverted commas in just this way (Lesser and Stallybrass). The speeches in question are the pieces of advice that Carambis (the Polonius figure in Q1) gives to his son Leartes and his daughter Ofelia. This is exactly the way Alexander Pope uses inverted commas in his 1725 edition of Shakespeare's works. At the end of volume 6 Pope supplies an index of "Speeches. The most considerable in Shakespeare" (Shakespeare 1725: 6: sigs. Kkkk2–Llll1), ranged under headings such as "Exhortatory," "Vituperative," and "Soliloquies" and cross-referenced to the preceding volumes by act and scene numbers. Some of these indexed speeches are marked in the text with left-hand inverted commas; most

A

But mad in craft. ["twere good you let him know
"For who that's but Queen, fair, sober, wise,
"Would from a paddock, from a Bat, a Gib,
"Such dear concernings hide; who would do so?
"No, in despight of sense and secrecie,
"Unpeg the basket on the houses top,
"Let the birds flie, and like the famous Ape,
"To try conclusions in the basket creep,
"And break your own neck down.

Qu. Be thou assur'd if words be made of breath,
And breath of life, I have no life to breath
What thou hast said to me.

Ham. I must to *England,* you know that.
Qu. Alack I had forgot,
'Tis so concluded on.

"*Ham.* There's letters seal'd, and my two School-fellows,
"Whom I will trust as I will Adders fang'd,
"They bear the mandate, they must sweep my way,
"And marshal me to knavery: let it work,
"For 'tis the sport to have the Engineer
"Hoist with his own petar, and't shall go hard
"But I will delve one yard below their Mines,
"And blow them at the Moon: O 'tis most sweet
"When in one line two crafts directly meet.
This man will let me packing.
I'll lug the guts into the neighbour room,
Mother good night indeed, this Counsellor
Is now most still, most secret, and most grave,
Who was in life a most foolish prating knave.
Come Sir, to draw toward an end with you.
Good night mother. [*Exit.*

ACT IV. SCENE I.

Enter King and Queen with Rosencraus and Guildenstern.
King. THere's matter in these sighs, these profound heaves,
You must translate, 'tis fit we understand them:
Where is your son?
Qu. Bestow this place on us a little while [*Exeunt Ros and Guild.*
Ah mine own Lord, what have I seen to night?
King. What *Gertrard,* how does *Hamlet?*
Qu. Mad

B

Himself the primrose path of dalliance treads,
† And recks not his own reed.
Laer. Oh, fear me not.

SCENE VI.

Enter Polonius.

I stay too long; — but here my father comes:
A double blessing is a double grace;
Occasion smiles upon a second leave.

Pol. Yet here, *Laertes!* get aboard for shame,
The wind sits in the shoulder of your sail,
And you are staid for there. My blessing with you;
And these few precepts in thy memory
See thou character. ' Give thy thoughts no tongue,
' Nor any unproportion'd thought his act:
' Be thou familiar, but by no means vulgar;
' The friends thou hast, and their adoption try'd,
' Grapple them to thy soul with hooks of steel:
' But do not dull thy palm with entertainment
' Of each new-hatch'd, unfledg'd comrade. Beware
' Of entrance to a quarrel: but being in,
' Bear't that th' oppos'd may beware of thee.
' Give ev'ry man thine ear; but few thy voice.
' Take each man's censure; but reserve thy judgment.
Costly thy habit as thy purse can buy,
But not exprest in fancy; rich, not gaudy;
For the apparel oft proclaims the man,
And they in *France* of the best rank and station
Are most select and generous, chief in that.
Neither a borrower, nor a lender be;
For loan oft loses both it self and friend:
A borrowing dulls the edge of husbandry.

This

† recks not his own reed, that is, heeds not his own lessons.

Figure 7A. William Shakespeare, *The Tragedy of Hamlet, Prince of Denmark as it is now acted at His Highness the Duke of York's Theatre* (1676), sig. I1. By permission of the Folger Shakespeare Library.

Figure 7B. William Shakespeare, *The Works of William Shakespear,* ed. Alexander Pope (1725), vol. 6, page 362. The Huntington Library.

are not. Surprisingly, none of Hamlet's soliloquies are so marked in the text—but Polonius's advice to Laertes is marked in just the way it is in the 1603 quarto. (See Figure 7B.)

De Grazia does not discuss the 1676 printing of *Hamlet*, but inverted commas to indicate *less* remarkable passages serve the same purpose as inverted commas to indicate *more* remarkable passages: in each case inverted commas mark the cut. The texts that result from these manipulations could be called cuts in their own right: the Smock Alley cut of *Hamlet* as opposed to Davenant's cut of the same play or Garrick's. Cuts cut both ways. They can end up as scraps on the cutting room floor, or in eighteenth-century anthologies such as *The Beauties of Shakespeare* and its digital equivalents on the web today.

=

To "cut off" a head, to "cut off" a speech, to "cut off" another's intent: the *off* in these idioms serves as a reminder of the dimensionality of cutting: cuts happen in space and time, and they require something moving through space and time. Most often that moving something is a human hand. Prepositions and adverbs are essential elements in the *OED*'s definitions of the cuts that occur most frequently in Shakespeare: to stab is "to make incision *in* or *into*" (*OED*, "cut, *v.*," I.1); to sever is "to make incision *through*" (II.7); to slash is "to pass *through* as in cutting" (IV.15); to carve is "to shape, fashion, form, or make by cutting" with an implicit *out* or *away* (VI.21); for a boat or a ship to cut the waves (IV.21) is to pass *through*; to fashion a beard or a garment is "to separate or detach [something] with an edged tool" (III.17) with an implicit *apart*, *away*, *off*, *out*, or *up*. Cutwork was a standard feature of clothing design, as witness several items in the Lord Admiral's Men's inventory of costumes: "one pair of white satin venetians cut with copper lace" and "one carnation-colored doublet cut, laid with gold lace" (Henslowe and Alleyn 1590–1600, MSS 1, article 30). ("Venetians" were a type of hose or breeches.)

Among the phrasal verbs catalogued at the end of the *OED*'s definition of "cut" are several that were current in late-sixteenth- and early-seventeenth-century English: "to cut *away*," "to cut *down*," "to cut *in*," "to cut *off*," "to cut *out*," "to cut *up*." The directionality and temporality of these phrases are registered also in special senses of "cut" as "to shape, fashion, form, or make by cutting" ("cut, *v.*" VI.23), including "to cut a caper," "to cut an antic," "to cut a flourish," "to cut faces" (all at "cut, *v.*" VI.25). The prepositions and adverbs that accompany cutting in all its permutations invite us to consider "cut" not as a thing but as a *phenomenon*. It is a noun that demands to be experienced, in first person, as an active-voice verb—or, better still, as movement between verb and noun, as a gerundive.

=

Acts of cutting invite us to consider five things:

(1) physics (stabbing, severing, slashing, carving, blinking, articulating sounds);
(2) psychology (perception of cuts and the role of cuts in cognition);
(3) materials (flesh, paper, words, cloth, wax cylinders and vinyl disks, celluloid film, video);
(4) instruments (knives, swords, scissors, tongue and teeth, binary codes); and
(5) the objects that cutting produces (speaking turns, omissions, retentions, quotations, prints from engravings, "the director's cut" in films, items collaged in multimedia performances).

It is the second of the five considerations, the psychology of cuts and cutting, that inspires my interest in the other four and guides my investigations.

I begin with the cuts that are most familiar to us—excisions of Shakespeare's texts in the service of theatrical performance, a practice regarded by many people as breaches in integral works of art—but my larger purpose is to install the cut as a critical concept, as an interest that can open up new, unexpected features in Shakespeare's texts and can provide the means for creating new works of art. The second chapter is concerned with cutwork as a fundamental practice in Shakespeare's art and in performances of his scripts. The third chapter, "Cut and Run," turns attention to cuts as units of perception. The fourth, "At the Cutting Edge," surveys the different kinds of cuts to which Shakespeare's works have been subjected in a variety of media, including engravings, photographs, cinema, and digital media. The final chapter, "The New Cut," returns us to the book's starting point: the fetishizing of cuts in "an age of distraction." As we shall discover, the length of cuts cannot be predicted from period, venue, and technology. Cinema is notorious for excising lines to make Shakespeare's scripts fit the visual medium, but Kenneth Branagh's 1996 *Hamlet* merges the longer second quarto text and the shorter folio text to present a "full text" that runs a little over four hours. Stage productions are supposed to be more generous in retaining Shakespeare's texts, but Tom Stoppard in *Fifteen-Minute Hamlet* and its more opulent successor *Dogg's Hamlet* cuts lines, speeches, and entire scenes with antic abandon.

=

On several fronts my approach here differs from existing treatments of cuts and cutting. By far, most criticism of cuts in Shakespeare is concerned with what has been excised and left unperformed in stage productions and films. The controversy stirred by the two editions of Erne's *Shakespeare as Literary Dramatist* indicates how incisively these issues strike a critical nerve. For stage performances, Alan Dessen's *Rescripting Shakespeare: The Text, the Director, and Modern Productions* offers a comprehensive survey of reasons for cutting, as well as a list of the most frequently cut scenes and sequences (Dessen 2002: 1–37). Peter Holland's essays "Film Editing" and "Shakespeare Abbreviated" extend these considerations to film (Holland 2000: 273–98, 2007: 26–45). For stage productions in earlier periods there is incidental information about cuts in work by Michael Caines for the eighteenth century and Richard Schoch for the nineteenth century, among many other scholars. Some of this material will be engaged in this book, but *Shakespeare|Cut* is not intended primarily as a history of theatrical and cinematic excisions.

Nor is it an act of homage to the cut in deconstructive theory, even as it remains grounded in the proposition that meaning-making depends on difference-marking. In his essay "The Scission" ("*La Coupure*"), Derrida considers the relationship of marking to cutting. The illusion of presence—my sense that I have a self who exists in *this* moment of time—requires some kind of severing or break whereby I step back and consider myself and set *now* apart from *then*: "The presence of the present only forms a surface, only enters squarely on stage, only institutes itself as something face-to-face—something present...in the play of this cut, this scission" (Derrida 1981: 303). More intuitively perhaps, all acts of reading, all interpretations of written texts, involve cuts:

this "scission" marks the text's interpretation...and also marks the arbitrary insertion of the letter-opener by which the reading process is opened up indifferently here or there, the cutting edge of writing which begins with the reading of some sentence clipped out from there or here, the chancy but necessary repetition of the already-thereness of some (other) text, the sharp blade of decision in general, of decided decision, of decision undergone as well as decision deciding (301).

Needless to point out, "decision" here is being invoked in its etymological sense from Latin, *de* + *cidere*, "off" + "to cut." In sum, "the pen, when you have followed it to the end, will have turned into a knife" (301).

With respect to historical time, my approach has much in common with Michel Foucault's concepts of genealogy and geological layering. In his essay "Nietzsche, Genealogy, History" Foucault attacks the once common assumption that the past is continuous with the present and that the goal of studying history is to "rediscover" ourselves in people and events of the past. No, a break is necessary—a "scission" in Derrida's terms: "History becomes 'effective' to the degree that it introduces discontinuity into our very being—as it divides our emotions, dramatizes our instincts, multiplies our body and sets it against itself...knowledge is not made for understanding; it is made for cutting" (Foucault 1984: 88). I will be paying attention to historical differences in the cuts to which Shakespeare's plays have been subjected, most especially to historical differences in the psychological effects of those cuts. The result is "effective history" in a sense that Foucault did not intend; hence, the subtitle of this chapter: "Forms and Effects."

My interest in the interspaces between cuts, developed most fully in Chapters 4 and 5, shares the same roots as Gilles Deleuze and Félix Guattari's insistence in *A Thousand Plateaus* and other works that creativity happens in spaces in between. The working together of these two authors demonstrates the principle. Deleuze in *Difference and Repetition* goes further to argue that it takes an act of violence to "awaken thought from its natural stupor" (139). As tools for cutting, swords, knives, scissors, shutters, recording needles, and keyboards provide that violence.

=

Fundamentally, *Shakespeare|Cut* is a project in historical phenomenology. Cutting of a sort is the starting point for phenomenology as a philosophical method. In the tradition of philosophical inquiry begun by Husserl, an object of inquiry is "bracketed," cut off from the received ideas that would explain that object. What a phenomenologist attends to instead is the *experience* of the object. That is just what I propose we do with cuts and cutting. The prepositions attached to the various meanings of the word *cut* indicate how open are cuts and cutting to phenomenological analysis. Prepositions inescapably involve the human body. In Michel Serres' phrase, prepositions literally "pre-position" the body: they set it up with respect to a given object in space and time (Serres 1997: 146).

With respect to cuts, five prepositions in particular pre-position us vis-à-vis Shakespeare's plays. We shall be singling out for attention not only cuts *to* Shakespeare's texts—cuts, that is, made by other people—but cuts *in* Shakespeare's texts. Lines, speeches, scenes, cross-cuts in narrative: all of these cuts are already inscribed in the texts with which readers, directors, and actors begin their own versions of cutwork. Cuts *from* Shakespeare's texts will likewise engage our attention in the form of quotations, scenes, and characters that have long enjoyed an imaginative life of their own, quite apart from the plays in which they originate. Finally, we shall move toward a fresh appreciation of cuts *with* Shakespeare as twentieth- and twenty-first-century artists collaborate with Shakespeare in ways that are not categorically dissimilar from artistic practices in Shakespeare's own time and place. The sense of *cut* as fashioning will be important to this endeavor. Taking a cue from early modern tailoring, I shall refer to acts of cutting and the resulting assemblage of cuts as "cutwork."

2

Cutwork

Cutting Out Plays and Putting Them On

> You could for a need study a speech of some dozen or sixteen
> lines, which I would set down, and insert in't? Could ye not?
>
> —Hamlet to the Players, *Hamlet* 2.2.542–4,
> in *Mr William Shakespeare's Comedies,*
> *Histories, and Tragedies* (1623), sig. oo4v

Hamlet greets the traveling players with a request for a cut. "We'll
have a speech straight," Hamlet declares. Which speech, the First
Player asks. One from a play Hamlet remembers the troupe performing, "an excellent play, well digested in the scenes" (2.2.433–4, 442)—
that is to say, well divided up and the resulting pieces well disposed
(*OED*, "digest, *v.*," †1.a). The play's well digested state does not stop
Hamlet from asking that it be cut apart. Thrilled with the player's
delivery of the speech, Hamlet asks if the troupe might play another
script, "The Murder of Gonzalo," and if he might add a new cut of a
dozen lines or so—in rhetorical terms, a *parenthesis*. A cut *from* a play
("The rugged Pyrrhus" speech suggests the play's subject was Dido
and Aeneas) is to be followed by a cut added *to* a play (the extra lines
Hamlet has in mind for "The Murder of Gonazlo"). It is altogether
fitting that differences among the first three printings of *Hamlet* seem to
be all about cuts as excisions—or could some of them be additions?
Cuts in another sense, cuts as collectibles, can be witnessed in manuscript commonplace books such as Edmund Pudsey's, where cuttings
from *Hamlet* are prominent. Hamlet's recitation of the opening two lines
of "The rugged Pyrhhus" (2.2.453–4) is a cut like the ones Pudsey has
made. In Hamlet's encounters with the players we find not just a play-
within-the-play (two of them, if we count the play on the fall of Troy

along with "The Murder of Gonzalo"), but an instance of *playwriting*-within-the-play. Putting on a play, Hamlet shows us, involves cutwork.

=

For Shakespeare and his contemporaries, at least four metaphors for script-construction were operative, each of them involving different modes of cutting. The most pervasive metaphor, inspired by classical rhetoric, took writing a play to be like writing an oration. Thinking of a script as an extended speech was perfectly natural in a theater in which speech was the dominant element in performance. *Dispositio* or "arrangement" of arguments was one of the five canons of Roman rhetoric. In the second metaphor for playwriting—constructing a building—cuts have a more problematic place. Ben Jonson devotes one of the longest passages in *Timber* to the proposition that constructing a play is like constructing a building: "We conclude the fable to be the imitation of one perfect and entire action; as one perfect and entire place is required in a building," Jonson declares (Jonson 2012: 7: 592). In the same passage in *Timber* Jonson introduces a third metaphor for play construction—the script as a body to be nurtured: "For as a body without proportion cannot be goodly, no more can the action, either in comedy or tragedy without his fit bounds" (7:594).

The fourth metaphor—and by far the most productive for the purposes of this book—is handed to us by Margaret Cavendish's epistle to her readers in *Plays Written by the Thrice Noble, Illustrious and Excellent Princess, the Lady Marchioness of Newcastle* (1662):

> I have heard that such poets that write plays, seldom or never join or sew the several scenes together; they are two several professions, at least not usual for rare poets to take that pains; like as great tailors, the master only cuts out and shapes, and his journey-men and apprentices join and sew them together; but I like as a poor tailor was forced to do all myself...(Cavendish 1662: sig. A5v).

Cavendish could be referring to the editorial drudgery involved in gathering the scripts together for publication, but the pieces she mentions are "each several scene," not each several play. Perhaps, too, her metaphor might be taken as an early instance of the "quilt-ing" technique claimed by some feminist critics to be distinctive to women writers. We can see the importance of cutwork in clothing design from the title-page illustration to the play *Greene's Tu Quoque* (1614), in which the comic protagonist Bubble sports a cutwork doublet. (See Figure 8.) Jonson anticipates Cavendish's metaphor in his verses "To the memory of my beloved, the author, Master William Shakespeare" in the First Folio. "Nature herself was proud of his designs," Jonson says,

> And joyed to wear the dressing of his lines,
> Which were so richly spun, and woven so fit,
> As since she will vouchsafe no other wit.

If lines are threads, plays are garments. Jonson celebrates Shakespeare as a kind of master tailor who works with the raw material of nature: "For though the poet's matter nature be,/ His art doth give the fashion" (Shakespeare 2005: lxxii).

Cavendish's image finds a latter-day counterpart in film editing. In the early days (1900–25), Walter Murch observes, an editing studio was like a tailoring shop: the editor wielded a big pair of scissors, and an assistant sutured the severed pieces of film before another assistant cemented them together (75). Machines took over these cutting and splicing tasks in the 1920s and '30s, but "the cutting room floor" remains an indelible image, even in an age of digital editing. Cavendish's cuts, like Murch's cuts, can be considered two ways. Cavendish apologizes for any remaining raw edges, implying that in the finished garment the seams ought not to be noticeable. With respect to film editing, Murch notes a difference in British and North American terminology: in the USA film is "cut," whereas in Britain and Australia it is "joined" (5). The emphasis in North American English is on separation; in British English, on bringing together.

Shakespeare anticipates Cavendish in recognizing the distinction between cutting and joining. The distinction in Cavendish turns on "cutting and shaping" on the one hand, carried out by a master tailor, versus "joining and sewing" on the other, done by journeymen. The extended joke about tailoring in *The Taming of the Shrew* 4.3 turns on the same distinction. One of the ways Petruccio devises to torment his new bride is to call in a haberdasher and a tailor and refuse, in Kate's presence, the cap and the gown that Grumio has ordered for her on Petruccio's behalf. When the tailor presents the gown, Petruccio exclaims,

Figure 8. Title page to John Cooke, *Greene's Tu Quoque, or The City Gallant* (1614). By permission of the Folger Shakespeare Library.

> O mercy, God, what masquing stuff is here?
> What's this—a sleeve? 'Tis like a demi-cannon.
> What, up and down carved like an apple-tart?
> Here's snip, and nip, and cut, and slish and slash,
> Like to a scissor in a barber's shop.
> Why, what o'devil's name, tailor, call'st thou this? (4.3.87–92).

Grumio refuses the tailor's bill by claiming that he ordered no such thing: "I commanded the sleeves should be cut out and sewed up again, and that I'll prove upon thee, though thy little finger be armed in a thimble" (4.3.141–4).

Taking my cue from Cavendish and from Shakespeare, I shall be pursuing in this chapter play-creation as "fashioning" in five kinds of cutwork: (1) costumes, (2) scene construction, (3) internally cued cuts, (4) print, and (5) the "new-modeling" of old plays.

=

Costumes, as we learn from the surviving inventories of the Admiral's Men's holdings, far outnumbered scripts, props, and musical instruments. The detail with which those costumes are itemized—for example, some cutwork "venetian" britches, one white satin, one carnation-colored, in the Lord Admiral's Men's possession—indicates not only the complexity of their construction (Hayward 2016) and their monetary value but also their importance to the business of personation. Costume, no less than language, could *make* character. The inventory identifies most garments not only by their color but by their cut: "venetians," "antics' coats" (presumably multi-colored patches), "pinked doublets" (with zigzag cuts), and hose cut to reveal variously colored panes of fabric beneath. Some of these costumes are associated with specific characters: "one green gown for Maid Marion," "Merlin['s] gown and cape," "Tamburlaine's coat with copper lace," "Tamburlaine's britches of crimson velvet," "Robin Hood's suit," "Tasso's robe," "Dido's robe," "Harry the V['s] velvet gown," "Harry the V['s] satin doublet laid with gold lace" (Henslowe and Alleyn 1590–1600: MSS 1, article 30). An actor inhabited a fictional person not only by inducing in himself that person's passions (Roach 1985: 23–57) and speaking that person's language, but also by putting on that person's costume. "Personation," the most usual sixteenth- and seventeenth-century term for what it is that actors do, catches perfectly the embodiedness of fictional identities on the stage.

Essential to putting on a play was putting on costumes. In a certain costume an actor cut a certain figure.

William Scott in *The Model of Poesy* (2013/1599) links styles of costume and styles of speech in just such terms. Dramatic language, he observes, is

> alterable according to the subject and circumstances (as it were, the fashion of the garment), suitable to every state, degree, and affection. And this is very aptly besides called *character*, for speech carries a certain stamp, impression, or image as well of the thing as of the nature or affection of the deliverer (Scott 2013: 50–1).

Citing J. C. Scaliger's *Poetics*, Scott coordinates high style in speech with "the courtier's gorgeous and rich garment" (56), middle style with "the citizen's neat habit" (57), and low style with "the plain-fashioned suit of the shepherd and ploughman" (57). The register of Tamburlaine's speech in Marlowe—speech perfectly coordinated with crimson velvet britches and copper-laced coat—illustrates Scott's observation. To judge from Scott's remarks, cutwork costumes were associated with courtiers certainly and citizens maybe. By Scott's criteria, the comedian Bubble in Figure 8 wears a costume a cut above his social station.

The situation gets interesting when cut and character do *not* match up, when there is a visible cut between the costume and the speaker. In Shakespeare the power of costume to make character is registered when Florizel in *The Winter's Tale* exclaims to Perdita, dressed as queen of the sheep-shearing feast, "These your unusual weeds to each part of you/ Does give a life" (4.4.1–2). In her reply Perdita may apologize that she is "most goddess-like pranked up" (4.4.10), but she does so in a verbal style that betrays how well her temporary costume *does* accord with her actual social status as daughter of the king of Sicily. Florizel, son of the king of Bohemia, illustrates the more usual effect of disguise in Shakespeare's comedies: a disparity between high style in speech and low style in dress. Edgar as Tom o'Bedlam is an exception—he displays low style in both—but *King Lear* is a tragedy, and in tragedy appearance and reality are coordinated differently than in comedy.

=

When Heywood, in his preface to *The English Traveler* (printed 1633), brags that there are 220 plays "in which I have had either an entire hand, or at the least a main finger" (sig. A3), he might have been thinking about holding a pair of scissors as well as a pen. Writing plays in Shakespeare's time was piece-work. The metaphor of play-as-garment helps us understand why separate writers got separate scenes, not separate characters or separate plot lines, when they worked on group-authored plays such as *Sir Thomas More* (BL MS Harley 7368). Counting the likely case of *Sir Thomas More*, Shakespeare participated in at least four such ventures: *1 Henry VI*, *Henry VIII* (*All Is True*), and *The Two Noble Kinsmen* are the others.

The divvying up of the scene cuts in *Sir Thomas More* was likely decided according to a "plat" or ground plan—a term taken over from building construction (Turner 2006: 216–44). In their physical appearance as well as their function these plats are a form of cutwork. The six plats of other plays that happen to survive were written up after the scripts were already in hand, since they contain cues for entrances and sound effects as well as some of the actors' names, but horizontal rules in the manuscripts indicate how each scene functioned as a cut (Kathman 2004, McMillin 1973). The best known of the surviving plats is one for "The Second Part of the Seven Deadly Sins," a play likely acted by Strange's Men between 1590 and 1592 (Henslowe and Alleyn 1590–1600: MSS 19, fols. 1r–3r). At least one of the plays with a surviving plat, a lost *Troilus and Cressida* for the Admiral's Men in 1599, is known to have been a collaboration between Thomas Dekker and Henry Chettle, two of the collaborators on *Sir Thomas More*.

A passage in George Puttenham's *The Art of English Poetry*, quoted by Turner, specifies a "plat" as a poet's starting point: "our maker or poet is to play many parts and not one alone, as first to devise his plat or subject, then to fashion his poem, thirdly to use his metrical proportions, and last of all to utter with pleasure and delight" (Turner 2006: 125). Dekker and Chettle in *Troilus and Cressida* and Anthony Munday, Dekker, Chettle, and likely Shakespeare and Thomas Heywood in *Sir Thomas More* would each have "fashioned" his allotted scene or scenes, each working as a master tailor on those particular pieces. The components would have then been sewn together just as Cavendish describes doing with her own work. In the case of *Sir Thomas More*, the sewer-together was perhaps Munday.

Horizontal strokes of the pen in the *More* manuscript divide one character's speeches from other characters' speeches. In Orlando's side these horizontal cuts between speeches end in cues, the last words of the preceding speech. In the plat of *The Second Part of the Seven Deadly Sins* the addition of vertical lines to the horizontal lines turn the summary of each scene into a rectangle, a visually separate entity. A third category of cuts in the *More* manuscript are lines that have been excised. In the scene attributed to Shakespeare (scene 6 in the Oxford text, digital image available at https://imagesonline.bl.uk/ as "May Day Scene"), two lines and part of a third in the midst of More's speech to the citizens (6.125–8) have been lined-through and a new phrase added to the ensuing line to patch the surviving text together. Whether the cancellation is Shakespeare's is not clear; the inserted phrase is in a different hand and a different ink. Grace Ioppolo attributes the cut to the book-holder but speculates that it may have been made with Shakespeare's consent (Ioppolo 2015). Whatever the case, we have in this cut to *Sir Thomas More* a documentary prototype for the cuts that have been made to Shakespeare's texts across the past four centuries: not only the excisions, but also the additions. Scene 6 is itself an added cut: it has been interpolated into a pre-existing manuscript of *Sir Thomas More*.

=

In the eyes of modern scholars, the stylistic cuts in *Sir Thomas More* are all too obvious. Would they have seemed so to the audience at the Globe if the play had been performed? Or might the variety of cuts have been part of the play's appeal? The two plays Shakespeare jointly authored with John Fletcher—*All Is True* and *The Two Noble Kinsmen*—illustrate this process of cutting and stitching and raise questions about the effects of that process in theatrical performance. Most modern scholars have supposed that the intended effect in collaborative plays was seamless continuity, and yet the prologues to both plays invite spectator-listeners to attend to the cuts. What you are about to see and hear, say both Prologues, is a sequence of scenes. "Such noble scenes as draw the eye to flow/ We now present," says the Prologue to *All Is True* (Pro. 4–5). Chaucer as the original teller of the tale is invoked by the Prologue to *The Two Noble Kinsmen*: "You shall hear/ Scenes, though below his art, may yet appear/ Worth two hours' travail" (Pro. 27–9). Computer-assisted analysis using multiple variables has confirmed that some of those scenes were fashioned by Shakespeare and some by Fletcher (Elliott). The word "scenes" in both prologues may suggest a number of things: not just subdivisions of the script, but also of the stage and tiring house, fictional locations, big dramatic effects, even the act of acting (Smith 2013: 103). However they may be framed, "scenes" are what the listener-spectators are cued to notice. Scott, let us remember, calls acts and scenes "cuts" (77–8).

How can we be so sure that cuts between hands, shifts in style as in subject, were not something that audiences actually listened for and appreciated? The mixture of clowns and kings that Sidney laments in *A Defense of Poetry* suggests an English delight in such discontinuities. Certainly the title page to the 1634 quarto of *The Two Noble Kinsmen* plays up the play's collaborative status, as "*Written by the memorable worthies of their time; M[aste]r John Fletcher, and M[aste]r William Shakespeare, Gent.*" (Shakespeare and Webster 1630: title page). Jeffrey Masten has read the brackets on each side of the authors' names as evidence of "textual intercourse" (Masten 1997). If that be so, how much the more interesting the Prologue's opening declaration "New plays and maidenheads are near akin" (Pro. 1). Textual intercourse requires, in multiple senses of the word, cuts.

=

Whether or not "hand D" in the *Sir Thomas More* manuscript is William Shakespeare's hand, the layout of the manuscript suggests how Shakespeare and his contemporaries might consider speeches as well as scenes as varieties of cuts. Horizontal lines in the manuscript separate not only scenes but also speeches within scenes. Beau-Chesne's and Baildon's *cut* pen (see Chapter 3) has become a *cutting* pen. In its presentation of speeches the "book" of *Sir Thomas More* resembles what the actors' "sides" would have looked like had production of the script gone forward. Shakespeare in production, as Tiffany Stern and Simon Palfrey have demonstrated, was *Shakespeare in Parts* (Palfrey and Stern 2011). Of the surviving examples of "sides" from Shakespeare's time, a sheet of Edward Alleyn's part for the title role in Robert Greene's *Orlando Furioso* (Henslowe and Alleyn 1590–1600: MSS 1, Article 138, fol. 8r) is the best known. Actors would have received only their own lines, with brief cues at the start of each speech.

In Alleyn's part, horizontal lines invite the user to think of each speech as a cut. So would the speeches have seemed as Alleyn memorized his lines. So would they have seemed as he listened onstage for his cues. So would they have seemed to everyone who heard the speeches in what modern linguistics knows as "speaking turns." For Shakespeare and his contemporaries, acts of personation happened in a series of cuts.

Scripts may have been acted continuously, one set of actors may have hurried onstage as actors in the preceding scene were leaving, but Shakespeare's scripts, like those of his contemporaries, are full of internally cued cuts that audiences cannot escape noticing. These internally cued cuts figure in five forms: (1) speaking turns, (2) speeches "aside," (3) announced changes in fictional location, (4) multiple focal points in a single scene, and (5) "discoveries."

=

Cuts as natural units in words and lines will occupy us in Chapter 3. Beyond those most basic of cuts, cuts between speaking turns figure as the most obvious cuts in Shakespeare's scripts. We can see and hear them with special acuity in Shakespeare's early scripts, in which one-line exchanges (classical poetics knows them as *stichomythia*) alternate with long speeches that amount, in some cases, to free-standing orations. The likeliest source of inspiration for these arrangements are the scripts of Seneca (Smith 1988: 203–8). Take, for example, the speeches that attend the on-stage murder of Edward, Prince of Wales, in *Henry VI, Part Three*. Prince Edward, abetted by his mother Margaret, provokes his stabbing death by speaking defiantly to the three York conspirators who have taken him prisoner: King Edward IV, Richard of Gloucester (the future Richard III), and George Duke of Clarence.

RICHARD OF GLOUCESTER
    By heaven, brat, I'll plague ye for that word.
PRINCE EDWARD
    Ay, thou wast born to be a plague to men.
RICHARD OF GLOUCESTER
    For God's sake take away this captive scold.
PRINCE EDWARD
    Nay, take away this scolding crookback rather.
KING EDWARD
    Peace, willful boy, or I will charm your tongue.
GEORGE OF CLARENCE (*to Prince Edward*)
    Untutored lad, thou art too malapert (*3H6* 5.5.27–32).

Prince Edward persists. In the ensuing murder King Edward invokes Margaret as yet another "railer":

KING EDWARD
  Take that, the likeness of this railer here.
      King Edward stabs Prince Edward
RICHARD OF GLOUCESTER
  Sprawl'st thou? Take that, to end thy agony.
      Richard stabs Prince Edward
GEORGE OF CLARENCE
  And there's for twitting me with perjury.
      George stabs Prince Edward, [who dies] (5.5.38–40).

The ritual quality of the exchanges is enhanced by the *stichomythia*, which reaches a climax in the final line, where two speaking turns occur within a single line:

QUEEN MARGARET
  O, kill me too!
RICHARD OF GLOUCESTER   Marry, and shall.
  He offers to kill her (5.5.41)

In all such instances the audience not only hears the cuts between speeches but also sees them as attention shifts from a speaker *here* to a speaker *there*. In the case of Act 5, Scene 5 of *Henry VI, Part Three*, those multiple focal points finally converge in the daggers or swords that pierce Prince Edward's body. What has been heard is realized in what is seen.

The *accelerando* effect of the one-line cuts is heightened by pauses for the long harangues and complaints at which Margaret the "railer" is so accomplished. The murder of her son provokes from Margaret an oration that anticipates Mark Antony's in *Julius Caesar*:

          O traitors, murderers!
  They that stabbed Caesar shed no blood at all,
  Did not offend, nor were not worthy blame,
  If this foul deed were by to equal it.
  He was a man—this, in respect, a child;
  And men ne'er spend their fury on a child (5.5.51–6).

And so on, until she invokes in her peroration the sense of "cut" as the thwarting of an intention or a speech or a life that we noted in Chapter 1:

> But if you ever chance to have a child,
> Look in his youth to have him so cut off
> As, deathsmen, you have rid this sweet young Prince! (5.5.64–6).

=

More common in Shakespeare's scripts, and more characteristic of his work throughout his career, are interior cuts in the form of movements "aside" and speeches "aside." As Alan Dessen and Leslie Thomson note, "aside" in early modern stage directions is always an adverb, never a noun (Dessen and Thomson 1999: 15). A change in spatial orientation vis-à-vis the spectator/listeners—a cut in location requiring a cut in attention—is essential to both actions. Hamlet cues his own standing-aside in the graveyard scene. The macabre verses he pronounces to Horatio ("Imperial Caesar, dead and turned to clay,/ Might stop a hole to keep the wind away" [5.1.208–9]) are interrupted by the arrival of Ophelia's funeral procession. "But soft, but soft, aside" (5.1.212), Hamlet cautions Horatio, and the two of them do indeed step aside to observe the procession, giving the spectators two groupings between which to look back and forth until Hamlet abruptly rejoins the main scene ("This is I,/ Hamlet the Dane" [253–4]) and, according to Q1, leaps into Ophelia's grave. As for speeches aside, Hamlet is a master of the genre—his very first speech in the play, "A little more than kin and less than kind" [1.2.65], is marked as "*aside*" in many modern editions—and he exploits that gift to the full in his soliloquies, one of which ("To be or not to be; that is the question" [3.1.58ff]) may technically be a speech aside if Ophelia, planted by Polonius and Claudius to intercept Hamlet, remains present on stage.

=

Aurally cued changes in fictional location constitute a third category of internally indicated cuts in Shakespeare's scripts. The Chorus's prologue and four subsequent interruptions of the action of *Henry V* in the folio text may not correspond to five discrete acts, but cuts these interruptions remain, and the Chorus's speeches emphasize that fact by calling attention to shifts in fictional location and in time. Time as chorus in Act 4 of *The Winter's Tale* serves the same function: he might just as well appear with a pair of shears as an hourglass. More often than not, however, the location cuts built into Shakespeare's scripts have to be inferred.

The sense of a cut is keener when the ensuing scene begins with special sound effects (*flourish, alarum*, etc.) or with a directly or indirectly announced change in fictional location ("Unto Southampton do we shift our scene" [*Henry V*, 2.0.42]; "Well, this is the forest of Ardenne" [*As You Like It* 2.4.13]). Evidence of the scissors is especially sharp in rapid shifts between "excursions" in battle sequences such as in *Henry IV, Part One*, 5.3—5.4—5.5; *Macbeth* 5.6—5.7—5.8—5.9—5.10—5.11; and *Coriolanus* 1.4—1.5—1.6—1.7—1.8—1.9—1.10—1.11. It could be argued that these shifts from one part of a battle to another, though marked as separate scenes in the folio and in most modern editions, would have been experienced in the theater as a single continuous entity—that is to say, as cuts *within* a scene, as cuts within cuts.

=

In a fourth category of internal cuts the spectator-listeners are confronted in the same scene with two or more simultaneously present focal points, each with its own dialogue, requiring the audience to shift attention from one to the other. A particularly striking example is the scene in *Troilus and Cressida* where Cressida is wooed by Diomedes while Troilus and Ulysses observe on one side and Thersites provides a running commentary on the other, giving the audience three focal points to look at and three sets of speeches to hear. The distractions these cuts invite in the spectator-listeners' perceptions are suggested in the dialogue. "Troilus, farewell," Cressida says when Diomedes has left; "One eye yet looks on thee,/ But with my heart the other eye doth see" (5.5.109–10). Troilus attests the same distraction when he exclaims repeatedly to Ulysses, "This is and is not Cressid" (5.5.149). As for Thersites, his quips throughout the scene establish an acerbic alternative to Troilus's romanticism, a cut that is visual as well as verbal.

Multiple focal points are most obvious in plays-within-the-play. The effect, in Shakespeare at least, is inevitably disruptive. In their verse form the plays-within-the-play in *Love's Labour's Lost*, *A Midsummer Night's Dream*, and *Hamlet* are instances of cutwork. The fourteeners of the Nine Worthies in *Love's Labour*, the varying meters of "Pyramus and Thisbe" in *Dream*, and the tetrameter of the Prologue to "The Mousetrap" in *Hamlet* are all examples of what James VI and I in *The Essays of an Apprentice in the Divine Art of Poesy* (1585) refers to as "cut verse"—that is, verse with varying numbers of feet. Further cuts are inserted by the onstage audience. In *Love's Labour* and *Dream* the audiences' cutting remarks produce in the players the effect described in Sonnet 23: "As an unperfect actor on the stage/ Who with his fear is put besides his part, So I…" (23.1–3). Take, for example, Costard, the first of the Nine Worthies to come before the King, his friends, and the French ladies in *Love's Labour's Lost*:

COSTARD (*as Pompey*)
    I Pompey am—
BIRON   You lie, you are not he.
COSTARD (*as Pompey*)
    I Pompey am—
BOYET   With leopard's head on knee.
BIRON
    Well said, old mocker. I must needs be friends with thee.
COSTARD (*as Pompey*)
    I Pompey am, Pompey surnamed the Big.
DUMAINE   'The Great'.
COSTARD   It is 'Great', sir—
    (*As Pompey*) Pompey surnamed the Great (5.2.541–7).

The play of "Pyramus and Thisbe" in *Dream* is cut to shreds in the same way. It is in this context that we should interpret Middleton's quip that a would-be gallant "must sit out the breaking up of a comedy or the first cut of a tragedy" (Middleton 2007: 173).

Even Hamlet does not refrain from cutting the tragedy he himself has arranged to have performed. The object of his verbal thrusts is only once the actors and their play. The three-line Prologue—"For us and for our tragedy/ Here stooping to your clemency,/ We beg your hearing patiently" (3.2.142–4)—inspires a quip that might come from Biron or Hippolyta:

HAMLET   Is this a prologue, or the posy of a ring?
OPHELIA   'Tis brief, my lord.
HAMLET   As woman's love (3.2.145–7).

As this exchange illustrates, the recipients of Hamlet's cuts are not the players or the play-within-the-play, but his fellow spectators.

In the plays-within-the-play in *Love's Labour's Lost*, *A Midsummer Night's Dream*, and *Hamlet* we encounter once again the second most frequent sense of "cut" in Shakespeare's scripts: a thwarting or cutting off of someone else's speeches and actions. Only body parts are cut—off, and into—more often. As with Hotspur's death in *Henry IV, Part One*, cutting *off* and cutting *into* are closely allied: comically, in the case of "Pyramus and Thisbe"; tragically, in the case of the sword fight that concludes *Hamlet*.

=

When a curtain is added to a play-within-the-play a fifth kind of cut is physically marked. "*Here Prospero discovers Ferdinand and Miranda playing at chess*" (*Tempest* 5.1.174 *sd*): the *dis-* in "discovers" carries the etymological trace of cutting, in the sense of "asunder" (*OED*, "*dis-, prefix*" 1. a) and "between, so as to separate or distinguish" (1.b). Physically, Prospero's act of discovery involved the pulling aside of a tapestry or painted cloth. In the statue scene of *The Winter's Tale* the fabric is specifically called a "curtain": "Do not draw the curtain," Leontes cries when Paulina threatens to cut off his vision of Hermione's statue (5.3.59). "I'll draw the curtain," Paulina warns again when Leontes persists in wanting to touch the illusion beyond the cloth (5.3.68).

Shakespeare's increasing use of such "scene-cuts" in his later scripts has been attributed to the availability of more elaborate stage machines and artificial lighting in the Blackfriars Theatre, as well as to the sophisticated tastes of the theater's patrons. If so, discovery scenes constitute a prime example of "the latest cut" in play fashions. Also part of that fashion, apparently, were musical interludes. In some printed scripts known to have been acted at the Blackfriars (Francis Beaumont's *The Knight of the Burning Pestle*, for example) the musical interludes between the acts are explicitly cued. If masques can be regarded as a genre distinct from stage plays and if music, artificial lighting, and *tableaux vivants* as technologies distinct from verbal declamation in the open air, "discoveries" in Shakespeare's late plays begin to look like the new media of their time—the early modern equivalent of the video projections in stage productions by the Wooster Group in *Hamlet* (2005) and *Troilus and Cressida* (2012) and the intermedial cutwork visited upon Shakespeare's *Roman Tragedies* (2007–14) by Ivo van Hove's Toneelgroep Amsterdam.

=

In addition to coordinating speech styles with costumes, Scott in *The Model of Poesy* uses the term "cuts" to refer to acts and scenes in drama. These divisions are, according to Scott, one of the features that distinguish plays (impersonated in action) from heroic poems (narrated in third person):

> [N]ow, these kinds being by action or personating not by narration, the division of them according to the discrete quantity differs likewise from the other of the heroic, and they are cut into acts and scenes…. An act is such a part as comprehends some convenient passage of the device where things are carried in one tenor without evident change…. Again, each act is subdivided into scenes, which are distinguished by some change of persons and speakers (Scott 2013:77–8).

Scott acknowledges that "acts" and "scenes" are terms taken over from Latin drama. Despite the evidence laid out in T. W. Baldwin's *Shakspere's Five-Act Structure* (1947), the consensus today among most scholars is that division of scripts into acts was not part of Shakespeare's modus operandi as a playwright, with the possible exception of the folio text of *Henry V*, in which a Chorus introduces cuts in the action five times—but without ever identifying the ensuing action as an "act" and, indeed, without appearing each time the folio text marks an act. The Chorus that introduces Act 2 in modern editions—"Now all the youth of England are on fire" (2.0.1)—appears in the folio embedded in the midst of what is marked as Act 1, bumping up by an act the Choruses that modern editions assign to Acts 3 and 4 and leaving the folio's Act 4 with no Chorus at all. A five-act structure is less prominent in the play's design than modern editions would suggest. More typical of Shakespeare's printed texts is the 1600 quarto of *The Chronicle History of Henry the Fifth*, in which acts and scenes are not marked at all.

Most of the cuts so central to the experience of plays in performance are hardly noticed in print. Speeches and scenes—entities ripe for being cut in part or *in toto*—already call attention to themselves as cuts. In describing scenes as "cuts," Scott is doubtlessly thinking of printed texts with act and scene divisions clearly marked—often with ruled lines between them, as in the Shakespeare First Folio—but cuts were as perceptible to spectator-listeners in Shakespeare's lifetime as ruled lines would have been to readers, perhaps even more so. The original meaning of the term "scene," after all, was what could be seen on the *scaena* at a given moment. In academic texts of Terence, a new scene was marked every time anyone entered or exited the *scaena* regardless of whether the action and dialogue were continuous (Smith 2013: 98). A cleared stage— all persons involved in the fiction having exited—made a cut between scenes not only visible but, in the momentary silence, audible.

=

Seen in historical perspective, the cutwork in recent productions of Shakespeare's scripts is nothing new. Excisions of text, additions of speeches and scenes, and rearrangements of existing elements were already common theatrical practice during Shakespeare's career and have continued to the present day (Ioppolo 1991). The metaphor of script-as-garment helps us understand the place of cutting and adding to "new-model" or "remodel" or old plays. (The former term, according to the *OED*, dates from the 1640s; the latter term, from the Restoration [*OED*, "new-model, *v.*"; "remodel, *v.*"].) New-modeling has clearly been carried out in the case of the B-text of *Doctor Faustus*. The shorter A-text, published in 1604, has been identified by most scholars with the play as it was originally acted by the Lord Admiral's Men between 1594 and 1597; the longer B-text, published in 1616, with a later revival, presumably incorporating the "additions in *Doctor Faustus*" for which Henslowe paid William Bird and Samuel Rowley the considerable sum of £4 on November 22, 1602 (Henslowe and Alleyn 1590–1600: MSS 7). For the 1616 printing there were cuts as well as additions to the A-text: 36 lines were excised, and 676 lines were added (Marlowe 1993). The 1619, 1624, and 1628 reprints of the B-text advertise the additions on the title page, even as they credit the long-dead Marlowe as the writer: *The Tragical History of the Life and Death of Doctor Faustus. With New Additions. Written by Ch. Mar.* As with *The Two Noble Kinsmen*, cutwork is foregrounded.

Given the example of *Doctor Faustus*, it is all the more a pity that there was no quarto edition of *Macbeth* between the play's likely first performance in 1606 and its printing in the 1623 folio. At 2,084 lines (by Erne's count) the text is considerably shorter than any other Shakespeare tragedy, and several scenes (3.5 and parts of 4.1) have been attributed to Middleton (Erne 2013: 165, Middleton 2007: 1165–9). Would a quarto edition have advertised Middleton's cuts and additions? In the case of the folio version of *Macbeth*, as for the B-text of *Doctor Faustus*, we confront a new "cut" in the sense of "the shape to which, or style in which a thing is cut; fashion, shape (of clothes, hair, etc.)" (*OED*, "*cut, n.²*," III.17.a). Refashioning an old play by cutting and adding was not unlike refashioning an old garment by giving it "the latest cut." Fielding in *The Author's Farce*, as we observed in Chapter 1, has fun with this analogy when he has the theater impresario Marplay Junior quip that he and his father "are a couple of poetical tailors; when a play is brought us, we consider it as a tailor does a coat, we cut it, sir, we cut it: and let me tell you, we have the exact measure of the town, we know how to fit their taste" (Fielding 1750: sig. B1).

In early modern plays, as in early modern garments, "the latest cut" called attention to its newness. Whether that attention was extended from the "joining" to the "cutting" remains an open question. Did audiences watching performances of the B-text of *Doctor Faustus* look out for which cuts were Marlowe's and which were William Bird's and Samuel Rowley's? Probably not. The title pages to the second, third, and fourth printings mention only "additions," and they credit Marlowe as the play's sole author. What about Fletcher's cuts and Shakespeare's cuts in *The Two Noble Kinsmen*? The question here is trickier, since both men's names are stated on the title page of the 1634 quarto, and Fletcher's comes first, as we might expect, since Fletcher's work for the stage was the more recent. (Fletcher's *Rule a Wife and Have a Wife* had been acted by the King's Men probably in 1624 and his collaborative play with Philip Massinger, *The Elder Brother*, probably in 1625, the year of Fletcher's death.) We should be aware, then, that even in Shakespeare's time cuts in play construction could be showcased or not. The same holds true in later centuries for cutwork that takes up pieces of Shakespeare and "repurposes" them toward new ends—including new stage productions.

=

In a striking image Peter Brook, whose playful, gymnastic production of *A Midsummer Night's Dream* (1970–3) immediately made audiences, directors, actors, and scholars rethink the possibilities encoded in the

2,102 lines of *Dream*, has envisioned the hundreds of thousands of words in Shakespeare's dramatic corpus as a single "skein" of fabric, unrolling in time:

> [I]f we're very bold, and think not in very constricting verbal terms, "he's an author, he wrote plays, the plays have scenes" and so on, but think much more broadly and say "this creator created an enormous skein of interrelated words", and if we think of a chain of several hundred thousand words unfolding in a certain order, the whole making an extraordinary fabric, I think that then one begins to see the essential point. And that is that this fabric reaches us today, not as a series of messages, which is what authorship almost always produces— it is a series of impulses that can produce many understandings (qtd. in Berry 1977, 115).

To extend the metaphor, we might imagine the visual evidence of stage productions as pattern books. They come in three varieties: (1) marked-up printed texts, like the Smock Alley sheets from the third folio (see Figure 6); (2) playhouse editions, like the 1676 "players' quarto" of *Hamlet* (see Figure 7A) and Bell's editions of Shakespeare's plays, advertised on the title pages as being printed "as they are now performed at the Theatres Royal in London: regulated from the prompt books" from the 1770s and later (see Figure 17); and (3) the miscellaneous category of documents lumped together as "prompt books."

As Charles Shattuck notes in his catalogue of *The Shakespeare Promptbooks* from the 1620s to 1961, the third category of documents are

> tricky, secretive, stubborn informants. They chatter and exclaim about what we hardly need to know…They fall blankly silent just when we most hope to be told where the actor stood or how he looked or what he did…. They tell lies, as anybody knows who ever produced a play and failed to write into the book his own last-minute revisions or the happy inspirations that come to the actors midway in a run of performances (Shattuck 1965: 3).

In their very variety, these marked texts, workbooks, preparation copies, souvenir albums, and memorial books give visual testimony to how stage productions are inevitably an assemblage of cuts. Some of the surviving documents are working drafts from the theater, but many are albums of texts, diagrams, finished drawings of scenes, costume designs, even swatches of fabric that have been assembled after the fact. Multiple illustrations, for example, exist for the spectacular Siege of Harfleur in Charles Kean's production of *Henry V* in 1859. The one shown in Figure 3 represents a working design; two others in the Victoria and Albert Museum's Department of Prints and Drawings (see http://collections.vam.ac.uk/, accession numbers D.1720 to 1760–1901), post-production records.

The cutting and sewing metaphor for play production becomes a physical reality in a prompt book for David Garrick and George Coleman's *Florizel and Perdita ... Alter'd from The Winter's Tale* (1758), now in the Folger Shakespeare Library's collection. Garrick and Coleman cut a long passage by sewing eight pages together with needle and thread. (See digital image at https://folger.edu/luna/.) The prompt book that David Garrick put together for his last performance as Hamlet in 1772–3 is quite literally an assemblage. This is the production about which Garrick confessed to a friend in France, "I have played the devil this winter, I have dared to alter *Hamlet*" (qtd. in Stone 1934: 893). What Garrick mainly did was eliminate most of the fifth act, so that the mad scene cuts straight to the final scene (Stone 1934, 890–921, Burnim 1961: 152–73). The prompt book for the production (now Folger PROMPT Ham. 16; see images at https://folger.edu/luna/) displays multiple kinds of cuts—indeed, cuts upon cuts. Garrick's pen-and-ink cuts are made on top of cuts from two already cut texts of *Hamlet*. The printed pages—the matrix, we might say—come from the 1747 printing of a text prepared in 1718 by the actor Robert Wilks (from 1708 to 1732 he was the best known Hamlet on the London stage) and his friend John Hughs. Wilks presumably dictated the cuts and the retentions; Hughs edited the resulting text, using Nicholas Rowe's edition of the complete plays, published in 1709. Pasted on top of the Hughs-Wilks text in Garrick's promptbook are two snippets from another edition of the play, by H. Woodfall, pblished in 1767.

=

Whatever the status of the earliest printed texts of Shakespeare's plays, actors and directors across the past four hundred years have found many reasons for cutting words, lines, speeches, scenes, even entire acts and refashioning the resulting pieces. With respect to productions today, cuts in service of a director's concept may get the most critical attention, but, as Alan Dessen points out in *Rescripting Shakespeare* (1999), cuts are made by and large for practical reasons: reducing the running time, dealing with verbal difficulties by eliminating them, adjusting casting requirements by dropping minor characters or combining several of them into one, and adjusting original stage practices to contemporary playing spaces (Dessen 2002: 3). Historically, other reasons for cutting have included eliminating morally offensive jokes and avoiding political provocations.

Equally important are historical changes with respect to (1) the actor's art, (2) rhetoric and syntax, (3) scenography, and (4) narrative structure. Each of these concerns has received systematic treatment in its own right. Joseph R. Roach's survey of changing ideas about "the science of acting" in *The Player's Passion* (1985) has been extended into the twentieth century, with specific reference to Shakespeare, in Sharon Carnicke's chapter on "Modern and Contemporary Approaches to Acting" (2016). Changing fashions in rhetoric and syntax are the subject of Russ McDonald's *Shakespeare and the Arts of Language* (2001) and A. C. Partridge's *Tudor to Augustan English* (1969), Russell Jackson's chapter "Shakespeare Their Contemporary" (2012), and Dirk Delabastita's chapter on "Shakespeare without Sweat" (2016). On scenography, historical changes have been charted by Richard Southern in *Changeable Scenery* (1952) and other books, and for the twentieth century by Christopher Baugh in *Theatre, Performance, and Technology* (2005) and a chapter on "Scenery" with specific reference to Shakespeare (2016). Narrative structure in Shakespeare's scripts has been studied, though without reference to changes across the plays' production history, by Emrys Jones in *Scenic Form in Shakespeare* (1971) and James E. Hirsh in *The Structure of Shakespearean Scenes* (1981).

It remains for us here to consider how these changes are realized in cutwork. As we shall discover, none of the four changes—the actor's art, rhetoric and syntax, scenography, narrative structure—alone explains why certain cuts were made in a given production. Rather, all four changes tend to work together. *Hamlet* offers a convenient reference point, and not only because Hamlet himself carries out cutwork within the fiction: the three early printed versions of the script involve different forms of cutwork, the play's production history is unusually well documented (with entire books on the subject by Anthony B. Dawson and Robert Hapgood), and the climactic scene features cuts in several of the senses that we catalogued in Chapter 1,

including an *aposiopesis* in the incomplete pentameter of Hamlet's last
line in the folio text:

    O, o, o, o!   *He dies* (5.2.311).

In setting up this final line with "The rest is silence" (5.2.310), Hamlet
(via Shakespeare) is perhaps quoting Henry Peacham's *The Art of
English Poesy* (1589). *Aposiopesis* is Englished by Peacham as "the figure
of silence, or of interruption" (Puttenham 2002: 250).

A *fourth* version of Hamlet, in terms of production history at least, is
recognized by Hapgood (in Shakespeare 1999) in the "players' quarto"
of 1676. That edition, as Hapgood demonstrates, has proved to be just
as important as the other three early printings. Cued by inverted
commas in the 1676 quarto, later redactors have held their pens at
the ready to mark cuts that are still being excised in productions today:
lines from Horatio's speeches and Marcellus's in 1.1, Claudius's public
declarations in 1.2 and elsewhere, Laertes' exchanges with Ophelia in
1.3 and Polonius's with Laertes (including "And these few precepts in
thy memory/ See thou character" [1.3.58–59]), the traveling players'
remembered excerpt from "Aeneas and Dido" in 2.2, Hamlet's advice
to the players in 3.2, the performance of "The Murder of Gonzago"
later in the scene, Hamlet's harangue of Gertrude after the Ghost's
appearance in 3.4, the mad Ophelia's excursions into bawdy in 4.5,
and speeches by and about Fortinbras throughout the latter part of the
play. Left out entirely in the 1676 quarto, and still being left out of
some productions today, are Polonius's dialogue with Reynaldo in 2.1
and the reports by the ambassadors from Norway in 2.2. In many
productions, particularly in the nineteenth century, Fortinbras was cut
out of the script entirely. In aesthetic terms, re-modelings in the 1676
quarto and its successors have served to bring out Hamlet's prominence, to distance characters such as Claudius and Polonius, and to
distance even more Fortinbras and the political framework his cam-
paign provides for Hamlet's story.

=

From oratory in the seventeenth century to "nature mechanized" in
the eighteenth to Romantic organicism in the nineteenth to method
acting in the twentieth: the changes in acting styles that Roach and
Carnicke have mapped are accompanied by changes in cutwork.

Oratory was the earliest determiner of cuts. *Hamlet* is one of the first Shakespeare plays Samuel Pepys records seeing when London's theaters reopened in 1660, and cuts are already in evidence. "To the Opera," Pepys records for August 24, 1661, "and there saw *Hamlet, Prince of Denmark*, done with scenes very well, but above all, Betterton did the Prince's parts beyond imagination" (Salgādo 1975: 49). There are two crucial plurals in this simple statement: "scenes" and "parts." We shall consider "scenes" later. With the phrase "the Prince's parts"—*parts* in the plural—Pepys is implying that he experienced Thomas Betterton's performance of the title role as a series of pieces or cuts. Did Pepys know about the physical documents, the "parts" or "sides," that actors used to learn their roles? Or was he listening and looking for the play's big moments? Or both?

Whatever the answer, the effect Pepys describes would have been enhanced by cutwork in the script that the Duke's Company, headed up by William Davenant, likely used on this occasion. In their production histories of *Hamlet* both Dawson (1995: 23) and Hapgood (Shakespeare 1999: 11) assume that the script was a version of the text published fifteen years later as *The Tragedy of Hamlet, Prince of Denmark as it is now Acted at His Highness the Duke of York's Theatre*, with Betterton's name opposite Hamlet's among "the persons represented" (Shakespeare 1676: sig. A2v). As we noted in Chapter 1, the preface to this edition alerts readers that "such places as might be least prejudicial to the plot or sense, are left out upon the stage" (sig. A2) and are indicated by inverted commas down the left margin. (See Figure 7A.) By Dawson's count, more than eight hundred lines out of 3,800 are so marked—nearly a quarter of the total (Dawson 1995: 23).

In some respects at least, Betterton's acting of the cut-up text may have replicated Richard Burbage's performances from sixty years earlier. Davenant claimed that Betterton had learned the role of Hamlet from Joseph Taylor, who had learned it from Shakespeare himself. As John Downes tells the story, albeit half a century later, "*Hamlet* being performed by Mr. Betterton, Sir William (having seen Mr. Taylor of the Blackfriars company act it, who being instructed by the author Mr. Shakespeare) taught Mr. Betterton in every particle of it" (Downes 1708: sig. C3). Every "particle." That term could, of course, refer to inflections, volume changes, movements, and gestures, but it may also be a synonym for Pepys's term "parts," indicating that even Richard Burbage's original performance moved from big moment to big moment, from major speech to major speech, from "part" to "part," from cut to cut. The "players's quarto" of 1676 suggests as much. With respect to excisions, what turns out to be least prejudicial to the plot or sense are the speeches and scenes that detract from Hamlet's "parts." Even though the 1676 "players' quarto" is based on a 1637 reprint of the 1604 quarto, it incorporates excisions from the folio text, including, curiously it would seem, Hamlet's final soliloquy, "How all occasions do inform against me" (J.23ff in the Oxford text). As later actors and directors have discovered, that particular cut has the effect of enhancing Hamlet's final "part" as a man of action once he has returned from England.

Eighteenth-century changes in the actor's art inform the cuts that David Garrick customarily took during his long experience with the role from 1742 to 1776, an astonishing thirty-four years. Annotations supplied by Francis Gentleman to *Bell's Edition of Shakespeare's Plays: As they are now Performed at the Theatres Royal in London: Regulated from the Prompt Books of Each House* (1774), in which Garrick's later productions are noticed, suggest that the idea of a speech as a "part," as a free-standing oration, persisted into the eighteenth century, despite the emphasis on the speaker's "naturalness." Gentleman lauds "To be or not to be" as a model for orators: "There never was so much philo-sophical reasoning expressed so nervously, in so narrow a compass, by any author, as in this excellent, nay we may say unparalleled soliloquy, which gives a good orator great latitude for the exertion of his abilities" (Shakespeare 1774: 3:176). More idiosyncratically, cuts in Garrick's acting facilitated his celebrated ability to make sudden transitions, in particular his alacrity in moving from "analogic flow," in Roach's coinage, to moments of stasis (1985: 73–5). Figure 9 shows Garrick in four static postures, each distinctive to one of the Shakespearean protagonists Garrick played throughout his career. Eighteenth-century aesthetics knew these postures as "attitudes," "points," or "starts." The four "attitudes" shown in Figure 9 would have been immediately recognizable by Garrick's contemporaries, as we know from the ubi-quity of the postures in paintings and engravings of Garrick's perform-ances. We shall examine these "character-cuts" in Chapter 4.

To "point" a speech an actor would step out of the fiction and direct the speech straight to the audience, often going downstage to do

Figure 9. "Mr. Garrick in Four of His Principal Tragic Characters," anonymous engraving (1750–70), copy originally owned by Charles Burney. © Trustees of the British Museum.

so (Worthen 1984: 62–3). The *OED* does not recognize this particular meaning of "point," but it seems related to both rhetoric (*OED*, "point, *v.*[1]," IV.17, "to give force, sharpness, or sting to; to lend prominence, distinction, or poignancy to," noted as *now rare*) and punctuation (II.6.a). Perhaps it also refers to gesturing with hand and finger (III.8.b), as readers of printed texts often did with the marginal notation known as a "manicule" (Sherman 2008). The theatrical term "starts" suggests pointing, but with an element of surprise or shock added to suspended time (*OED*, "start, *n.*," 3.a). Georg Christoph Lichtenberg, who saw Garrick in action as Hamlet—or, rather, in *in*action—provides a firsthand description of this effect. According to Lichtenberg, at the appearance of the Ghost in 1.1, Garrick

> stands rooted to the spot, with legs apart, but no loss of dignity, supported by his friends…His whole demeanor is so expressive of terror that it made my flesh creep even before he began to speak…At last he speaks, not at the beginning, but at the end of a breath, with a trembling voice (qtd. in Burnim 1961: 160).

So long did Garrick hold the attitude that some witnesses of his earliest performances in the role, before this attitude became a trademark, wondered whether Garrick was in need of a cue from the prompter (Burnim 1961: 160).

In the organic Romantic acting of the early nineteenth century Betterton's and Garrick's noble prince became a poet who brought to the stage "the spontaneous overflow of powerful feelings" that William Wordsworth in the Preface to *Lyrical Ballads* (1800) takes to be the mark of "all good poetry" (¶6). Garrick's carefully paused "starts" became Edmund Kean's emotionally charged "stops." Stops, like starts, are a form of cutting. In general, audiences were swept away by Kean's innovations, but the reviewer of a London performance of *Hamlet* in 1814 protested not only Kean's emotional excesses but his cuts, in multiple senses of the word. Most reprehensible in the reviewer's ears were Kean's cuts to famous speeches, including the penultimate line of "O, what a rogue and peasant slave am I" (2.2.552ff). Kean apparently omitted "I'll have grounds/ More relative than this" (2.2.605–6) and cut straight to "The play's the thing/ Wherein I'll catch the conscience of the King" (2.2.606–7). A small thing, one might think. But to the reviewer Kean's cuts were acts of vandalism: "This, in the saucy jargon of the day, may be called "a new reading," but as it is a proceeding that is deeply injurious to common sense, we must enter our protest against such destructive novelties" (Salgãdo 1975: 243–4). Whether or not the reviewer was aware of the customary cuts—*different* cuts, to be sure, but cuts nonetheless—in earlier London productions of *Hamlet* is not clear. The reviewer seems to be judging Kean's performance against the printed text.

Edmund Kean's cuts in aural technique extended to the volume, pitch, and speed of his declamation. The 1814 reviewer takes these eccentricities to be symptomatic of a new style of acting that should be stopped in its tracks:

> He appeared to us to labor more sedulously to be singular in his manner, than just, which is a scenic vice that is gaining ground too rapidly. Many of his speeches are marred by a drawling sententiousness that fatigued the ear, and some of his words were too powerfully accented.... In pronouncing the word *contumely*, in the celebrated soliloquy, he chose to divide it into four distinct syllables, that seemed to hop after each other like limping relatives; as thus: – Con-*tu*-me-ly! This was another effort of new reading, and certainly did not pass off without exciting a burst of "bravos" from many of the auditors, who appeared to be loud in their acclamations, in proportion as he departed from the prescribed institutes of speech! (Salgãdo 1975: 245–6).

Another side of organic Romantic acting—a side that audiences and hostile reviewers alike did not see—was the introspection that went into the preparation of parts. Charles Macready, famous in Shakespeare production history for having brought to the stage for the first time in 175 years a version of *King Lear* without Nahum Tate's happy ending, lets us see this preparation technique in his diary for the years 1833–51. Cuts are central to the enterprise. Notations of incidents from Macready's private and social life are intercut in the diary with reflections on the roles he is preparing and attempting to perfect. The entry for April 22, 1835 is typical in recording the sleep, the withdrawal from the waking world, that Macready customarily brought to his preparation: "With an earnest desire of acting Hamlet well, lay down on the bed after dinner striving to keep it in my mind" (1.225). Macready's diary entries about his preparation of the role of Lear are even more specific about the importance of reflection, sleep, and, in some cases, dreams. Cuts between sleeping/dreaming and waking/ acting represent, in my view, something new in nineteenth-century acting.

Cuts in a more conventional sense figure in Macready's account of his performance of Hamlet. "Ernest" and "earnestness" are repeated words in the diary entry for April 22, as Macready reflects on a performance that evening (in Norwich) that was less than satisfactory to him. He thinks back over the performance scene by scene. In 1.2 he felt himself to be better than usual, "more direct, and with more meaning and true feeling" (Macready 1912: 1.225). "The scene with Horatio etc." (presumably 1.1) "still requires study and earnestness" (1.225), as does Act V. "Earnestness" I take to be emotional directness. Other scenes (the interview with the Ghost, the exchanges with the players) will require not only further study but "rearrangement" (1:225); the closet scene, "a little revision and correcting" (1:226). A reference elsewhere in his diary (1:370) aligns rearranging with cutting, which suggests that excising lines and moving them around were part of Macready's "study" and that they were enacted to achieve "earnestness." Material evidence of Macready's Hamlet is considered at some length by Hapgood in Shakespeare 1999: 26–30.

In nineteenth-century acting, cuts to the script in the form of pauses helped heighten the illusion that one was witnessing a spontaneous confession of feeling and not, as with Betterton, an artfully calculated oration. The effect was carried even further at the end of the nineteenth century by Henry Irving in his celebrated Shakespeare performances at the Lyceum Theatre. Cuts in unexpected places were central to Irving's technique. Of Irving's Hamlet in 1880 Henry James complains:

> The great trouble with the Hamlet was that it was inordinately slow—
> and this, indeed, is the fault throughout of Mr. Irving, who places
> minutes between his words, and strange strides and balancings between
> his movements. Heat, rapidity, passion, magic—these qualities are the
> absent ones, and a good general description of him is to say that he is
> picturesque but diffuse (James 1948: 140).

For us, in hindsight, the most important cut in acting styles occurred at the very end of the nineteenth century and in the early years of the twentieth. George Bernard Shaw, reviewing Johnston Forbes Robertson's performance in the role of Hamlet at the Lyceum Theatre in 1897 (Irving was out of town), recognized the shift that was happening. Forbes Robertson's style, Shaw declares, is "classical," Irving's "romantic." "What I mean by classical," Shaw writes,

> is that he can present a dramatic hero as a man whose passions are those which have produced the philosophy, the poetry, the art, and the statecraft of the world, and not merely those which have produced its weddings, coroner's inquests, and executions. And that is just the sort of actor Hamlet requires (Salgādo 1975: 255).

Forbes Robertson (whose delivery was reportedly soft and even) represented a character with integrity, in the literal sense of that word as "wholeness." Irving—"instinctive, imaginative, romantic"—moved from big moment to big moment: "You will see him weeping bucketsful of tears over Ophelia, and treating the players, the gravedigger, Horatio, Rosencrantz and Guildenstern as if they were mutes at his own funeral" (255). With respect to cuts as excisions, Forbes Robertson's classical acting involved restoration of lines, speeches, scenes, and characters that had been cut in earlier productions. Shaw expresses astonishment at seeing Reynaldo, Voltimand, and Cornelius on stage. "Just as the time for their scene arrived, my eye fell on the word 'Fortinbras' in the programme, which so amazed me that I hardly know [*sic*] what I saw for the next ten minutes" (254).

More decisive still was the production of *Hamlet* that Konstantin Stanislavsky and Leopold Sulerzhitsky directed at the Moscow Arts Theatre in 1912. Gordon Craig was brought in as scenic designer and proposed an abstract concept (to be discussed below) that was only partly realized in the production. Stanislavsky's "System" in its earliest iteration (there were, as Carnicke [2016] points out, later revisions through the 1930s) required actors to achieve the same kind of through-conceived quality—"flow," perhaps—that Shaw admired in Forbes Robertson's Hamlet. Paradoxically, that flow was achieved through cutwork. In a letter to the famous actress Olga Knipper two years before *Hamlet* was at last realized on stage, Stanislavsky expresses delight that she may be interested in joining the production. Craig wanted her to play Gertrude. To judge from Stanislavsky's letter, Knipper has heard about his new System and wants to know more:

> You want to work on the costumes—I would be pleased.
> You want to know about psychology and circles?..
> In short, choose what's on your mind.
> If you want to work—believe me, I'll do everything in my power (qtd. in Senelick 2014: 280).

Ultimately, Knipper did not participate in MAT's *Hamlet*.

In his System, Stanislavsky was bringing together elements of yoga, eurhythmics, and experimental psychology (Carnicke 2016: 2:1437). The "circles" mentioned in the letter to Knipper are "circles of attention" from yoga, meditative practices that encourage concentration. Rhythmic bodily exercises were carried out to help the actors feel Shakespeare's verse. "Psychology" in the letter to Knipper refers to Stanislavsky's practice of working with the actors, scene by scene, to determine their "inner desires" in that scene. In effect, scenes become the major cuts, just as speeches had been for romantic actors. Stanislavsky would further cut each scene into sections and direct the actors to determine their inner desires in that section and mark the script with what they had discovered (Senelick 1982: 132). In these marks we can observe yet a third set of cuts in the System: a psychological equivalent of the commonplaces that Comenius instructed his seventeenth-century students to find in books and indicate with pen-and-ink. (See Chapter 1 and Figure 4.) "Then we marked the 1st scene in *Hamlet* (2nd part)," Stanislavsky writes in a letter,

> and the actors even performed it while I was there. Of course, it was all shallow, but the important thing is that they all suddenly came to life. Moreover, all of them suddenly, according to the tasks I had assigned, performed various external images. The Hamletics seemed to be convinced by the system (Senelick 2014: 304).

The section of 1.1 that Stanislavsky refers to here is presumably the Ghost's first appearance (1.1.38ff).

Romantic acting, with its different agenda for making cuts, continued from the nineteenth century well into the twentieth. Stanislavsky saw John Barrymore play Hamlet in New York 1923 and pronounced him "far from ideal, but very charming" (Senelick

2014: 417). It was, however, Stanislavsky's System and its development in various strands of The Method, inspired by the Moscow Art Theatre's tours in American in 1923–4, that ultimately made romantic acting seem shallow and old-fashioned. The cut between interior and exterior experience that we saw developing in Macready reached its apogee in Method acting, which encouraged actors to find in themselves parallel experiences to those they were being asked to portray.

The style that resulted often involved significant pauses, cuts in continuity, that gave new meaning to Hamlet's declaration "But I have that within which passeth show" (1.2.85). A line that might earlier have meant "My feelings of mourning are deeper than my 'inky cloak'" (1.2.77) or even "I know who murdered my father" or "I have a plan for revenge" become in the System and in Method acting a gesture toward an interiority that cannot be fully articulated, an interiority that finds its expression in pauses, in palpable cuts between inner and outer. Stanislavsky commends the "external images" that his *Hamlet* actors were able to project. The resulting style—plain, sometimes halting, punctuated by inarticulate moments—was well suited to film but was difficult to reconcile with the prolixities of Shakespeare. Marlon Brando, trained as a Method actor, is reported to have said that "the most daunting aspect in playing Shakespeare was relying on the written text," because he had learned in Method acting to speak "in pauses, in gestures, in grunts and mumbles, even in silence" (Claudia Roth Pierpont, qtd. in Carnicke 2016: 2:1440).

The house style of the Royal Shakespeare Company, developed during the 1960s under voice coach Cicely Berry and directors Peter Hall, Trevor Nunn, and Terry Hands and later exported to the National Theatre, combines Stanislavsky's sense of the script as a musical score (including eurhythmics as training in speaking verse) with the Method's insistence on an inner search. The question is: where do the cuts in the text and the cuts in delivery occur? Different directors and different actors working in the RSC tradition have provided different answers. A pronouncement Hall made in 1958 has guided his work as a director into the twenty-first century: "A Shakespeare play like an operatic score gives one the end product, a complex image." Hall acknowledges the interiority in modern acting, but he insists that actors begin with the language on the page: "You must work from that back to the actor and from that the actor finds the realistic human motives which make him able to sing or say the poetic impression" (qtd. in Cole and Chinoy 1976: 424). For Hall, regarding Shakespeare's scripts as musical scores has meant pausing slightly at the end of each line of verse (Hall 2003). In this practice we observe, not for the last time in *Shakespeare|Cut*, how an internal cut can paradoxically enhance the sense of flow. Trevor Nunn has taken a different tactic: "When you approach the text of *Hamlet*, the cutting virtually is the production," Nunn told Ralph Berry in an interview in the 1970s. "What you decide to leave in is your version of the play" (qtd. in Berry 1977: 71).

=

Cutwork has been guided by yet another set of changes. Rhetoric and syntax—from *copia* and periodic syntax in Shakespeare's own time to polished elegance in Restoration drama to the chiastic structures favored in the later seventeenth and eighteenth centuries to the paratactic plainness we find most comfortable today—dictate different kinds of cuts at different times in the history of Shakespeare production.

In 2015 the Oregon Shakespeare Festival announced that it had commissioned thirty-six playwrights to "translate" Shakespeare's plays into the idiom of twenty-first-century English in a multi-year project called "Play on!" No cutting of scenes would be allowed, but words and phrases would be cut and replaced with more readily understandable equivalents. "It is…worth noting," the OSF's website explained in making the announcement,

> that most theaters already make textual choices when they produce Shakespeare; for instance, productions often reconcile quarto and folio manuscripts, trim lengthy plays or rearrange tricky ones, and replace words that have become antiquated past comprehension. In fact, we believe that every age, while hewing close to Shakespeare's original texts on one path, creates a parallel path of experimentation, exploration, and changing the language (Oregon Shakespeare Festival 2015).

The fact that such practices had been going on for four centuries—though seldom declared so boldly and seldom on this scale—was recognized by Daniel Pollack-Pelzner writing in *The New Yorker*. If there is a radical cut in OSF's "Cut on!," it consists in pursuing to its logical conclusion cutwork with rhetoric and syntax that started in the late seventeenth century.

With *Hamlet* we can witness cutting and rearrangement in the service of rhetorical style as early as the "players' quarto" of 1676. What comes as a surprise are the considerable cuts and rearrangements made in Hamlet's own parts, particularly in his soliloquies. Only "To be or not to be" (3.1.58ff) is retained intact. One explanation for these changes to what for us are sacrosanct speeches has to do with changing notions of rhetoric and syntax. Take, for example, Hamlet's first soliloquy, "O that this too too solid flesh would melt" (1.2.129ff). For us, the tortured syntax, the stops and starts, of Hamlet's sentences are evidence of a hyperactive, distracted mind. For Pepys and Pope, the syntax was an embarrassment. It needed to be changed. And so it was in the 1676 quarto. The speech is trimmed into something more compact and deliberate than audiences today are used to hearing. A third of the soliloquy's thirty-one lines go missing altogether.

In the excisions (marked with inverted commas in most instances but not all) and the relineations of the 1676 version we have an unusually clear example of how changing models of style and syntax can govern the new-fashioning of Shakespeare's scripts. In Hamlet's soliloquies people like Pepys wanted to hear finished, elegantly framed verses, not the syntactical confusions and rushes from one thought to another. Chiastic syntax is what Pepys and his contemporaries sought, and the revisers of *Hamlet* have given them that, even pointing up the isocolon between "So excellent a King" and "So loving to my mother" by separating them into two short lines. Unmarked in the printed text is an elision of the phrase "that was to this/ Hyperion to a satyr" (1.2.139–40) that spoils the effect in the second quarto and folio printings. Also gone without a trace are colloquial interjections such as the "O God! O God" (1.2.132) before "How weary"; the "Fie on't, ah fie, fie!" (1.2.135) before "'Tis an unweeded garden"; the "Heaven and earth,/ Must I remember?" (1.2.142–3) and the "Why…" (1.2.143) before "She would hang on him"; and the emphatically repeated "even she" (1.2.149) before "Heaven? a beast that wants discourse of reason." For Restoration taste, what Hamlet needed was lines written by John Dryden. With *The Enchanted Island* (1667) and *All for Love* (1678), actors like Betterton—and auditors like Pepys—got their wish.

Alexander Pope's lack of interest in Hamlet's soliloquies, noted in Chapter 1, begins in this context to make more sense. In his edition of Shakespeare's plays (1725) Pope included "soliloquies" as a heading in his index of "Speeches. The most considerable in Shakespeare," but he did not single out any of Hamlet's soliloquies in the main text with inverted commas—a mark that Pope reserved for especially remarkable speeches. The honor of inverted commas was, however, bestowed on Polonius's "And these few precepts in thy memory/ See thou character" (1.3.58ff), despite the speech's omission on the Restoration stage and possibly in Pope's time as well.

In the nineteenth century spontaneity and "earnestness," as we have observed already, produced the cuts in diction and syntax in Edmund Kean's performance that so infuriated the reviewer. His son Charles' performance in the role, first at Drury Lane in 1838 and afterward at the Princess's Theatre, continued the father's practice of cutting up the text in his delivery. John Forster, reviewing the Drury Lane performance, opines,

> It is not difficult to trace to their source the majority of Mr. Kean's mistakes in this arduous performance. It will be found, we think, that his chief power with an audience lies in effect of emotion and of sudden gusts of passion, and his own consciousness of this is betrayed in a habit of emphasizing his level passages too much, of throwing them into startling contrast by long pauses, and of laying forceful and pathetic stress on lines that need no such aid (qtd. in hamlet-shakespeare.com).

The American actor James Henry Hackett—a much applauded Falstaff—agreed: "Charles Kean's Hamlet discovers various proofs of a defective ear, by sundry false emphases, bad cadences and misplaced pauses" (qtd. hamlet-shakespeare.com).

Cuts in the service of changing norms of rhetoric and syntax continued in the twentieth century. The ideal of "natural speech," first realized in the theater by Ibsen and Chekhov, favored parataxis and simplicity of diction—the very opposites of the periodic syntax and inventive diction of Shakespeare. Polonius's response to "The rugged Pyrhhus" speech, not even half way through, says it all: "This is too long" (2.2.501). A variety of ways of meeting these challenges has been tried. In its ambition to translate Shakespeare's texts into the idiom of contemporary English the Oregon Shakespeare Festival's

"Play on!" project merely represents an extreme. The festival's public statement about the project is true: cutting words and phrases, replacing them with others, cutting to make texts clearer has been going on since 1676, if not before. Most Shakespeare productions in the twentieth century have simply been more discreet about making cuts: substituting a modern word where the original would be obscure to contemporary listeners, excising "difficult" passages altogether, allowing one metaphor in a speech to stand in for the string of metaphors that often follows in the original text. The founders of the Folger Shakespeare Library, Henry Clay Folger and Emily Jordan Folger, were especially hostile to cuts in performances. "Cut! Cut! Cut!" Emily would write in the journal she kept (Grant 2014: 34). By this criterion, the Folgers must have approved very few performances of the texts they so assiduously collected.

=

Among the reasons for making cuts to Shakespeare from the seventeenth century through the late nineteenth, scenography may be the most obvious. When Pepys notes in his diary for August 24, 1661 that he "saw *Hamlet, Prince of Denmark*, done with scenes very well," he is referring to the movable illusionistic scenery, a true novelty in England in 1661 (Shakespeare 1999: 11). Each scene would have figured as a visual cut, particularly if the set involved "shutters" that could be pulled aside to reveal a new painted scene beyond.

Scenery for Shakespeare productions was never more elaborate than in the nineteenth century, when a passion for historical accuracy and big effects produced ever more elaborate productions. In the preface to the printed edition of *Hamlet, Prince of Denmark Arranged for Representation at the Royal Princess's Theatre…as Performed on Monday, January 10, 1859*, Kean calls particular attention to the costume he wore. The fact that Hamlet is a Christian and England a tribute-state to Denmark means the fictional time must be sometime in the 900s or 1000s. Therefore,

> the costume of the tenth and eleventh centuries may be selected for the purpose. There are but few authentic records in existence, but these few afford reason to believe that very slight difference existed between the dress of the Dane and that of the Anglo-Saxon of the same period (Shakespeare 1859: n.p.).

Figure 10A. W. Kohler, "Charles Kean in the Character of Hamlet," mezzotint (1838). By permission of the Folger Shakespeare Library.

Figure 10B. Design for Act 1, Scenes 1 and 4, for Charles Kean's *Hamlet* (1859). By permission of the Folger Shakespeare Library.

Figure 10A shows Kean in this supposedly historically accurate garb. He had been wearing something like it since 1838, becoming the first Hamlet to wear a period costume (Shakespeare 1999: 109). The no less historically accurate scenery amid which Kean spoke his strangely paused lines can be sampled in Figure 10B. Kean's posture in the left-hand image suggests that he has just encountered the Ghost in 1.4: with upraised hands he reprises one of Garrick's famous "starts" from nearly a hundred years before. The scenery, despite its archeological correctness, is very much of Kean's mid-nineteenth-century moment.

Truncations of speeches, the excision of Reynaldo and Fortinbras, and, above all, the discreet cuts in all of Hamlet's soliloquies except "To be or not to be" likewise hark back to Garrick's time, indeed Betterton's. "O that this too too solid flesh would melt" (1.2.129ff) is trimmed of many of its exclamations and false starts and is supplied with much more logical punctuation. With Kean, as with Betterton and Garrick, the end of the soliloquy loses many of the cuts in syntax that make the original seem improvised and overpowering. The new cuts, signaled more often by /:/ and /;/ than by / – /, were calculated to allow Kean to make his own rhetorical stops and emphases within syntax that was more regular than Shakespeare's original. More important than these changes in cuts to rhetoric and syntax, in logistical terms at least, were the cuts between scenes necessary to accommodate the scenery within which Kean spoke and moved.

Compared with *The Merchant of Venice*, with its shifts in fictional location from Venice to Belmont and back to Venice and then back to Belmont, *Hamlet* is a tractable script. Many nineteenth-century producers of *Merchant* solved the problem by eliminating Act 5 entirely. Squire and Marie Bancroft in their production of 1875 set a precedent of consolidating the scenes in Venice and in Belmont (Shakespeare 2002: 20) so as to reduce the number of set changes. To judge from watercolor designs for Kean's *Hamlet* now in the Folger Library, the producers chose to emphasize a few grand scenes, each with its distinctive set. The first is "Elsinore. A platform before the Castle. Night" for what Kean's published text marks as 1.1 and 1.4 (the battlement scenes). (See Figure 10B.) The second is "A room of state in the palace" for 1.2 (the first court scene); "A room in the castle" for 2.2 (Claudius's first consultation with Rosencrantz and

Guildenstern, Hamlet's taunting Polonius, the arrival of the players); "A room in the castle" for 3.1 (Claudius's second consultation with Rosencrantz and Guildenstern, Ophelia set as decoy, "To be or not to be"); "A room in the castle" for 4.1 (a much cut version of the rapid events that the Oxford text marks as 4.1 through 4.7); and "A room in the castle" for 5.3 (the sword fight scene). The third grand scene is "The Queen's chamber" for 3.3.

The status of the other drawings in the Folger collection is less clear. Were they realized as three-dimensional sets, or as painted drops? In at least two cases they must have been drops. That must certainly have been the case with "A more remote part of the platform" for 1.5, whither Hamlet follows the Ghost, without a pause, from 1.4. The drawing for 1.5 in the Folger shows the same view as in Figure 10B, but from a notional vantage point several hundred feet to the left. After the play-within-the-play in "A room in the castle" in 3.1 the scene shifts to "Another room in the same" in 3.2. The short dialogue between Claudius and Polonius in this scene almost certainly takes place in front of a painted drop, allowing time for the set behind to be shifted to "The Queen's chamber" in 3.3. About the remaining scenes—"A room in Polonius's house" for 1.3 and 2.1 and "A church-yard" in 5.1—the situation is less clear. In more than a few cases the concentration on a few massive scenes was facilitated by excising lines and speeches and cutting entire scenes in Shakespeare's original. The seven scenes in the Oxford text's Act 4, for example, are amalgamated into just one scene in "A room in the castle." Fortinbras's entry in 4.4 is eliminated, as is Horatio's dialogue with a servant and a sailor in 4.6, not to mention large swaths of text in the remaining scenes. In sum, the cuts in Charles Kean's *Hamlet* take three forms: excisions to the text in the interest of brevity, alterations in rhetoric to heighten Kean's romantic acting style, and cuts to facilitate scene changes.

By the beginning of the twentieth century William Poel and the various acting companies he founded (the Elizabethan Stage Society is the most famous) had demonstrated how much smoother it was to perform Shakespeare's scripts with no illusionistic scenery at all. That tradition continues today in theaters-in-the-round and black boxes all over the world. A different but equally influential example was set by Gordon Craig's designs for Stanislavsky's production of *Hamlet* with the Moscow Arts Theatre in 1912. Drawings and a three-dimensional model for Craig's single abstract set, a piece of sculpted cutwork with interior and exterior spaces, survive in the Victoria and Albert Museum (see accession numbers E.3275-1922 and E.146-1922 at http://collections.vam.ac.uk/). As with Stanislavsky's concept for the acting, Craig's scenography was designed to externalize internal experience, to treat the theatrical space as a psychological space and not a fictional location. If Craig himself had been directing the production, that idea would have extended to all the characters except Hamlet. "Craig is staging *Hamlet* as a monodrama," Stanislavsky writes in a letter dated 1909, when work on the production was just beginning:

> He regards everything through the eyes of Hamlet. Hamlet is the ghost; everything else around him is crude matter.... The whole court and its pomp are imagined by Hamlet in the guise of monstrous gold courtiers. In the course of his musing he hears trumpets, the sound of bells (Senelick 2014: 259).

Craig's original concepts, for the scenery and for the monodrama, were not realized, but movable screens in the 1912 production established a model for fluid, non-realistic staging that continues to dominate stage productions of Shakespeare's plays today. Cuts between scenes, in this concept, are de-emphasized.

=

It is one thing to cut out scenes and rearrange the remainder to make smooth cuts from one illusionistic set to another; it is another thing again to cut and rearrange to accommodate new expectations about narrative structure. In a general way, changes in narrative structure can be correlated with changes in syntactic structure. The periodic syntax of Shakespeare's sentences is reflected in the "periodic" layout of his plots. There may be a progression toward moments of climax or stasis, but scene follows scene like the clauses in a complex sentence. A sequent scene often qualifies, amplifies, or restates in different terms what has come before. Beginning in the late seventeenth century, the rationale for narrative structure, like tastes in rhetoric and syntactic structure, changed. A new desire for linearity and symmetry made periodic narrative structure as well as periodic syntax seem inelegant. In the nineteenth century a looser, more organic style in syntactic structure—the pauses and unexpected emphases of Kean, Irving, and others are signs of that change—was also realized in narrative cuts that removed interruptions, dilations, and diversions in favor of fewer but emotionally powerful scenes. The twentieth and early twenty-first centuries have witnessed two conflicting trends: on the one hand, a return to original staging practices and the earliest scripts, beginning with Poel's productions (he directed *Hamlet* three times between 1881 and 1914), and, on the other, a fascination with cuts and cutting in Modernist and Post-modernist aesthetics. We shall investigate the latter phenomenon in Chapter 5.

We can observe the chronological changes in narrative structure by considering some examples from *Hamlet*. The sequence of scenes marked 2.2. 3.1., 3.2., and 3.3 in the Oxford text (which follows the folio version of the script) does have a linear logic: from Hamlet's inner anguish over Claudius's guilt in 2.2 to public exposure of Claudius's guilt in 3.2. Along the way, however, that progression is qualified, amplified, and held back by the entrance of the players in 2.2, which is followed by the spying and posturing in 3.1, climaxing in "To be or not to be," which is followed in turn by Claudius's aborted confession in 3.3 (visually observed by Hamlet but perhaps not over-heard by him), which is followed finally by the play-within-the-play in 3.3. The move from inner knowledge to external proof is structured like a periodic sentence, with intervening clauses. Another example comes after the stage direction "*Enter Fortinbras with an army over the stage*" (4.4. *sd* in both the 1604 quarto and the folio texts). In the 1604 quarto this scene is actually observed by Hamlet, prompting his soliloquy "How all occasions do inform against me" (Additional Passage J 4.4.23ff in the Oxford text). The folio text preserves For-tinbras's passage over the stage, but cuts Hamlet's direct observation of the scene as well as the soliloquy the sight inspires.

The 1676 "player's quarto" of *Hamlet*—the one likely used by Betterton—in general follows the 1604 quarto, but the brief entry of Fortinbras and his army in 4.4 is cut, as well as Hamlet's soliloquy "How all occasions do inform against me." In these cuts the 1676 quarto anticipates most acting texts of *Hamlet* from Betterton through the nineteenth century and indeed into our own day. Garrick was quite unusual in retaining it for his 1772–3 production. John Caird, who directed a production at the National Theatre in 2000, with

Simon Russell Beale in the title role, said in an interview for the RSC edition of *Hamlet* that he regards the play as "at heart a domestic and philosophical drama, not a history play," a concept in which Fortinbras has no place. Caird even wonders if "the political scenes" might be later additions to the script (Shakespeare 2008: 211). In the 1676 quarto Fortinbras does in fact make a speaking appearance in the play's last lines, but most productions of the eighteenth and nineteenth centuries end with "The rest is silence" (5.2.310) or perhaps some brief words from Horatio.

Cutting out Fortinbras's entry and Hamlet's soliloquy in 4.4 helps to remedy what Francis Gentleman, annotator of Bell's edition (1774), judges to be a miscalculation on Shakespeare's part: "The fourth act is much more languid than any other, in the piece; Hamlet has too little, the King and Laertes too much, to say" (Shakespeare 1774: 3:207). The omission of Fortinbras's entry and Hamlet's soliloquy are pointedly commended by Gentleman:

> The author has here introduced a very unessential scene, unworthy of the closet or the stage, therefore properly consigned to oblivion; though *Hamlet*'s soliloquy, in Mr. *Garrick*'s alteration, is preserved not censurably—in the original state of the play, the whole is quite superfluous; beside, the Prince seems to take a violent resolution, yet is no more heard of till we find he has been shipwrecked (3:197).

"Superfluous" to what? To the linearity that Gentleman clearly desires. Combined with cuts to individual speeches and the fortunate absence from the 1604 quarto of the diversionary scene in which Horatio confers with a servant and a sailor (4.6), the excision of Fortinbras and Hamlet's soliloquy turns the "languid," periodic structure of Act 4 into a through-written sentence that begins with Claudius and Gertrude wondering what to do about Hamlet (4.1) and ends with Claudius and Laertes laying plans to kill him (4.7). News of Ophelia's death at the end of 4.7 seals the deal, and closes the sentence. Without his soliloquy, Hamlet remains the direct object of the sentence, not the speaking subject. He reassumes his role as chief speaker in the graveyard scene (5.1) and retains that role until the interrupted sentence of his death.

Charles Kean's production of 1859 cuts Act 4 even more severely in terms of represented events (no Fortinbras, no "How all occasions do inform against me") as well as the lengths of speeches, especially those of Claudius and Laertes. The criterion here seems to have been keeping Hamlet to the fore as much as possible, to keep him at the center of the narrative structure. In this regard we should not discount the influence of nineteenth-century novels. Among the single-hero novels published in 1859 were George Eliot's *Adam Bede* and George Meredith's *The Ordeal of Richard Feverel.* Quite another principle informs the fractured structures of the Wooster Group's *Hamlet* (2005) and Annie Dorsen's *A Piece of Work* (2009), which will be considered in Chapter 5. In terms of structure, both productions demonstrate extreme parataxis, the placing of elements side by side so as to play up discontinuities looms large.

=

If we fasten on Margaret Cavendish's metaphor for play construction and think of *Hamlet* as a costume that has been new-modeled and re-modeled hundreds of times over, we might think of the "inky cloak" of the 1599–1600 production as synecdoche for the cutwork that has kept the play up and moving for four hundred years. In the history of "putting on" *Hamlet,* the ink in Hamlet's cloak has invited actors and directors to use their pens as tailors use scissors, to recut the skein of Shakespeare's fabric, refitting earlier cuttings to the shapes of the times. In Shakespeare's own time black clothing was associated with mourners, blocked lovers, and melancholy men, all of which Hamlet is—or seems to be:

> Seems, madam? Nay, it *is.* I know not 'seems'.
> 'Tis not alone my inky cloak, good mother,
> Nor customary suits of solemn black,
>
> …
> That can denote me truly. These indeed "seem",
> For they are actions that a man might play…(1.2.76–8, 83–4).

Ever an incisor with words, Hamlet himself invites us here to make connections between "seems" and "seams."

3

Cut and Run

Perceptual Cuts in Hearing, Seeing, and Remembering

Nay, if our wits run the wild-goose chase, I am done:
For thou hast more of the wild goose in one of thy wits,
than I am sure I have in my whole five.

> —Mercutio to Romeo, *Romeo and Juliet* 2.3.66–8,
> in *Master William Shakespeare's Comedies,*
> *Histories, and Tragedies* (1623), sig. ff1v

There is a curious thing about running: it seems to be all about speed, but it actually happens in increments. When you run, you feel forward motion, *rapid* forward motion. It took the invention of photography to catch the increments in that seemingly continuous action. The sequential photographs that Eadweard Muybridge made of running men between 1872 and 1885 illustrate this sequential action in stop-time images captured by multiple cameras stationed along the runner's path. (See Figure 11.) The increments seem to disappear when the images are captured by a motion-picture camera—but only when those images succeed one another in the viewer's vision at a speed of at least 24 frames per second (25 in Britain) (Murch 2001: 94). However the eye may perceive it, the running time of a film is in fact a series of cuts. When the subject is running, we have film "footage" in more ways than one. Sixteen-millimeter film works out to 40 frames per foot of film; thirty-five-millimeter film to 32 frames per foot. The pixels in digital video, when the re-*solution* is low, are even more obviously cuts rather than flow.

As Daniel C. Dennett so succinctly puts it, consciousness is *not* a "plenum," a space completely filled with matter. Rather, "consciousness is gappy and sparse, and doesn't contain half of what people think

Figure 11. Eadweard Muybridge, *Animal Locomotion* (1887), vol. 1 plate 68. Muybridge Online Archive.

is there!" (Dennett 1992: 366). All human perceptions are quick oscillations between *this* and *that*. Any sensation, whether it is experienced through sight, hearing, taste, smell, or touch and through a combination of two or more senses, is converted into an electrical current through the firing of a chain of neurons (Horowitz 2012: 94–131). (You can hear what it sounds like at https://www.youtube.com/watch?v=8bxpz-YEuao.) Rapid alternation between neural events, much amplified, presents itself as a crackle.) In this respect, our understanding of sensation and perception differs drastically from that of Shakespeare and his contemporaries. They imagined the body's communication system to be an aerated fluid called *spiritus* (Park 1988: 464–84). In effect, they thought of sensation and perception as fluid states, like the water that Tadder presents as a medium in Figure 1. Truth to tell, that is how most of us *experience* sensations and perceptions when we are not *thinking* about them in a science class or in the pages of a book like this one. Like Shakespeare and his contemporaries, we experience a plenum. But sensation and perception have been demonstrated in scientific observation to operate like the sword that Henry V brandishes in Tadder's image: they happen in a series of cuts, most of them so small we don't notice.

Take vision. If changes in the field of vision occur faster than about fifteen to twenty-five times a second, we can't perceive the changes: we experience them as continuous. That perceptual gap makes it possible for film, television, and digital media to deliver the illusion of a fluid state. Hearing is even more extreme. The hair cells in our ears can detect and transmit vibrations oscillating at up to five thousand times per second. At that rate, we can't even begin to feel the cuts, but they are there, first in the air, then in our nerves (Horowitz 2012: 98). Similar cutwork happens in memory-making: we *re*-member things that have been "*dis*-membered" by time's sword. This chapter is concerned with the cutwork involved in hearing, seeing, and remembering Shakespeare's scripts, with particular attention to the creative work that happens in the cuts.

=

On the page, Shakespeare's scripts are measured in numbers of lines, most of them having, as we say, five "feet"; on the stage, scripts are measured in minutes or hours, in "running time." Feet on the page become sands through the hourglass. In both cases, scripts are said "to run." Benedick in the throes of love recalls Leander, Troilus, and other famous lovers "whose names yet run smoothly in the even road of a blank verse" (*Much Ado about Nothing* 5.2.32–3). John Gower, introducing the last scene of *Pericles*, declares, "Now our sands are almost run;/ More a little, and then dumb" (Sc. 22.1–2). Our own sense of a play having a running time has more to do with reels of film than with hourglasses. It has been possible since the early eighteenth century to speak of a play or a production "running" for so many nights or so many weeks, but "to run" in the sense that a play, a film, or a video lasts a predetermined time is dated by the *OED* no earlier than 1905, and the reference then is to a motion picture (*OED*, "run, *v.*," III.58.a–b). Sands run smoothly through an hourglass, but camera cuts and director's cuts inform statements that a particular stage production of *Much Ado*, say, has a running time of two hours and twenty minutes. That association with cutting is altogether appropriate, since too many lines and too many minutes are prime excuses for cuts to Shakespeare's scripts in contemporary stage performances, films, and videos. If Lukas Erne (2013) is correct, such cuts were standard performance practice even in Shakespeare's time.

Even without cameras, the dynamics of running remain constant. "To go with quick steps on alternate feet" is the most immediate, most physical meaning of the word *run* (*OED*, "run, *v.*," I.1.a). The "alternate" calls attention to the rhythm in that action. The tongue of a loquacious person runs (I.1.b.[b]); thought runs in, into, forward, and back (I.28.a-e); the eye runs along, down, and over (I.35.a–b); speech runs on (II.42.b.[b]); memory runs to or back to (III.55.b); but they all do so in alternations, in a series of cuts, now here, now there. Running is at bottom a matter of alternations, and so is perception. To "discern" something is to distinguish between one thing and another. Seeming continuities in perception turn out to be, on closer inspection, a series of vibrations. Particularly is this case with listening and vision. Cuts as a factor in perception and in the creation of objects for perception invite us to consider the perceptual cuts cued in Shakespeare's scripts and how those cuts have been realized in various media. Let us begin with a search for the shortest cut of all.

=

That shortest cut is a second or a fraction of a second. What happens when lines are converted into running time? At 2,535 lines, *Much Ado about Nothing* is about average among the versions of Shakespeare's scripts printed in the First Folio (Erne 2013: 165). The actual mean is 2,735 lines, but as Erne points out, the comedies run shorter, the history plays and the tragedies longer (166). According to Erne's statistics, the extremes are marked by *Richard III* at 3,570 lines in the folio version and *The Comedy of Errors* at 1,753 lines. The Prologue to *Romeo and Juliet* famously refers to "the two hours' traffic of our stage" (Pro. 12). For the 2,989 lines of *Romeo and Juliet*, that works out to 2.4 seconds per line, not accounting for entrances and exits, stage business, rhetorical pauses, or interruptions by the audience. To get a sense of just how fast that would be, we can compare the 4 to 4.2 seconds per line that recent productions by the Royal Shakespeare Company have averaged, according to Erne (164). You might want to calculate your own pace by timing how many seconds it takes you to declaim aloud the Prologue's first quatrain:

> Two households, both alike in dignity
>   In fair Verona, where we lay our scene,
> From ancient grudge break to new mutiny,
>   Where civil blood makes civil hands unclean
>   (*Romeo and Juliet* Pro. 1–4).

Like me, you are likely to come close to the RSC's 4 to 4.2 seconds per line. Try repeating the exercise at twice the speed and you will discover the near impossibility of two hours' traffic across 2,989 lines. "Traffic" in the sense of "intercourse, communication" (*OED*, "traffic, *n.*," 3. *fig.*, marked "*Now rare*") nicely catches the running action involved in staging a play on the actors' part and taking in a play on the audience's part. One of the ways you can "run," then and now, is with a boat or ship and a sail (*OED*, "run, *v.*," I.19.a), the primary means of marine, intracoastal, and river commerce in early modern England. In running plays the Lord Chamberlain's Men were also, in a commercial sense, trafficking in plays.

Thinking of Shakespeare's language in terms of seconds, not minutes or hours, introduces a factor that has not, to my knowledge, been considered in connection with cuts to Shakespeare's scripts: the timing of human perceptions. Bringing together evidence from neuroscience, psychology, and linguistics, Vyvyan Evans in *The Structure of Time* explores the periodicity in perception (Evans 2005: 3–32). According to the studies that Evans assembles, cognition occurs not in a continuous stream of consciousness, but in a series of "perceptual moments" in which simultaneous input from various areas of the brain converges in "multi-unit bursts" (23). Perceptual moments are in effect "aha!" moments, even if seldom remarked as such by the person who is experiencing them. Each "burst" is separated from other such moments by a gap, "a silent interval" (22). Human perception may *feel like* the continuous "stream of consciousness" named by William James and pursued in Modernist writing, but physiologically it operates as a series of cuts between and among discrete sensations. According to the studies that Evans surveys, each perceptual moment lasts between a fraction of a second to an outer limit of about three seconds.

James conceptualized consciousness as a continuous line, but in *The Principles of Psychology* (1890) he drew a graph showing how meaning is made in rises and falls of that line, through changes in "the objects or contents of the thoughts" (James 1890: 280). (See Table 2.) James divides the thought "The pack of cards is on the table" into four segments. A few years later Ferdinand de Saussure in his lectures on linguistics re-conceptualized James's continuous changes as discrete cuts. (See Table 1 in Chapter 1.) These demarcations of *conscious* experience in James and Saussure happen *unconsciously* in the firing of neurons.

=

In the context of this book, we might think of perceptual moments as "attention-cuts." At 2.4 seconds per line, the pace of speaking implied by the Prologue to *Romeo and Juliet* suggests that each line of the play might constitute an attention-cut. Individual phonemes and words could be perceived in a fraction of a second, at the lower limit of a

Table 2. William James, "The Stream of Consciousness," from *Principles of Psychology* (1890). Public domain.

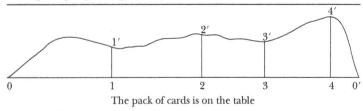

The pack of cards is on the table

perceptual moment; the entire line in 2.4 seconds, just below the upper limit of a perceptual moment. The process of attending to sound waves and decoding them is of course much more complicated than these measures would indicate—the movement from individual phonemes to the semantic sense of an entire line involves many factors, including the listener's memory—but the neurological research cited by Evans invites us to consider a pentameter line as a basic cut in Shakespeare's scripts, perhaps *the* basic cut. Considered thus, each separate line in the Prologue to *Romeo and Juliet* would cue a perceptual moment. In phenomenological terms, each can be "bracketed," each can be discerned by the ears as a separate unit:

{Two households, both alike in dignity}
    {In fair Verona, where we lay our scene,}
{From ancient grudge break to new mutiny,}
        {Where civil blood makes civil hands unclean.}

In this relatively early script, with its preponderance of end-stopped lines, the syntax supports such perceptual cutting.

We need something more, however, to get at the contextualizing and the cross-referencing that accompany the decoding of a line of verse. Judith Anderson in *Words That Matter: Linguistic Perception in Renaissance English* (1996) would encourage us to think of individual words as units. Wallace Chafe in *Discourse, Consciousness and Time* (1994) would suggest units both wider and deeper through his concept of "focal consciousness." "At any given moment," Chafe observes, "the mind can focus on no more than a small segment of everything it 'knows.'…Consciousness is an active focusing on a small part of the conscious being's self-centered model of the surrounding world" (Chafe 1994: 28). When spoken language is the object of the mind's focus, multiple factors come into play: not just semantic sense, but overall pitch level, changes in voice quality, acceleration and deceleration, pauses, contours of terminal pitch. For this language-specific type of focal consciousness Chafe proposes the term "intonation unit." With respect to time he sets the upper limit of an intonation unit at about two seconds (61–2).

If the Prologue to *Romeo and Juliet* is any indication, each line of verse in the play constitutes an intonation unit. Andrew Gurr and others have remarked, however, that 2.4 seconds per line pushes the limits of human possibility for both speakers and listeners (Gurr 1999; Erne 2013: 161–68, Urkowitz 2012). If that is so, we need to look at the unit of perceptual cuts as being shorter than a line. The RSC's current pace invites us to do just that. In this case, the two-second "brackets" are cued by caesurae in the verse:

{Two households,} {both alike in dignity}
        {In fair Verona,} {where we lay our scene,}
{From ancient grudge} {break to new mutiny,}
        {Where civil blood} {makes civil hands unclean.}

In the last two lines internal oppositions ("ancient"/"new," "grudge"/ "mutiny," "blood"/"hands") positively invite these two-second cuts in perception. In the last line, however, complications upset this regular rhythm: "blood"/"hands" cues discernment, but "civil"/"civil" invites cross-over, and "unclean" emerges from the alliterating [k] sounds as a conclusion that unsettles the preceding alternations. We end up, perhaps, with cuts of 2 seconds/2 seconds/1 second, thus:

{Where civil blood} {makes civil hands} {unclean.}

Considered in terms of aural perception, cuts in Shakespeare's speeches occur in smaller units than the lines and individual words that current performance practice would lead us to assume.

A further consideration is the importance of cultural factors in determining how long an attention span happens to be. Material media, user skills, and goals all help to determine the attention span required in a given situation. Jonathan Crary in *Suspensions of Perception: Attention, Spectacle, and Modern Culture* puts forth on page one the axiom that "the ways in which we intently listen to, look at, or concentrate on anything have a deeply historical character" (Crary, 1991: 1). Attention spans vary widely: from one culture to another, at different moments in history, in sync with different occasions, and in different configurations with different art forms.

=

Prominent among things that can be said to "run" are liquids (*OED*, "run, *v.*," II.41–7). To the eyes, and in the ears, of his contemporaries, Shakespeare's lines seemed to possess that flowing quality. "Honey-tongued Shakespeare," John Weever addresses him in an epigram of 1595 (Ingelby, Toulmin Smith, and Furnivall 1909: 1:24). "The sweet witty soul of Ovid lives in mellifluous and honey-tongued Shakespeare," Francis Meres writes in 1598 (1:46). Shakespeare's "honey-flowing vein" is praised by Richard Barnfield the same year (1:51). What all three writers most likely had in mind were the verses in Shakespeare's Ovid-inspired narrative poem *Venus and Adonis*, first published in 1593 and reissued thrice by the time Meres and Barnfield were writing. The same flowing quality characterized Shakespeare's dramatic verse, according to Ben Jonson. Shakespeare's wit, says Jonson, "flowed with that facility that sometime it was necessary he should be stopped" (Jonson 2012: 7:522).

In the air of the theater, as well on the page, Shakespeare's flowing speeches in fact required constant cuts. Linguists have known for more than a hundred years that what we hear as a series of discrete words when someone speaks is in fact a continuous stream of sound. The speaker's larynx, tongue, teeth, and lips do not shape each phoneme as a separate entity and then stop; rather, one sound flows into another as the speaking apparatus adjusts for what is coming next. The stream stops only when the speaker pauses or takes a breath. The linguistic name for this process is coarticulation (Lieberman and Blumstein 1988: 126–7). Spectrographic analysis, using a device that turns sound waves into visual spectra, lets us see with our eyes a phenomenon we hear with our ears. Take, for example, the first two lines of Hamlet's first soliloquy, "O that this too too solid flesh would melt,/ Thaw, and resolve itself into a dew" (1.2.129–30). (See Figure 12.) The spectrograph reveals a continuous flow of sounds that coalesce at certain "peaks" into complex frequencies. An auditor actively listens for the peaks and perceives them as separate phonemes, filtering out sounds that do not signify (Lieberman and Blumstein 1988: 140–61). In effect, a listener makes cuts in the continuous stream of sound, and does so in fractions of a second, just as happens in William James's "stream of thought." (See Table 2.)

Because of coarticulation, the unit that listeners bracket is not phonemes like

[o:] [ð] [a] [t] [ð] [I] [s] etc.

but syllables like

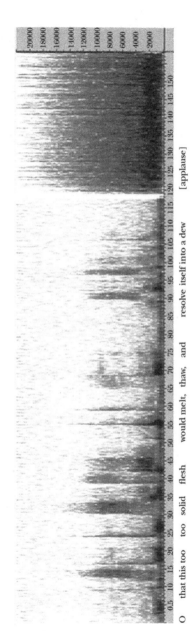

Figure 12. Spectrograph of *Hamlet* 1.2.130–1.

{o}{that}{this} etc.

Thanks to the monosyllabic nature of most English words, in most cases a word becomes the basic cut in speech perception. Only the two-syllable *sol-id* breaks the pattern in Hamlet's line. If it takes a modern speaker, on average, four seconds to declaim a ten-syllable line of verse—and, by implication, a listener four seconds to decode the speaker's sounds—the shortest cut in aural perception becomes about half a second, at the lower limit of Chafe's intonation units. A phrase would occupy the upper end at two seconds, as with each of the two phrases here:

{o that this too too solid flesh} {would melt}

Or an actor might deliver the line in three units, each falling comfortably within Chafe's one- to two-second "intonation unit":

{o} {that this too too solid flesh} {would melt}

Or perhaps

{o that this} {too too solid flesh} {would melt}

A listener would, then, take in the entire line in a single perceptual moment, but that moment would be complexly textured with the cuts and cross-cuts of multiple intonation units. As the spectrograph reveals, Hamlet's utterance becomes slower and more flowing toward the end (at least in the recorded speaker's enunciation) on the liquid words "melt," "thaw," and "dew."

The multiple cuts in Shakespeare's speeches—even his most flowing speeches—are registered on the printed page in the separateness of letters of the alphabet, in the spaces between words, and in punctuation. Compare the spectrograph of sounds in Figure 12 with the printed words beneath. Before the fourth century CE, as M. B. Parkes observes in *Pause and Effect: An Introduction to the History of Punctuation in the West,* Greek and Latin were written in *scriptio continua,* with spaces between graphemes but not between words (Parkes 1993: 19). Inscriptions on surviving Roman buildings and monuments take this form. An educated reader would know where to put the longer spaces between words, between syntactic elements, and between complete statements, just as young men and women preparing for bar mitzvah and bat mitzvah ceremonies still learn to do with the Hebrew scriptures. Cuts in *scriptio continua* were dictated by a rhetorical understanding of punctuation that did not give way until the seventeenth century to the logical scheme that we claim to abide by today.

In the rhetorical scheme, *commata* (commas), *cola* (colons), and *sententiae* (sentences) were understood to be breath-units, not logic-units (Parkes 1993: 4). As breath-units they represented pauses of varying lengths, cuts that show up in a spectrograph as blank spaces, as in the one that separates "flesh" from "would" in Hamlet's two lines. Jonson in *The English Grammar* recognizes punctuation marks as breath-units. After going through all the parts of English syntax Jonson concludes the treatise with a consideration "Of the distinction of sentences":

> There resteth one general affection of the whole, dispersed thorough every member thereof, as the blood is thorough the body, and consisteth in the breathing, when we pronounce any sentence. For, whereas our breath is by nature so short that we cannot continue without a stay to speak long together, it was thought necessary, as well for the speaker's ease, as for the plainer deliverance of the things spoken, to invent this means whereby, men pausing a pretty while, the whole speech might never the worse be understood (Jonson 2012: 7:400).

If Shakespeare's hand is indeed hand D in the manuscript of *Sir Thomas More* (now BL MS Harleian 7368), Shakespeare likewise thought of punctuation marks primarily in terms of cuts to the flow of speech. Scene 6 is very lightly punctuated, with only a few commas to mark momentary pauses and one *positura* (`',`) to mark the end of a verse paragraph (Parkes 1993: 306).

George Puttenham, in *The Art of English Poesy* (1589), remarks, vis-à-vis caesura, that "clear distinction of voices" is the most important mark of a "civil" language: "the most laudable languages are always most plain and distinct, and the barbarous most confused and indistinct. It is therefore requisite that leisure be taken in pronunciation, such as may make our words plain and most audible and agreeable to the ear" (Puttenham 2002: 163). Among the ornaments that Puttenham takes up later in the treatise is "*Brachylogia*, or the Cutted Comma":

> We use sometimes to proceed all by single words without any close or coupling, saving that a little pause or comma is given to every word. This

figure for pleasure may be called in our vulgar the Cutted Comma, for that there cannot be a shorter division than at every word's end (298).

The example that Puttenham offers is a paratactic list of vices:

Envy, malice, flattery, disdain,
Avarice, deceit, falsehood, filthy gain (298–9).

In certain moments Shakespeare's scripts register a reflexive awareness of the flowingness of speech and of cuts that interrupt that flow. The most obvious example is the misplaced punctuation in Peter Quince's speaking of the prologue to "A tedious brief scene of young Pyramus/ And his love Thisbe" in *A Midsummer Night's Dream* (5.1.56–7). Quince cuts his speech in all the wrong places:

> {We do not come as minding to content you,}
> {Our true intent is.} {All for your delight
>   We are not here.} {That you should here repent you
> The actors are at hand}…. (5.1.114–6).

The audience know exactly what is wrong:

THESEUS   This fellow doth not stand upon points.
[That is to say, he does not come to a stop at periods or full stops.]
LYSANDER   He hath rid his prologue like a rough colt: he knows not the stop (5.1.119, 120–1).

Cuts often figure as well in transcriptions of vernacular speech, as contractions, as sounds cut out. The effect here is just the opposite of Quince's awkward stops. Contractions enhance the sense of flow and quicken the tempo: they make speeches run. Justice Shallow, in *Henry IV, Part Two*, offers endearing examples whenever he gets excited. His account of "the little quiver fellow" who could muster his troops in Shoreditch like nobody else is a particularly eloquent example. Shallow's speech devolves from sentences into words into phonemes. Even "he" contracts into "a," spinning the speech on its way:

and a would manage you piece thus, and a would about and about, and come you in, and come you in. 'Ra-ta-ta!' would a say; 'Bounce!' would a say; and away again would a go; and again would a come. I shall ne'er see such a fellow (3.2.278–83).

For a listener, the enhanced speed crams many more words into the intonation unit than is the case in verse. If he were speaking verse, one could imagine Shallow in moments like this quite easily speaking a line in 2.4 seconds.

=

The subtlest and most sustained engagements with cuts in speech occur in that language-obsessed play *Love's Labour's Lost*. In their macaronic mania, Don Armado, Holofernes, and Nathaniel are constantly cutting from English to Latin to English to Italian to English, introducing stops that work like Peter Quince's vagrant punctuation in *A Midsummer Night's Dream*. While the curate Nathaniel reads Biron's intercepted sonnet to Rosaline, the schoolmaster Holofernes extemporizes a speech that jumps from Virgil's Latin to his own pompous ·English to an Italian proverb to the sol-fa musical scale, punctuating the flow of language at each turn with full stops:

> "*Facile precor gelida quando pecas omnia sub umbra ruminat*", and so forth. Ah, good old Mantuan! I may speak of thee as the traveller doth of Venice:
> *Venezia, Venezia,*
> *Chi non ti vede, chi non ti prezia.*
> Old Mantuan, old Mantuan—who understandeth thee not, loves thee not. (*He sings.*) Ut, re, sol, la, mi, fa (*Love's Labour's Lost* 4.2.92–9).

When Nathaniel proceeds to read Biron's sonnet aloud, Holofernes upbraids him, "You find not the apostrophus, and so miss the accent" (4.2.120–1). That is to say, you ignore the elisions, you pronounce sounds that should be cut, and so get the rhythm wrong. It is in the speeches of vernacular fellows like Costard and Dull, however, that most of the contractions in *Love's Labour's Lost* are to be found, just as in the speeches of Shallow in *Henry IV, Part Two*. Dull combines these colloquial contractions with misconstrued cuts between syllables when he hears Holofernes' Latin "*haud credo*" ("I can scarcely believe") as an English phrase. What kind of deer did the Princess kill?

> NATHANIEL   But, sir, I assure ye it was a buck of the first head.
> HOLOFERNES   Sir Nathaniel, *haud credo.*
> DULL   'Twas not a 'auld grey doe', 'twas a pricket. (4.2.9–12)

This is petty stuff, mere snips here and there, compared with the fancy cutwork of the lovers' speeches.

Game-playing is one metaphor for the lovers' verbal sparring. "Well bandied, both," the Princess says after Rosaline and Catherine have exchanged ten one-liners: "a set of wit well played" (5.2.29). If the "set" here is tennis, spectator-listeners like the Princess and Maria would have cut their visual and aural attentions from one player to another five times. The "cut" involved in such bantering of wits is explicitly mentioned in the play, beginning with Maria's description of Longueville to the other ladies in Act 2, Scene 1. His only fault

> Is a sharp wit matched with too blunt a will,
> Whose edge hath power to cut, whose will still wills
> It should none spare that come within his power (2.1.49–51).

The metaphor is sustained. Dull is dull because in his "undressed, unpolished, uneducated, unpruned, untrained, or rather unlettered" state (4.2.16–18) he lacks edge. Armado praises an exchange of quips between Holofernes and Mote as "a quick venue of wit; snip, snap, quick, and home" (5.1.56–7), as if they were wielding rapiers or swords. Especially sharp, according to Boyet, are "the tongues of mocking wenches." They are

> as keen
> As is the razor's edge invisible,
> Cutting a smaller hair than may be seen,
> Above the sense of sense… (5.2.256–9).

Biron recognizes as much when the lords' disguises as visiting Russians has been exposed and he has no choice but to surrender to Rosaline:

> Thrust thy sharp wit quite through my ignorance,
> Cut me to pieces with thy keen conceit… (5.2.398–9).

The cutwork in *Love's Labour's Lost*, its incessant play with listeners' aural perceptions, is more elaborate and more sustained than in any of Shakespeare's other scripts.

"Let me hear a staff, a stanza, a verse," Holofernes asks when Nathaniel is ready to read aloud Biron's intercepted sonnet to Rosaline. Moving from longer units to shorter units, Holofernes insinuates here a series of verse-cuts that might be heard as perceptual moments. In the event, the cut-up text of *Love's Labour's Lost* is even more intricate than Holofernes' list would suggest. The tennis-matches of wit among the lovers (or are they sword-fights?) reach a climax in Act 5, Scene 2, when the lords, disguised as Muscovites, invite the ladies to dance. The ladies refuse. Instead, the couples dance around each other in words. One meaning of the verb *cut* in early modern English, as we have observed, was to perform an action, gesture, or display of a striking kind, one possibility being "to cut a caper" (*OED*, "cut, *v.*," VI.25). The verbal caper the couples cut in this scene moves from shared half-lines (5.2.217, 220, 225, 229, etc.) to shared couplets (5.2.222–3, 224–5, 226–8, 230–1 etc.) to shared quatrains to entire sonnets. Cuts of intonation units are interlayered in these speeches with cuts in speaking turns with cuts in verses and stanzas, to produce an intricate piece of cutwork not unlike the fabric in Bubble's doublet in Figure 8.

An exchange between Longueville and Catherine illustrates the effect. Longueville, let us recall, is said by Maria to have an especially sharp wit. Bracketing the intonation units, the speaking turns, and the four- and two-line stanzas, as in Table 3, can help us see how cuts and cross-cuts work their aural magic. Catherine and Longueville "part words" in multiple ways. In doing so they in fact speak a sonnet, though the cuts and cross-cuts between the speakers complicate a sonnet's usual perceptual units of three quatrains and a couplet, giving listeners an aural experience that is more like a canon or a fugue with one part cutting in and now another. In the end looms the butcher's knife, a token of the cutting technique that has made the entire bravura performance possible.

=

How hard can a problem be? According to Mote in *Love's Labour's Lost*, you might measure the difficulty in winks. When Mote quizzes Armado on what the "deuce-ace" means in cards, the Spaniard gives a characteristically periphrastic reply: "It doth amount to one more than two." Mote cuts that down to plain English: "Which the base vulgar do call three.... Why, sir, is this such a piece of study? Now there is 'three' studied ere ye'll thrice wink" (1.2.46–51). Modern psychology and neuroscience have confirmed Mote's way of measuring problems: blinking may feel like a reflex action, but the frequency of blinking increases under stress and decreases during periods of concentrated mental activity (Gregory 1997: 44). You blink less when your attention is more sharply focused than normal, whether the object is physically present or just being thought about. An adult

Table 3. Delivery and perception cuts in *Love's Labour's Lost* 5.2.242–55.

CATHERINE

{{What,} {was your visor made} {without a tongue?}}

LONGUEVILLE (*taking Catherine for Maria*)

{{I know the reason, lady,} {why you ask.}}

CATHERINE

{{O, for your reason!} {Quickly, sir, I long.}}

LONGUEVILLE

{{You have a double tongue}{within your mask,}}

{{And would afford my speechless visor} {half.}}

CATHERINE

{{'Veal', quoth the Dutchman.} {Is not veal a calf?}}

LONGUEVILLE

{{A calf,} {fair lady?}}

CATHERINE

{No,} {a fair lord calf.}}

LONGUEVILLE

{{Let's part the word.}

CATHERINE   {No,} {I'll not be your half.}}

{{Take all and wean it,} {it may prove an ox.}}

LONGUEVILLE

{{Look how you butt yourself} {in these sharp mocks!}}

{{Will you give horns,} {chaste lady?} {Do not so.}}

CATHERINE

{{Then die a calf} {before your horns do grow.}}

LONGUEVILLE

{{One word in private with you} {ere I die.}}

CATHERINE

{{Bleat softly, then.} {The butcher hears you cry.}}

blinks about ten to twenty times a minute, less frequently when concentrating on something, such as when reading a book, listening to a speech, or watching a film or a stage production.

Such cuts in visual perception seem to have been very much on Shakespeare's mind. In early modern usage, the word *wink* covered Mote's quick closing of the eyes (*OED*, "wink, *v.¹*," †I.a), but it could be extended in time and broadened in scope to include many other experiences. Let us proceed from shorter intervals to longer. "Was this the face/ That like the sun did make beholders wink?" asks the imprisoned Richard II, looking in a mirror (*Richard II* 4.1.273–4). The wink here is a momentary cutting off of vision (*OED* 2.a), though more marked than Mote's three quick blinks. More marked still, and perhaps lengthier, are the knowing glances (*OED* 8) that Helena accuses her friends of sharing in *A Midsummer Night's Dream*. You "Make mouths upon men when I turn my back," she complains, "Wink each at other, hold the sweet jest up" (3.2.239–40).

Still more emphatic, and longer in duration, is the metaphorical closing of one's eyes to reprehensible behavior (*OED* 5.a) that King Harry describes in *Henry V* in the scene where he judges Scrope, Grey, and Cambridge:

> If little faults proceeding on distemper
> Shall not be winked at, how shall we stretch our eye
> When capital crimes, chewed, swallowed, and digested,
> Appear before us? (2.2.53–6).

Later in *Henry V*, in the wooing scene, multiple senses of "wink" come into play. Help me conjure up the spirit of love in Princess Catherine, King Harry asks Burgundy. To do that, Burgundy jokes, you will have to conjure up Cupid, but "a maid yet rosed over with the virgin crimson of modesty" (5.2.93–4) will find it "a hard condition" (5.2.96) to contemplate "a naked blind boy" (5.2.95).

KING HARRY   Yet they do wink and yield, as love is blind and enforces.
BURGUNDY   They are then excused, my lord, when they see not what they do.
KING HARRY   Then, good my lord, teach your cousin to consent winking.
BURGUNDY   I will wink on her to consent, my lord, if you will teach her to know my meaning (5.2.297–304).

In Burgundy's final quip, to wink is to signal a command, direction, or invitation (*OED* †7.a).

In the now-obsolete senses of sleep or doze (*OED* †3) "to wink" far exceeds our modern "blink" with respect to both continuity and content. (We still have, to be sure, the phrase "to catch a few winks.") As for continuity, hear Biron in *Love's Labour's Lost* as he runs through the list of rules—each more outrageous than the last— that the King is proposing for his academy:

> And then to sleep but three hours in the night,
> And not be seen to wink of all the day,
> When I was wont to think no harm all night,
> And make a dark night too of half the day (1.1.42–5).

As for the content of winking, Shakespeare fashions an entire sonnet on the experience:

> When most I wink, then do mine eyes best see,
> For all the day they view things unrespected;
> But when I sleep, in dream they look on thee,
> And, darkly bright, are bright in dark directed (43.1–4).

Ordinary expectations about visual perception are reversed here: with his eyes open the lover finds nothing in the daylight world to "respect" in the obsolete sense of pay attention to (*OED*, "respect, *v.*," †3,a), whereas in the dark, in dreams, he sees better than ever the object he adores.

The longest wink of all in early modern English is death, as Leontes proclaims in his fit of jealousy in Act 1, Scene 2 of *The Winter's Tale*. Camillo, he suggests, could prove his loyalty by poisoning Polixines:

> Who mayst see
> Plainly as heaven sees earth and earth sees heaven,
> How I am galled, mightst bespice a cup
> To give mine enemy a lasting wink...(1.2.316–19).

=

Taken altogether, Shakespeare's playful ways with the word *wink* articulate a two-faceted understanding of visual perception: Shakespeare recognizes that vision operates as a series of cuts made by closing one's eyelids at the same time that he finds compelling content in the black-outs. We encounter here the double senses of "cut" that we noticed in Chapter 1: the significance of a cut can consist in the things cut apart from each other or in the spaces created by the act of cutting—or in both. Contemporary neuroscientific research has demonstrated the truth of Shakespeare's intuition. A typical person blinks fifteen to twenty times a minute. If each blink lasts 0.3 to 0.4 seconds, the total time in the dark each day (or perhaps in the skin-toned twilight) amounts to as much as 10 percent of an individual's waking hours. In the course of a normal lifetime a person might spend as much as five years in the twilight, not including sleep-time, before the final wink of death.

When the eyes are focused on an object for an extended period of time the rate of blinking decreases to as little as three to four times per minute, and the rhythm of the blinks is not random. Reading a text, we tend to blink after finishing a sentence; listening to a speech, when the speaker pauses. Researchers at Osaka University in Japan have demonstrated in a series of experiments that the same thing happens when watching a video: subjects tend to blink at the same time. These synchronized blinks usually occur at the end of an action sequence or when a character has disappeared from view. Occupying up to 15 percent of viewing time, black-outs are not negligible phenomena. Briefly closing our eyes, the researchers concluded, allows us to process what we have seen and return to the visual field with focused attention. Measurements of brain activity during the experiments demonstrated that blinks decreased activity in the dorsal attention network but activated the default-mode network (DMN), which is implicated in internal processing (Nakano et al. 2013: 702–6).

Cuts in the form of blinks are not, then, totally under the viewer's control. Shakespeare's scripts in written form and their performance onstage and in films and video actively control how often a perceiver makes cuts in the seeming flow of experience. Game designer Will Hell-warth has seized on eye-blinks as a design principle in his award-winning videogame "Close Your" [*sic*] (http://www.closeyour.com/#about). Face-recognition software on the user's computer picks up how often the player blinks, speeding up the animated life-story onscreen as the player starts blinking more often in response to the cuts. The effect is cumulative, like a ball rolling downhill. As the blinks speed up, the life-story gets faster and faster, making the whole life seem to pass by in a flash. (One might wish the same thing were possible in a boring stage production.)

What the Osaka researchers seem not to have taken into account about videos is the influence of camera-cuts in cuing blinks. According to Walter Murch 2001, whose reflections on film editing we considered in Chapter 1, camera-cuts may, however, be cued by blinking habits on the part of actors and spectators. When he was editing *The Conversation* (1974), Murch noticed that the cuts he had chosen to make often coincided with frames in which the protagonist Gene Hackman blinked (Murch 2001: 59). Murch cites the work of psychologist John A. Stern in positing the blink as a unit of comprehension. Considered this way, a blink has as much to do with thought on the spectator's part as it does with the disposition of people and objects in visual space. In an interview that Murch quotes, Hackman demonstrated film-cuts to the interviewer thus: "Look at that lamp across the room. Now look back at me. Look back at that lamp. Now look back at me again. Do you see what you did? You *blinked*. Those are *cuts*." (60, emphasis original).

Murch's own take on cuts is more subjective:

> it seems to me that our rate of blinking is somehow geared more to our emotional state and to the nature and frequency of our thoughts than to the atmospheric environment we happen to find ourselves in. Even if there is no head movement [from one object to another]…the blink is either *something that helps an internal separation of thought to take place*, or it is *an involuntary reflex accompanying the mental separation that is taking place anyway*.…So we entertain an idea, or a linked sequence of ideas, and we blink to separate and punctuate that idea from what follows. Similarly—in film—a shot presents us with an idea, or a sequence of ideas, and the cut is a 'blink' that separates and punctuates those ideas (62–3, emphasis original).

It is a film editor's job to foster this mental process: "We must render visual reality discontinuous, otherwise perceived reality would resemble an almost incomprehensible string of letters without word separation or punctuation" (63).

Thinking of cuts in Murch's subjective terms helps to explain what happens in live performance in a theater when no camera intrudes to direct a spectator's gaze. Blocking and lighting do, of course, invite if not compel certain ways of looking, but ultimately it is each spectator's internal experience that determines the timing of the blinks. As Murch insists, an individual spectator's "emotional state" is as important to cuts in the visual field as the blocking and the pauses in delivery of lines that give the assembled spectators their cues. Shakespeare captures these dynamics in the long sequence of Act 5 of *The Winter's Tale* in which events that are happening offstage are narrated. Describing the events rather than representing them directly, Shakespeare finds occasion to reflect on visual perception in a way not dissimilar to his reflections on line-delivery in Hamlet's dialogue with the players. Consider the Third Gentleman's description of how news of Hermione's death was received by himself and by Perdita. Eyes figure prominently in this account, as objects vie for attention and tears close off vision:

> One of the prettiest touches of all, and that which angled for mine eyes—caught the water, though not the fish—was when at the relation of the Queen's death, with the manner how she came to't bravely confessed and lamented by the King, how attentiveness wounded his daughter till from one sign of dolour to another she did, with an "Alas", I would say bleed tears (5.2.81–8).

In emotional terms that Murch would recognize, the First Gentleman defines each revelation as being coordinated with a blink: "Who would be thence, that has benefit of access? Every wink of an eye some new grace will be born" (5.2.108–10). The multiple off-stage revelations in Act 5, Scene 2 of *The Winter's Tale* are reported as discrete perceptual moments, each charged with emotion and each set off from the others by a wink.

=

The most decisive cut in perception involves memory. Within the twinkling of an eye even the most powerful perception becomes a thing of the past. Time as Chorus in Act 4, Scene 1 of *The Winter's Tale* articulates this inescapable phenomenon. Time presents himself to the audience/spectators not as an *agent* of action but as an *observer* of action:

> Let me pass
> The same I am ere ancient'st order was
> Or what is now received. I witness to
> The times that brought them in; so shall I do
> To th'freshest things now reigning, and make stale
> The glistering of this present as my tale
> Now seems to it (4.1.9–15)

"Glistering" is itself a matter of winks, of oscillations of light now brighter now dimmer (*OED*, "glister, *v.*," *archaic*, a). All the preceding events of *The Winter's Tale* have become memories; the ensuing events remain expectations. Long before the Chorus speaks, however, the events of Acts 1, 2, and 3 have been cut off from glistering presence, syllable by syllable, blink by blink. The Chorus merely verbalizes a process that has already taken place—and that continues to take place in the Chorus's very act of speaking.

In Book 11 of the *Confessions*—the founding document of presentism—Augustine confronts just how ephemeral the present is. The past and the future have greater claims to existence, but they can be known only in a present moment that is always passing from the future to the past. "It is inexact language," Augustine reasons,

> to speak of three times—past, present, and future. Perhaps it would be exact to say: there are three times, a present of things past, a present of things present, a present of things to come. In the soul there are these three aspects of time, and I do not see them anywhere else. The present considering the past is the memory, the present considering the present is immediate awareness, the present considering the future is expectation (Magalhães and Oaklander 2010: 30).

With respect to the workings of memory, cognitive science confirms the intuitions of Augustine and Shakespeare. The three kinds of memory recognized in current investigations vary radically in extension, and they are locatable in different regions of the brain (Markowitsch 2005, Nyhus and Bardre 2015). Lasting less than a second, sensory memory involves brain tissue specializing in vision, hearing, touch, and other sensations. Considering how constricted Augustine finds the present to be, we may not be stretching a point to identify his "immediate awareness" with sensory memory. The duration of short-term memory is longer—but still limited to only a few seconds—and involves more complex networks of firing neurons. Evans's "perceptual moments" and Chafe's "intonation units" would seem to be varieties of short-term memory. Vastly greater in capacity, long-term memory involves networks across the entire brain and can last a lifetime. The content of long-term memory is still, however, *distributed* information: it is composed of separate units, differing in kind and stored in different areas of the brain. Even long-term memory is an assemblage of cuts from what was once a glistering present.

"Faculty psychology," as it is called, may long ago have been superseded, but early modern theories of perception are not as remote from cognitive science as we might assume. In a scheme going back to Aristotle's *De Anima*, Shakespeare and his contemporaries told themselves that sensations of sound and vision were fused in a kinesthetic "common sense," along with sensations of touch, smell, and taste. In that synesthetic state the sensations were received by imagination, which formed internal images of the external objects reported by the senses and passed those images along to fantasy, which combined them into *phantasmata*. Estimation then assessed whether these internal *phantasmata* were to be embraced by the perceiver or avoided. Memory completed the process by turning all of these experiences—sensations, images, *phantasmata*—into *past* experiences (Park 1988: 464–84). Sensations may be combined, transformed, and recombined in this model of perception, but essential to the whole process are cuts: continuous sensations become discrete objects of knowledge accessed through memory. The process was imagined to take only fractions of a second.

Another model of memory in early modern psychology was spatial. Memories were thought to be stored in different rooms in the mind. To retrieve a memory meant moving from room to room and locating the object being sought. That might take time. Hamlet seems to have such a model in mind when he tries to remember the speech he requests from the First Player, a speech recounting Aeneas's telling Dido the tale of Troy's fall:

> If it live in your memory, begin at this line—let me see, let me see:
> "The rugged Pyrrhus, like th'Hyrcanian beast"—
> 'tis not so. It begins with Pyrrhus—
> "The rugged Pryrrhus, he whose sable arms…" (2.2.450–5).

Marry, there it goes. Hamlet's memory is spatial, locational, and associative.

=

Eyewitness accounts of Shakespeare's plays in their original performances illustrate the workings of cuts, of fragments, in acts of *re-collection* very much like Hamlet's. In each case memories stored in various regions of the brain—visual memories, aural memories, kinetic memories—are reassembled in a present act of verbalization. Words supply the connective tissue for these separate memories, taking the place of the complex sensations touched off by the original performances.

John Manningham's diary entry concerning *Twelfth Night* on February 2, 1602 recalls just two scenes from the play, 2.5 and 3.4, and two distinct moments in each scene, at that. The content of Manningham's memories of the performance is primarily visual, though kinetic memory likely comes into play as Manningham particularly remembers Malvolio's gestures:

> A good practice in it to make the steward believe his lady widow was in love with him, by counterfeiting a letter as from his lady, in general terms, telling him what she liked best in him, and prescribing his gesture in smiling, his apparel, etc., and then when he came to practice making him believe they took him to be mad (Salgādo 1975: 23).

Kinetic memory is explicitly fused with visual memory and aural memory in Henry Jackson's account of the King's Men's performance of *Othello* at Oxford in September 1610:

> They also had tragedies, which they acted with decorum and fitness. In these they elicited tears not only with their speaking but also with their physical action. But that Desdemona, murdered by her husband in our presence, although she always pled her case excellently, yet when killed moved us more, while stretched out on her bed she begged the spectators' pity with her very facial expression (qtd. in Potter 2002: 28).

Simon Forman's memoranda about performances of *Macbeth* at the Globe on April 20, 1610, *The Winter's Tale* at the Globe on May 15, 1611, and *Cymbeline* at an unspecified location and date are often lamented for being too brief, for sticking closely to the plot of each play, for leaving out details, and for being too quick to extract a moral. The editors of *The Shakspere Allusion-Book*, usually so quick to find an allusion where more cautious scholars would hesitate, disdain printing any of Forman's "Book of Plays and Notes Thereof *per* Forman's for Common Policy": "The "notes" are nothing more than a short relation of the story of what he saw, and are in no way critical" (Ingelby, Toulmin Smith, and Furnivall 1909 1:228). Considered as acts of memory, however, Forman's notes are instructive. His account of

The Winter's Tale, for example, is cut into three discrete segments. Within each segment his memories are further cut into specific scenes and parts of scenes, each cast as a separately punctuated sentence or clause, as noted in square brackets in the extract below.

The first cut, concerned with the main plot, begins with the command "observe": a directive to cut, to look, to annotate. The series of specific visual memories that follows establishes visual perception as Forman's dominant mode:

> Observe there how Leontes, the king of Sicilia, was overcome with jealousy of his wife with the king of Bohemia, his friend, that came to see him [1.2.1–211]. How he contrived his death, and would have had his cupbearer to have poisoned him [1.2.212–351]: who gave the king of Bohemia warning thereof and fled with him to Bohemia [1.2.352–465].

The second cut is concerned with the oracle of Apollo's judgment and with the fulfillment of the oracle's conditions for a happy ending:

> Remember also how he sent to the oracle of Apollo [2.2.182–201], and the answer of Apollo—that she was guiltless and that the King was jealous, etc.; and how, except the child was found again that was lost, the King should die without issue [3.2.123–242]. For the child was carried into Bohemia and there laid in a forest and brought up by a shepherd [3.3]. The King of Bohemia's son married that wench [announced in 4.4.530 but not dramatized]. And how they fled into Sicilia to Leontes [5.1.123ff]. The shepherd, having shown the letter of the nobleman by whom Leontes sent away that child and the jewels found about her, she was known to be Leontes' daughter, and was then sixteen years old [5.2].

The third cut, the most circumstantial of all, is concerned with Autolycus's part in the play and introduces kinetic memories of the way the actor, likely Robert Armin, bore his body in performance:

> Remember also the rogue that came in all tattered like Coll Pixie [4.3.1–30]; how he feigned him sick and to have been robbed of all that he had [4.3.31–69]. How he cozened the poor man of all his money [4.3.70–122]. And, after, came to the sheep-shearing with a pedlar's pack and there cozened them again of all their money [4.4.219–321]. How he changed apparel with the King of Bohemia's son [4.646–843], and then how he turned courtier, etc. [5.2]. Beware of trusting feigned beggars or fawning fellows (Salgādo 1975: 33).

"Tattered" registers the visual impression that Armin/Autolycus made on Forman; "Coll Pixie," the kinetic impression of his movements as "a mischievous sprite or fairy" (*OED*, "colt-pixie, *n.*). Many commentators have called attention to the fact that Forman leaves out entirely the coming to life of Hermione's statue in 5.3, if indeed that scene was performed in the version of *The Winter's Tale* that he saw at the Globe. For the players, or more likely for Forman recalling other things, the statue scene did not "make the cut."

The parataxis in Forman's memory, its disposition into a series of cuts set side by side, shows up not only in the way continuous performance is cut into segments, but also in Forman's choice not to report those segments in linear chronological order. Segment one, concerning Leontes' story, does indeed precede segment two, concerning the oracle of Apollo. But segment three, concerning Armin/Autolycus, doubles back to an earlier moment in segment two. Perhaps Hermione's resurrection is not remembered because it does not conveniently fit into any one of the three existing segments. In his refusal to make connections—the habit that the *Allusion Book* editors found "in no way critical"—Forman illustrates the fundamentally disjointed nature of memory. Augustine catches that quality precisely: "When a true narrative of the past is related, the memory produces not the actual events which have passed away but words conceived from images of them, which they fixed in the mind like imprints as they passed through the senses" (Magalhães and Oaklander 2010: 29).

=

In its fluidity the live experience of a theatrical performance seems no different from other kinds of human experience. We can arrest and remember some of the sounds we hear, we can capture in the mind's eye some of the images we see. Technical equipment like digital recorders, cameras, and computers can help us in those tasks, but ultimately the shards of experience that we curate can never be put back together as the well-wrought urn that we encountered originally. Inevitably pieces are missing. The shards can function as synecdoche, perhaps, as parts that call up a whole, but the experience itself has dissolved into air, into thin air, or perhaps like Prospero's books the experience has been drowned "deeper than did ever plummet sound" (*Tmp.* 5.1.56).

What is needed to give the illusion of continuity to memory's cuts is a verbal narrative. Each of us supplies such a narrative when we recall a theatrical performance that we have witnessed. Or perhaps we don't. For me, David Warner as Hamlet with the RSC in 1967 is the visual/aural/kinetic memory of a tall figure slouched downstage delivering the character's famous soliloquies with such low energy that I, standing at the back of the stalls, could barely hear him. David Tennant in the same role with the RSC in 2008 is the visual/aural/ kinetic memory of a gymnastic performer who energized the stage space in every movement and every speech. I will confess that, in each case, all I can remember is a series of perceptual moments. Anything beyond that would, for me at least, have to be supplied by recourse to a printed program (Patrick Stewart, I discovered when I located my dog-eared copy of the program while writing this book, played the Second Player to Warner's Hamlet) or, in the case of Tennant's Hamlet, recourse to the 2009 video of the production (this time with Patrick Stewart as Claudius).

The workings of theatrical memory in all its aspects are considered by the contributors to *Shakespeare, Memory, and Performance* (Holland 2006), a collection about recollection. Among the topics considered are historical and cultural memory, early modern memory practices, memorization techniques on the part of players, location and media, technologies of recording, and memory in performance history. Reflective writers of performance history such as Joseph Roach are keenly aware that even collective memory is a matter of cuts:

> The theatre dies every night, and yet Shakespearean performance endures as both history and a living tradition. Performances yield up tangible evidence of their memorability. That evidence takes the form not only of play texts, documents, images, eyewitness accounts, architectural and archeological remains, prompt books, memoirs, reviews, and musical scores, but also of embodied practices, anecdotes, and lore (Roach 2016: 2:1545).

However radical a contemporary production of *The Winter's Tale*, for example, may be, it will inevitably contain cuts from earlier productions in the form of production concepts, modes of delivering particular speeches, blocking—not to mention traditional cuts to the script. To use a term usually associated with the web, a given production is made up of theatrical "memes." We shall explore in Chapters 4 and 5 the creative possibilities in this phenomenon. In the meantime, let us observe that the most radical cuts of all may be the ones in acts of criticism such as you are reading now. Criticism is cutwork.

4

At the Cutting Edge

Interfaces Between Figure and Life

> This figure, that thou here seest put,
> It was for gentle Shakespeare cut;
> Wherein the graver had a strife
> With nature, to outdo the life.
>
> —Ben Jonson, "To the Reader," in
> *Mr William Shakespeare's Comedies,*
> *Histories, and Tragedies* (1623), sig. A1

Since 1623, when Ben Jonson supplied these verses to accompany Martin Droeshout's engraved frontispiece to *Mr. William Shakespeare's Comedies, Histories, and Tragedies*, cuts have been standing in for life. (See Figure 13.) In Jonson's conceit, "life" and "figure" are separated not by a mirror as Hamlet would have it (*Ham.* 3.2.22), but by a cut. Paradoxically, that cut also *conjoins* life and figure. What turns separation into conjunction is an act of imagination on the part of a spectator/reader. Would that the graver could have drawn Shakespeare's wit as well as his face, Jonson laments:

> But since he cannot, reader, look
> Not on his picture, but his book (Shakespeare 2005: frontispiece).

Jonson inserts a chiastic cut between "picture" and "book," but the technology that produced both was, in 1623, two versions of the same process. Until the chemical technologies of photography and lithography came into use in the nineteenth century, it took physical cuts of some kind to turn life into figure. In woodcuts a knife was used to cut away areas of the wood's surface, leaving raised lines to receive the ink. In engravings like Droeshout's portrait, a sharp pointed tool

Figure 13. Martin Droeshout, engraved title page portrait for *Mr. William Shakespeare's Comedies, Histories, and Tragedies* (1623), detail. Public domain.

(a burin) was deployed to incise lines and/or dots to catch the ink. In the case of woodcuts, it is the raised lines that delineate the image; in the case of engravings, the cut-away lines or stippled dots. The detail cuts in Figures 16A and 16B allow us to examine the burin's cut-away lines up close. As with all forms of cutting, significance can reside in either the *removed* material (engravings) or the *remaining* material (woodcuts). In both cases, meaning-making happens not only in the cuts themselves, but in the cuts between the cuts.

The printed text of the First Folio was, like Shakespeare's portrait, a species of cutwork. A piece of movable type was produced by tracing the image of the letter onto the head of a rectangular piece of steel, then cutting and filing away the metal to leave the letter standing out in high relief. This "punch" was then hammered into a piece of copper, creating a depressed "matrix" that could be used as a mold and filled with metal alloy to produce the piece of type. The result, even though it was molded, retained the form and substance of a chiseled sculpture: it possessed a "body" and a "face" (Moxon 1958: 135–50). When impressed on sheets of paper, raised type reversed the cut, creating depressions in the paper to receive the ink. If the edges of a piece of type were sharp enough and the pressure hard enough, the paper could be cut through and the ink would "bleed." With respect to the propagation of Shakespeare's works, Jonson's trope of the cut can be traced from 1623 to the latest digital project today.

Paper, wood, copper, photographic negative, wax cylinder, celluloid film, 1 | 0 electronic signals: each of these physical media presents different opportunities for cutting and requires different tools for doing so. The tools are not just means to an end: they facilitate certain kinds of cuts, resulting in different kinds of cutwork. Each of the tools used to make the cuts—pen-knife and goose quill, type-punch, woodcutter's knife, burin, shutter, stylus, cutting and splicing machine, computer keyboard—provides a physical means for turning "life" into "figure," but the figure in each case models a distinct way of reading life. New media model new ways of turning life into figure but also of turning figure into life. There is a reciprocal relationship between cutting tools and cuts in perception.

In this chapter I shall be pursuing two goals: to survey the technologies that have produced the cutting edge between life and figure, and, in the process, to observe the kinds of figures that have been made with those cuts. Throughout I shall be particularly attentive to how the cuts have refigured "life" and caused people to apprehend Shakespeare's plays and poems in new ways. "Shakespeare" after sound recording, for example, is different from "Shakespeare" before. The technologies I will take up in chronological order, beginning with the writing and printing technologies available in Shakespeare's lifetime and proceeding via woodcuts, engraving, photography, sound recording, and film to the digital technology of our own time. In the process I shall be distinguishing nine types of cuts: line-cuts, speech-cuts, scene-cuts, character-cuts, actor-cuts, author-cuts, sound-cuts, camera-cuts, and digital-cuts. With each of the cutting technologies we confront, yet again, the paradox noted in Chapter 1, that a cut can incise an object of special attention or excise it for discarding. Each kind of technology, furthermore, involves its own interspace between cuts, inviting different kinds of imaginative acts on the creator's part and the perceiver's part. Each type of cut involves one or more varieties of the attention-cuts that we surveyed in Chapter 3.

=

As a script in which knife and pen figure prominently, *The Merchant of Venice* offers a suggestive example of early modern writing technology and the kinds of cuts that pen and ink facilitate in manuscripts. Knife and pen are physically present in the trial scene, as Shylock, earlier derided as a "cut-throat" (1.3.110), sharpens his knife on his shoe-sole (4.1.120–3). Although Graziano calls attention to this act ("Not on thy sole, but on thy soul, harsh Jew,/ Thou mak'st thy knife keen" [4.1.122–3]), some Shylocks, seeking to downplay their savagery, have chosen to whet their knives more circumspectly, on the floor for example (Shakespeare 2002: 218). Shylock's complaint to Antonio "You call me misbeliever, cut-throat, dog" (1.3.110) insinuates multiple associations for the knife. Lines in another play, in Othello's suicide speech "I took by th' throat the circumcisèd dog/ And smote him thus" (5.2.364–5), establish an association of Shylock's knife with circumcision. The cut to Antonio's breast might then figure as the mark on the "upper stratum" of the Christian's body for the mark on the "lower stratum" of Shylock's Jewish body: a turning of the stigma against the man who has stigmatized Shylock.

In *The Merchant of Venice* the pen that writes the bond comes before the knife; in the writing technology of early modern culture, it came *after*. Writing was taught separately from the skill of reading, so many people in Shakespeare's England could read but not write (Cressy 1–18). Writing began with a knife. The often reprinted writing manual *A Book Containing Diverse Sorts of Hands* by Jehan de Beau-Chesne and John Baildon (first edition 1571) starts with instructions on how to make ink, how to prepare the paper, how to make a pen from a goose quill, and how to make a good penknife:

> Your pen knife as stay in left hand let rest,
> The metal too soft, nor too hard is best:
> Too sharp it may be and so cut too fast:

> If it be too dull, a shrewd turn for haste:
> For whetstone, hard touch that is very good,
> Slate or shoe sole is not ill but good
> (de Beau-Chesne and Baildon 1602: sigs. A2–2v).

More detailed instructions are provided in John Brinsley's *Ludus Literarius: Or, the Grammar School* (1612), where the violence that precedes the act of writing is made explicit. First you choose a quill. Taking in hand your knife, you then

> cleave it straight up the back; first with a cleft, made with your pen-knife: after with another quill put into it, rive it further by little and little, till you see the cleft to be very clean:…After, make the neb and cleft both about one length, somewhat above a barleycorn breadth, & small; so as it may let down the ink and write clean. Cut the neb first slant downwards to make it thin, and after strait overthwart (Brinsley 1612: sigs. E3–E3v).

We should regard the student in Comenius's study (see Figure 4) as having performed this cutting action before he proceeds to make inked cuts with his pen.

A knife like the one Shylock readies to cut Antonio's flesh was involved in writing the bond between them and is used, in more ways than one, in the act of redeeming that bond. Nerissa, in her guise as judge's clerk, likely uses pen and paper to transcribe the entire proceedings as they happen. In modern productions Nerissa often appears carrying a stack of legal books, but writing down the proceedings is one of the things that sixteenth-century clerks did in court (*OED* "clerk, *n.*," 6.b). In the play's last scene Graziano explains how he was forced to give away Nerissa's ring after Bassanio had handed over Portia's to "Balthasar": "then the boy his clerk,/ That took some pains in writing, he begged mine" (5.1.181–2). After the judgment Nerissa is explicitly ordered to "draw a deed of gift" whereby Shylock will hand over his fortune to Lorenzo and Jessica (4.1.391), but she has probably been writing all along.

In the bond and in Nerissa's scribal duties we encounter, within the fiction and through performance, three varieties of cutwork: at least one line-cut (the phrase "Nearest his heart" [4.1.251] is quoted by Shylock from the written bond), multiple speech-cuts (Nerissa probably writes down the litigants' words as they speak), and a major scene-cut (her transcript frames "the trial scene" as an entity). If in fact Nerissa writes out all the proceedings, she re-enacts how the trial scene came to be written in the first place, as we observed in Chapter 2. Before there was a trial scene on stage there were manuscripts that planned out the whole affair: Shakespeare's own draft or drafts of the entire script, fair copies for the censor and for the book-holder who would manage entrances and exits, sides containing only a single character's lines for the actors' use in learning their parts, a plat for visualizing the layout of scenes amid the flurry of activity in the tiring house.

Within the fiction of *The Merchant of Venice* we might infer yet another kind of cut being made with pen and ink. Portia/Balthasar's interpretation of Venetian law and of the bond's precise wording depends on habits of close reading taught in early modern schools. According to Brinsley and other pedagogical authorities, a student's attention should be directed toward diction and syntax on the one hand and memorable thoughts on the other. In both cases, pen and ink were used to cut a text into parts. With respect to diction and syntax, Brinsley would direct a student "to *mark* the sentence well, and to observe all the points in it, both commas and colons; or less distinctions, and middle distinctions" (Brinsley 1612: sig. N4, emphasis added). The words "sentence," "commas," "colons," "distinctions," and "mark" are all invoked here as synecdoche. Literally, Brinsley is talking about "sentence" as a unit of writing, but meta-phorically as a thought worth taking away; about "commas" and "colons" as punctuation marks, but also as the contents of the units so marked; about "distinctions" as syntactical units, but also as ethical principles; and, above all, "mark" as taking notice, but also as using a pen—a knife-sharpened pen—to give these attention-cuts visible presence. Elsewhere in *Ludus Literarius* Brinsley advises a scheme of single and double underscorings for syntactic units.

More widely in use by early modern readers were conventional marks for indicating *sententiae* as memorable thoughts. The student in Comenius's woodcut of "The Study" can serve as a model for Balthasar at his law books. (See Figure 4.) Comenius's text describes how the student "sitteth alone, addicted to his studies, whilst he read-eth books," shown in the woodcut as laid out on the desk before him, and "picketh all the best things out of them...and marketh them...

with a dash or a little star in the margent" (Comenius 1659: sigs. O4v–O5). In *Merchant* the letter to the Duke from Bellario of Padua commends Balthasar's learnedness by declaring, "We turned o'er many books together" (4.1.154–5). Balthasar's astute reading of the Venetian statutes and Shylock's bond might have involved not only dashes, asterisks, and pointing hands, but also the inverted commas that we noted in Chapter 1. (See Figure 7B.) Certainly Balthasar seems to be quoting the law precisely as he cancels Shylock's bond. In *The Merchant of Venice* physical cuts made on paper with pen and ink are translated into ethical distinctions.

=

The two main "hands" in early modern writing technology, "secretary" and "italic," are regimes that both separate and conjoin. The writing hand cuts between letters even as it connects them. In that respect, the intermedial strokes are like coarticulation in speech. (See Chapter 3.) In print, on the other hand, the cuts between letters are emphatic. The interspace must be filled in by the reader, perhaps through coarticulation as the reader sounds the letters sub-vocally. With respect to lines and speeches, the cuts in print are more emphatic still. The horizontal lines between speeches in *The Book of Sir Thomas More* become blank spaces in print, and the speech cues are often typeset in italics or all caps, giving them more prominence. The addition of marked cuts between scenes and acts completes a process of cutting that begins at a micro level, with spaces between letters.

All the surviving plays by Mr. William Shakespeare, with the exception of the scenes attributed to him from the manuscript *Book of Sir Thomas More*, were submitted to the cutting technology of print between 1594 and 1623. Only the presumably lost play *Love's Labor's Won* has come down to us in pristine uncut condition: no pages, no ink, no excisions or rearrangements for productions, *no play*. It is the perfect example—the only one, in fact—of a completely uncut Shakespeare text. The presumably lost play *Cardenio* is quite the opposite: it exists *only* in cut-up form, in the "new-modeled" play *Double Falsehood* from the early eighteenth century (Shakespeare 2005: 1245). As for *The Merchant of Venice*, it was twice cut up in print, with different results each time.

When the manuscript (or manuscripts) of *The Merchant of Venice* first came to be set in type, in the 1600 quarto of *The Most Excellent History of the Merchant of Venice. With the extreme cruelty of Shylock the Jew toward the said merchant, in cutting a just pound of his flesh*, the trial scene was, as with all the quartos issued in Shakespeare's lifetime, printed continuously with the rest of the text (sigs. G3–I1), with no sign of its being a separate entity. The 1600 quarto of *The Most Excellent History of the Merchant... As it hath been divers times acted by the Lord Chamberlain his Servants* preserves the sense of flow present in the ink that was used to write out the script in the first place, and it registers on the page the continuity of performance in the theater. In the 1623 folio version of *The Merchant of Venice*, in a book explicitly addressed "To the great variety of *readers*" (sig. A3, emphasis added), visible cuts between the play's parts are prominent: the trial scene is set apart from the rest of the text not only by the heading "*Actus Quartus*" (sig. P4v) but also by ruled lines. The next heading in the text, "*Actus Quintus*" (sig. Q1v), serves to cut off the trial scene at the end. *The Merchant of Venice* is typical of many of the folio's plays in being marked haphazardly—in this case, only cuts between acts are indicated graphically (Smith 2013: 99). With the trial scene, it so happens that the entity being cut apart from the rest of the script coincides with what the printers Isaac Jaggard, William Blount, and/or their compositors chose to mark as an act.

The horizontal rules before and after *Actus Quartus* (sig. P5v) in the folio *Merchant* are a species of "paraph," the general term for marks made to distinguish one piece of writing from another. "Paragraphs" are the most familiar form. No less prominent in contemporary textual studies are "paratexts": elements added alongside (*para-*) a given text, including footnotes, marginal notes, running heads, page numbers, even title pages and book covers. Originally, a paraph was a flourish at the bottom of a signature, used to distinguish and authenticate the signature. Among the most famous is Queen Elizabeth's:

Paraphs were used in pen-and-ink technology (we observed in Chapter 2 how horizontal lines separate speech-cuts in the manuscript *Book of Sir Thomas More*), but they came into greater prominence in print, first as a graphic and then as an indention taking the place of the sign. The inverted commas in the 1676 quarto of *Hamlet* (see Figure 7A) and in Pope's 1725 edition of Shakespeare's plays (see Figure 7B) function as paraphs, as do the horizontal lines that Pope used to relegate unworthy lines and passages in Shakespeare's text to the bottom of the page. All forms of paraphs are cuts.

=

"Cool" media and "hot" media: Marshall McLuhan's distinction in *Understanding Media* (1964) is interesting to think about in connection with pen-and-ink technology versus print. McLuhan's distinction is made according to how much participation a particular medium invites on the part of the perceiver: "Any hot medium allows of less participation than a cool one, as a lecture makes for less participation than a seminar, and a book for less than a dialogue" (McLuhan 1964: 25). McLuhan regards printed books as a hot medium, and I would agree. A playhouse manuscript in the form of the "book" of the play or an actor's "side" requires much more participation than a printed text does. In the "cooler" medium of manuscript it is the writer and the user, not a typesetter, who does the cutting.

Nerissa's pen-and-ink cut of the trial scene in *Merchant* was enacted whenever an early modern reader chose to write down extracts from Shakespeare's texts. In transcribing cuts from Shakespeare's printed texts into their own manuscript "tables," they were, in McLuhan's terms, moving Shakespeare's words from a hot medium into a cool one. Or, rather, back again. All of the verbal cuts from Shakespeare that occur in surviving manuscript miscellanies of the late sixteenth and early seventeenth centuries come from printed sources: *Venus and Adonis* (1593), *The Rape of Lucrece* (1594), and sonnets published in the anthology *The Passionate Pilgrim* (1599), including versions of three sonnets written by the suitors in Act 4, Scenes 2 and 3, of *Love's Labour's Lost*. But extracts from fourteen of Shakespeare's plays also figure in these collections (Beale 1980–3: 1:452ff), and they too come from printed texts. An example is Edmund Pudsey's manuscript book datable to 1609–12 (now Bodleian MS Eng. poet.d.3 and Shakespeare Birthplace Trust ER 82/1/21) containing pen-and-ink cuts from six Shakespeare plays, many of them altered slightly from the quarto texts. *Hamlet* gets the most sustained attention, but Pudsey writes out five one- and two-line speech-cuts from *The Merchant of Venice* and sorts them into passions ("austere," "peevish"), rhetorical occasions ("protests"), topics ("laws"), and figures of speech ("simile") (Savage 1887 unpaginated).

Line-cuts and speech-cuts dominate Shakespeare cuts in manuscripts, but there is one famous instance in which a penman has added character-cuts in the form of costumed figures. A single manuscript sheet with an inscribed date of 1595 (Marquess of Bath, Harley Papers, vol. 1, fol. 159v, Foakes 1985: no. 25) includes three speech-cuts from *Titus Andronicus*, which had been printed a year before the inscribed date, plus a frieze-like drawing of seven characters from the play. (See Figure 14.) Two inscriptions on the sheet, one of them in a contemporary hand, attribute the cutwork to Henry Peacham, who declares in his book *The Complete Gentleman* (1622) that from childhood he has liked to draw people's faces (Foakes 1985: 50). The speech-cuts come from two different places in the printed text: an exchange between Tamora and Titus (sig. B1, Oxford text 1.1.104–21) and, joined by a two-line bridge put together by the writer, a speech from Aaron (sigs. I2–I2v, Oxford text 5.1.125–44). As for the drawing, most scholars have taken it to be a scene-cut. But which scene is it? The speech-cuts from Tamora and Titus, as well as the assembled characters and their postures, would seem to indicate 1.1, but two significant details from stage directions in the printed text of the scene—a crowd of Romans "*as many as can be*" (1.1.69 *sd*) as well as a black-draped coffin containing the bodies of two of Titus's sons—are absent in the drawing. Aaron figures in the drawing, but his speech-cut comes from another scene entirely: 5.1. These discrepancies have led scholars to several conflicting conclusions: (1) that the speech-cuts were added beneath the drawing by someone else, (2) that Peacham or whoever made the drawing was *remembering* a theater performance rather than *recording* it, or (3) that the drawing does not refer to Shakespeare's play at all (Foakes 1985: 48–51; Schlueter 1999). It is also possible that the draftsman may never have seen *Titus Andronicus* in performance but was recording what he imagined as he read the printed text and what he remembered as he drew.

Whether or not the speech-cuts were added later, whether or not they come from the same hand, what we see in Figure 14 is not a scene-cut but a series of character-cuts. In its combination of speech-cuts and character-cuts, the drawing accords with woodcut illustrations on title pages of plays printed in quarto. The most famous is the

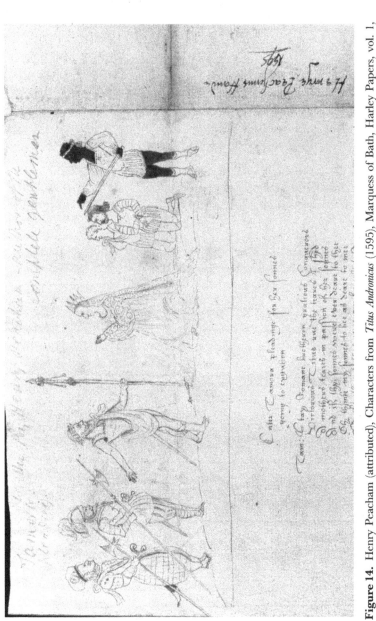

Figure 14. Henry Peacham (attributed), Characters from *Titus Andronicus* (1595), Marquess of Bath, Harley Papers, vol. 1, fol. 159v. Reproduced by permission of the Marquess of Bath, Longleat House, Warminster, Wiltshire, Great Britain.

1615 edition of Thomas Kyd's *The Spanish Tragedy* (Foakes 1983: no. 44, see http://luna.folger.edu/), which shows character-cuts and line-cuts (in the form of banderoles that seem to issue from the characters' mouths) but combines elements from more than one scene, all within the same picture space. Most definitely it is character-cuts, not a scene-cut, that we see on the title page to *The Wits* (1672, see http://luna.folger.edu/), an engraving that includes characters labeled "Sir J. Falstaff" and "Hostess," on the same platform with characters from other plays by other writers. At the back of the platform, stepping out from behind a curtain, is the comedian Bubble from John Cooke's play *Greene's Tu Quoque, or The city gallants* (1614, Foakes 1985: no. 43; see also Figure 8 [this volume]). Bubble is the only character-cut supplied with a banderole line-cut: his signature complement "Tu quoque. To you sir" ("And you. To you, sir"), which he happily says to anyone, in any situation. Seen in these contexts, the sheet attributed to Peacham would seem to combine character-cuts and speech-cuts rather than being a scene-cut.

=

From 1600, when speech-cuts from Shakespeare's poems and plays were included in John Bodenham and Anthony Munday's *Bel-vedére* and Robert Allott's *England's Parnassus*, until 2005, when YouTube was launched, print provided the main technology for disseminating line-cuts, speech-cuts, and eventually scene-cuts from Shakespeare's texts. A year earlier, complete sonnets by Shakespeare, including some embedded in *Love's Labor's Lost* (see Table 2), had been printed in *The Passionate Pilgrim*, with a title-page attribution of the entire anthology to "W. Shakespeare." Both *Bel-vedére: The Garden of the Muses* and *England's Parnassus; or, The Choicest Flowers of our Modern Poets* are organized like manuscript commonplace books, with line-cuts and speech-cuts ranged under such headings as "Angels" ("——If Angels fight/ Weak men must fall, for heaven still guards the right. *W. Shakespeare*"), "Affection" ("Affection is a coal that must be cooled,/ Else suffered, it will set the heart on fire…. *W. Shakespeare*"), "Audacity" ("Things out of hope are compassed oft with venturing,/ Chiefly in love, whose leave exceeds commission…. *W. Shakespeare*"), and so on (Allott sigs. B2, B4, B4v). *England's Parnassus* includes line-cuts and speech-cuts from *Venus and Adonis, The Rape of Lucrece, Romeo and Juliet,*

Richard III, and *Richard II* (Rumbold 2016: 2:1688–94). The subtitles and the prefatory remarks in both anthologies present the texts as "flowers" that have been found in a garden, cut, and gathered for the reader's delight and utility. The term "anthology" derives from the Greek word *anthos*, "flower" (*OED*, "*anthology, n.,*" etymology), so an *anthologia* is a collection of "flower-words." On the extensive cultural history of the *florilegium* metaphor before, during, and after Shakespeare's time, we can turn to a study by Jessica Rosenberg, forthcoming at the time of this book's publication.

More line-cuts and speech-cuts from Shakespeare appeared in John Cotgrave's *English Treasury of Wit and Language* (1655), but it was in the eighteenth century that cutwork with lines, speeches, and scenes from Shakespeare became a cultural phenomenon. The index of "Speeches. The most considerable in Shakespeare" in Pope's edition of 1725, noted in Chapter 1, is organized by topic, like *Bel-vedére* and *England's Parnassus* a century earlier. The "starts" and "points" in Garrick's performances of Richard III, Hamlet, Macbeth, and Lear (see Chapter 2 and Figure 9) were also influential in the printing of speech-cuts and scene-cuts. Collections of great moments in English drama like *Thesaurus Dramaticus* (1724), reprinted many times during the eighteenth century as *Beauties of the English Stage* and *Beauties of English Drama*, established the precedent for William Dodd's *The Beauties of Shakespeare* (1752), the multiple editions of which are organized not by theme as in the *Thesaurus Dramaticus* but by play and act. Usually (but not always) a moral tag precedes each passage that Dodd has chosen. The Rev. Dodd's anthology was still in print 130 years later.

Scene-cuts rather than speech-cuts finally make a sustained appearance in the third (1784) and later editions (1791, 1797, 1800) of another, separate enterprise with the same title: *The Beauties of Shakspeare* (first edition 1783). In this case the thematically organized speeches of the older anthologies are supplemented with "A selection of the most interesting scenes in Shakspeare's plays" (Shakespeare 1784, sig. P6), including six from *Hamlet*. All in all, the so-called "detached scenes" (sig. A2) in *The Beauties of Shakespeare* take up half the book. Once established in the eighteenth century, books of scene-cuts became a commodity in nineteenth- and twentieth-century publishing (Rumbold 2016, Márkus 2016). In these eighteenth-century anthologies an underlying structural principle has been preserved, but the metaphor is no longer a garden, as in *England's Parnassus*. Instead, the whole enterprise comes under the aegis of "William Shakespeare" as national bard. The collected cuts function as synecdoche for Shakespeare's genius. As Zoltán Márkus has observed, in such circumstances speech-cuts and scene-cuts become author-cuts: "Quotations tend to collapse the characters who utter the lines in their respective plays with the author.... It is noteworthy, therefore, that quotations are vehicles of commemorating and celebrating the cultural status of the author, but they are also acts of forgetting, suppressing, and rupture" (Márkus 2016: 2:1695).

=

In our own time, so-called "cuttings" still have a vital function in drama schools. Among the print resources available to acting and directing classes are *Short Scenes from Shakespeare: Nineteen Cuttings for the Classroom* (Samuel Selden and William-Alan Landes 1993), *Scenes from Shakespeare: Fifteen Cuttings for the Classroom* (Michael Wilson 1993), and *More Scenes from Shakespeare: Twenty Cuttings for Acting and Directing Practice* (Michael Wilson 1999). The term "cuttings" suggests press clippings from newspapers and magazines, but also at play perhaps are at least three ideas from cinematography: "cuts" as changes in camera angle, "cuts" as edited versions of a film ("rough cut," "director's cut," etc.), and "cuts" as deleted scenes that end up on "the cutting room floor."

Even more than printed anthologies of scenes, cuttings imply a distinctive way of approaching Shakespeare's texts: not as through-written plays, but as amalgamations of speeches and scenes. More than *six hundred* scenes and monologues from Shakespeare and his contemporary playwrights are catalogued in Kurt Daw and Julia Matthews' *A Guide to Scenes and Monologues from Shakespeare's Stage* (1998). Compared with complete plays, where so many things are going on, cuttings invite concentration. John Russell Brown in *Shakes-cenes: Shakespeare for Two* (latest edition 2000) goes so far as to discourage reading the entire play: "An earlier reading may help in a general way, but the task in hand is to act only the lines of one short duologue and to bring those comparatively few words to life in as complete a manner as possible" (Brown 2000: 7). The goals of such concentration are two things in particular: character-development and, in Brown's words, "bringing to life." The procedures of Method acting (see Chapter 2) inform all of these anthologies, in particular the assumption that the actor playing a dramatic role needs to find and convey a backstory beyond the lines in a given scene. The thirty-five cuttings in Robin J. Holt's *Scenes from Shakespeare: A Workbook for Actors* (1985) "were chosen because the characters' intentions are relatively clear in the text" (1).

The origins of books of cuttings, like anthologies of speech-cuts and scene-cuts more generally, can be traced to the eighteenth century. The earliest example is probably *The Sentimental Spouter: or Young Actor's Companion* (1774), a pocket-sized book containing a treatise on oratory and acting and "a collection of the most celebrated scenes, speeches, and soliloquies, selected from the most admired tragedies and comedies," including twenty-three scenes from Shakespeare. What the young actor spouts are sentiments. The thirty-nine cuts have been chosen to give the volume's purchaser material for acting out the major passions, including gravity, perplexity, hope, joy, courage, boasting and threatening, grief, anger, pity, love successful and unsuccessful, jealousy, rage, fear, remorse, and despair—hence the "sentimental" in the title, "Characterized by or exhibiting refined and elevated feeling" (*OED*, "sentimental, *adj.*," 1.a). The balcony scene from *Romeo and Juliet* (love successful) leads off the collection; Iago's fanning of Othello's burning jealousy in *Othello* 4.1 concludes it. Again, a structural principle organizes the cuts: the commonplaces and the synecdoche of earlier anthologies have been replaced by actors' passions.

=

The combination of print and title-page woodcuts in the likes of *Greene's Tu Quoque* in 1614 (see Figure 8) and the reprint of *The Spanish Tragedy* the next year invite us to consider woodcuts as part of print technology. Physically speaking, they are: an inked woodblock has to be pressed forcefully to deliver an impression on paper. Phenomenologically, however, woodcuts ask to be read differently from the printed texts they accompany. They give us a visual version of events rendered in the words. They insinuate connections with particular lines, speeches, and scenes, but above all else they cut characters from the fiction and present them to us in arresting visual form. The cut of Bubble on the title page of *Greene's Tu Quoque* is a striking example. For a potential purchaser and a ready reader of John Tryndle's quarto, the text that ensues *is* the character. None of the scenes is as important as the character, and none of the words as important as the line "Tu quoque. To you sir" that issues on a banderole out of Bubble's mouth. Foakes wonders if what we see in the woodcut is not just Bubble, but a likeness of the actor Thomas Greene, who was famous for the part (Foakes 1985: 102–3). If so, we have here the earliest instance of an "actor-cut" of the sort that became universal in eighteenth-century engravings.

We may also have in title-page woodcuts the prototype for single-panel caricatures, "strip" comics, comic books, manga, and graphic novels: all forms of cutwork that have accommodated Shakespeare. An eighteenth-century invention that flourished in the century that followed, caricatures included exaggerated likenesses of Shakespeare himself, as in examples by Silvester Harding, William Heath, George Cruikshank, and Max Beerbohm (Haynes 2016). Neil Gaiman's "Sandman" series numbers 13 (1990), 19 (1990), and 75 (1996) and Conor McCreery and Anthony Del Col's "Kill Shakespeare" series (2010–14) stand as famous examples of Shakespeare comics. (A survey and analysis of Shakespeare in comics, manga, graphic novels is offered in Mykelbost 2016.) In physical terms, the caricatures may be engraved, the earlier comics lithographed, the manga and later comics digitally created and reproduced, but phenomenologically they all engage viewer/readers in similar ways. In both their strip and book form, multi-panel comics are, in McLuhan's terms, a "cool" medium in which viewer/readers insinuate themselves into the interspace between cuts, in this case a space known as a "gutter." Scott McCloud describes the effect thus: "Nothing is seen between the two panels, but experience tells you something must be there. Comic panels fracture both time and space, offering a jagged, staccato rhythm of unconnected moments. But closure allows us to connect these moments and mentally construct a continuous, unified reality" (McCloud 1993: 67).

=

The first illustration of a fiction by Shakespeare is usually taken to be the engraved frontispiece opposite the title page to *The Rape of Lucrece...By the incomparable master of our English poetry, Will: Shakespeare Gent.* (1655). (A digital image can be seen at http://folger.edu/luna/.) Attributed to England's first native-born master engraver William Faithorne, the cut contains (1) an author-cut of Shakespeare based on the folio, (2) character-cuts of Lucrece and Tarquin, (3) a scene-cut of Lucrece about to cut into her breast while Tarquin strides toward her, and (4) a two-line speech-cut "The Fates decree, that it is a mighty wrong/ To womankind, to have more grief than tongue." All the cuts—author-cut, character-cuts, scene-cut, and speech-cut—coalesce in a powerful image. The illusion of a theatrical scene-cut is heightened by drapery in the upper right and a column from what might be a *scenae frons* on the left, but there is no such scene in Shakespeare's poem (Tarquin is long gone when Lucrece decides to commit suicide), and the speech-cut comes not from Shakespeare but probably from the editor John Quarles, who supplies a continuation of the story in which Tarquin is arraigned and receives punishment. Confronted with this engraved frontispiece, we find ourselves in exactly the position we face vis-à-vis the scene-cut in Peacham's drawing of *Titus Andronicus* and the title page to the 1615 edition of *The Spanish Tragedy*: two scenes in the text have been fused into one.

The distinction of first illustration of a Shakespeare *play* (as opposed to Quarles's illustration of a Shakespeare *fiction*) may actually belong not to a printed book, but to a broadside ballad. *A New Song, Showing the Cruelty of Gernutus a Jew* (1620, Pepys 1.144–45, English Broadside Ballad Archive 20063) may be a "residual" or "spin-off" of Shakespeare's play (Smith 2006: 193–217). (See Figures 15A and 15B.) Many details in the ballad do not match the play—the Jew's name, for example, and the fact that it is a Judge, not a Portia-figure, who comes up with the decisive argument—but the ballad and the play share line-cuts and speech-cuts, especially when the protagonists are given direct speech. "Merry sport" (1.3.144) becomes "merry jest" (*Gernutus* fol. 1), and "Let the forfeit/ Be nominated for an equal pound/ Of your fair flesh" (1.147–9) becomes "For this shall be the forfeiture/ Of your own flesh a pound" (fol. 1). The relationship between *Gernutus* and *Merchant* is not unlike the relationship between Quarto 1 and Quarto 2 of *Hamlet*: the ballad gives its readers a cut from a verbally more sophisticated text.

Whether or not the ballad represents a version of the play, it nonetheless reminds us that woodcut illustrations on broadside ballads are for the most part character-cuts and scene-cuts that set a precedent for later illustrations of Shakespeare's plays. The woodcut on the left in Figure 15A is a character-cut that fits perfectly the ballad's

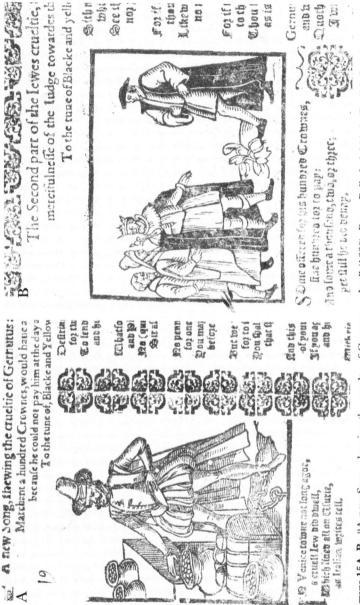

Figure 15A–B. "A new Song, showing the cruelty of Gernutus a Jew" (1620), Pepys Ballads 1.144–5, English Broadside Ballad Archive 20063, details showing a character-cut (left) and a scene-cut (right). Reproduced by permission of the Pepys Library, Magdalene College, Cambridge.

description of Gernutus's person and his props; the woodcut on the right, a scene-cut of the trial. The fact that both cuts may have been generic woodblocks that a printer could have moved around at will does not detract from the fact that establishing a character-type (wealthy merchant on the left, a king in judgment on the right), setting a scene, and giving a viewer cues for imaginative engagement are primary functions of ballad woodcuts (Marsh 2016)—and, indeed, of *all* early-modern images. The famous character-cut/scene-cut that appears on the title page to the 1615 edition of *The Spanish Tragedy* also adorns the ballad of "The Spanish Tragedy" published at about the same time (ESTC 214639, Roxburghe 1.364–5 and 1.390–1, English Broadside Ballad Archive 30246 and 30263).

Comparison between the woodcut of Thomas Greene's Bubble on the title page to *Greene's Tu Quoque* (see Figure 8) and the engraving of William Shakespeare on the title page to *Mr. William Shakespeare's Comedies, Histories, and Tragedies* (see Figure 13) will point up just how different the interface is between "figure" and "life." Both cuts stand in a similar relationship to the titles and the texts they accompany, but the engraving, made with burin-and-copperplate technology and rendered in finer detail, contains much more visual information than the woodcut does. Compared with the sparse lines in woodcuts, the inked lines in engravings are dense, the white spaces fewer. Notice in particular the lack of shadow in the woodcut of Greene's Bubble versus the modeling of Shakespeare's bald forehead, highlighted where it is struck by the same ambient light that the viewer shares. The result is a greater degree of life-likeness that requires less imaginative participation on the part of the viewer.

=

It was in the eighteenth century that engraved cutwork with Shakespeare came into its own. Nicholas Rowe's *The Works of Mr. William Shakespear, Adorned with Cuts*, published by Jacob Tonson in six octavo volumes in 1709, provides not just a frontispiece portrait (based on the Chandos portrait that had been owned and eulogized by John Dryden), but one engraving for each play. With just two exceptions—Peacham's drawing of characters from *Titus Andronicus* (1595?) and the engraved title page to *The Wits* (1672)—the cuts for the Rowe/Tonson edition are the earliest visual representations of scenes from

Shakespeare's plays. The cuts were designed by a relatively unknown young French artist, François Boitard, and engraved by the equally obscure Elisha Kirkall (Sillars 2016a, Blake 2016). In the case of *The Merchant of Venice* the cut depicts the trial scene. (See Figures 16A and 16B.) We have in these images "scene-cuts," not only because a particular scene has been detached from the play, but because cutting is the technology that has allowed the scene-cut to be reproduced. The detail in Figure 16B shows how physical cuts made by a burin in the copper plate have received the ink to produce the resulting cut-as-print.

What constitutes the "scene" in scene-cuts like this one? These earliest illustrations mark out two directions: one that leads to the stage and one that leads to the library. It takes only a glance at the cut for *Merchant* in Rowe's edition to see that, despite the drapery at the top, the image has only a tangential relationship to any particular stage production. After all, many of the plays adorned with a cut in Rowe's edition were never performed in the early eighteenth century (Whitfield 2013: 20–3). Rather, the images function as synecdoche for the play it accompanies. The cut is placed, not next to the scene it illustrates, but at the beginning of the play. The chosen moment represents what a reader of the text might imagine, not what a spectator might see on the London stage. Looked at before the reader begins the text, the cut functions as a preview of the play's decisive scene. Looked at after the reader has finished the text, the cut functions as a mnemonic device, a place-holder for the reader's memory of the play. Rowe's cuts have, as it were, two faces: one turned toward the text as public figure and one turned toward the reader's private imaginative experience.

=

Reciprocity between engraving as a cutting technique and the life it claims to represent can be witnessed in a print of "Mr. Garrick in Four of His Principal Tragic Characters" (1750–70). The copy in Figure 9, once owned by Charles Burney, shows Garrick in four iconic poses, each associated with a particular Shakespearean role. The Hamlet pose is corroborated from other prints, such as James McArdell's mezzotint of 1754 and Francis Hayman and Hubert Gravelot's *Hamlet* illustration for Charles Jennens' edition of five of Shakespeare's tragedies (he died before he could complete his planned edition of the complete works) in 1773 (digital images at http://folger.edu/luna/).

Figure 16A–B. Illustration for *The Merchant of Venice*, designed by François Boitard, engraved by Elisha Kirkall, for *The Works of Mr. William Shakespear…Adorned with Cuts*, ed. Nicholas Rowe (1709), showing the full image (left) and detail of Shylock (right).

Note in the four composite cuts in Figure 9 how Garrick has been
physically detached from any scenic context. In considering the interspace between engraving and theatrical performance, we run up
against the question of which came first: the "attitudes" that Garrick
struck in the theater, or the cuts, the perceptual moments, shown in
"Mr. Garrick *in* Four of His Principal Tragic Characters" (emphasis
added)? From one direction, the answer might be that Garrick in his
attitudes was making cuts *from* history painting; from the other direction, that the engraver of Figure 9 was cutting moments in live performances and inserting them *into* history painting. Either way, prints
like this one helped shaped audiences' perceptions in the theater.

John Boydell approached character-cuts and scene-cuts from both
directions when he commissioned paintings of famous scenes from
Shakespeare and set them up, for an admission charge, in a gallery in
Pall Mall. He followed Rowe and Tonson in calculating that the
images could serve both for public display, in his gallery, and for
private reading, in the form of illustrations to a projected new edition
of the texts. By 1789, when the Shakespeare Gallery opened, Boydell
had published single engravings showing actors such as David Garrick
in famous roles, but the images in his Shakespeare Gallery were
intended to encourage a British school of "history painting" to rival
France's, and very few of the images had anything to do with theater.
A printed catalogue, enlarged several times as new pictures were added
to the exhibition, allowed viewers to read the text of the scene in the
catalogue while they looked at the painting of the scene on the wall.

Cuts like "Garrick and Mrs. Pritchard in *Macbeth*" (1768), engraved
by V. Green after a painting by Zoffany and published by John
Boydell in 1776, are typical of these scene-cuts from the theatre.
(Digital images of these and other depictions of Garrick in action
are available at http://folger.edu/luna/.) The engraved image may
carry an inscription that specifies play title, act number, and scene
number, but most such prints would more accurately be labeled
character-cuts. William Hogarth's painting of Garrick as Richard III
(c. 1745), for example, was immediately engraved by Hogarth himself,
assisted by Charles Grignion, and issued as a large-format print
suitable for framing or binding with other prints. Hogarth's painting
and engraving may not represent the actual stage setting in which
Garrick performed the role in the 1740s, but it captures one of

Garrick's characteristic postures in that role. The distinction between scene-cuts and character-cuts is patent in some copies of Bell's 1774 edition, in which scene-cuts and character-cuts have been combined to produce a double frontispiece to each play. The opening in Figure 17 shows the graveyard scene in *Hamlet* on the left and Jane Lessingham in character as the mad Ophelia on the right. When we remember the origins of the word "character" in the Greek verb *charássein*—"to make sharp, to cut into furrows, to engrave" (*OED*, "character, *n*.," etymology)—the association of character and cut becomes all the stronger.

=

Character-cuts were part of a more general eighteenth-century penchant for detaching Shakespearean characters from the texts in which they figure and giving them a life of their own in critical analyses, paintings, prints—and even porcelain figurines (Caines 2013: 108–9, Vickers 1981: 11–21). The process accelerated in the nineteenth century. The images in Figures 18A, 18B, and 18C illustrate both a chronological and a technological sequence, as character-cuts move from engraving (Figure 18A) to a combination of engraving and photography (Figure 18B) to straight photography (Figure 18C). The first image in the sequence shows Charles Macklin, knife in hand, as Shylock (first performance 1741). "This is the Jew, that Shakespeare drew": the inscription is a testimonial to Macklin's acting attributed to Alexander Pope. In this particular print, the word "drew" acquires multiple meanings: as Shakespeare's writing, Macklin's characterization, and the engraver's cut. We can note also that Shylock "draws" his knife.

The engraver's cut is still present in the earliest widely circulated photographs of Shakespeare performed, a series of prints of famous actors published by John Tallis in the 1850s. Figure 18B shows Charles Macready in the role of Shylock (first performance 1839). The inscription advertises that Macready's likeness is taken "from a Daguerreotype by Paine of Islington," but engraving was necessary to make copies of what the camera's click had captured on a unique sheet of silvered metal (Sillars 2016b). The only difference from a standard engraving was that Tallis's engraver used a photograph rather than a drawing as a model for Macready's face. In Tallis's prints the cut between life and figure was sharper than it may have appeared. And so it is in photographs.

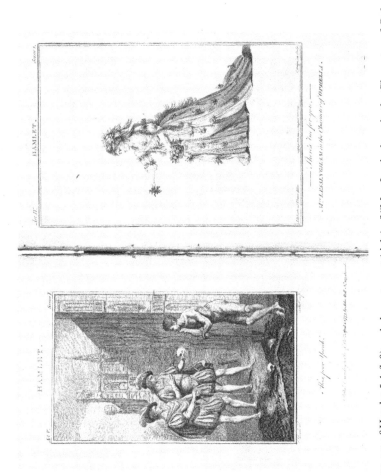

Figure 17. Scene-cut of Hamlet 5.1 (left) and character-cut (right) of "Mrs. Lessingham in the Character of Ophelia," from *Bell's Edition of Shakespeare's Plays* (1774). By permission of the Folger Shakespeare Library, PR2752 1774b copy 1 vol.3 Sh.Col.

Figure 18A. "Mr. Macklin in the Character of Shylock," engraving by John Lodge (1775). By permission of the Folger Shakespeare Library.

Figure 18B. "Mr. Macready as Shylock, *Merchant of Venice*, act I, scene 3 / from a daguerreotype by Paine of Islington" (mid-nineteenth century). Published by John Tallis and Company. By permission of the Folger Shakespeare Library.

Figure 18C. Charles Kean as Shylock and Patty Chapman as Jessica, albumen-print photograph by Martin Laroche (c. 1842). © Victoria and Albert Museum.

The photograph by Martin Laroche in Figure 18C shows Charles Kean as Shylock and Patty Chapman as Jessica from a production at the Haymarket Theatre in 1842. An albumen print made from a glass negative, the image predates Tallis's but could never have been reproduced in the numbers that engraving technology made possible. Cuts in mid-nineteenth-century theatrical photographs were both fugitive and slow. The slowness could be measured in feet as well as minutes. Until the very end of the nineteenth century, lighting requirements meant that actors had to decamp from the theater to a photographer's studio. One reason that a particularly large number of photographs were taken of Charles Kean and his company in Shakespearean roles at the Princess's Theatre from 1850 to 1859 is that Laroche's photography studio was only a few doors away on Oxford Street (Sillars 2016b). With their painted backdrops and standard props, most of Laroche's theatrical shots look not very different from the ordinary portraits he took with the same accoutrements, but a few seem to include pieces of scenery that may have been hauled down the road along with the actors' costumes. The backdrop in Figure 18C, with its Venetian pointed arches, could be one of these. In nineteenth-century theater stills we observe the "character-cut" of eighteenth-century engraving carried out with a different technology, but with the same purpose of cutting characters from their live theatrical contexts and giving them a life quite independent of Shakespeare's plays.

It was not until the end of the nineteenth century that camera and lighting technology permitted photographs to be taken in theatres, giving a record of what the stage actually looked like. The contrived poses of actors in twentieth-century theatre stills like those taken by Angus McBean from the 1930s through the 1950s look not so different from Garrick's character-cuts in the eighteenth-century print in Figure 9. Beginning in the 1960s, so called "rehearsal shots" attempted to capture the fluidity of live performance. Printed theater programs are now likelier to contain such shots than carefully staged theater stills (Sillars 2016b).

=

Ben Jonson's cut between "life" and "figure" would seem to be erased in photography. A click of the shutter, accompanied by a flash of light, arrests the ongoing-ness of life and turns it into a figure. Even in the mid-nineteenth century, when photograph-taking was a slow process, photography was patently faster than engraving or drawing. Because it eliminated the hand of an intermediary it also appeared to offer images taken directly from life. Still, the cut was there. "To *take* a photograph" was—and is—to use a machine to cut through the life-space in front of the photographer. The violence of such an action is even greater in the phrase "to *shoot* a photograph," which the *OED* dates to 1890 and regards as a subset of "to send missiles from an engine" ("shoot, *v.*," III, III.22.f). An image so taken becomes a "shot," likewise dated by the *OED* to the 1890s ("shot, *n.¹*," I.7). Our own terms of "image *capture*" and "screen *capture*" continue metaphors that began with photography in the nineteenth century. As a model for perception, the new technology of photography encouraged viewers to look for discontinuities where viewers in earlier times had seen continuities. In the theater, for example.

The very term "theater still" points to a fundamental opposition in photographs: a theater production is fluid action that a photograph *stills*. Tim Tadder captures that stilled fluidity in the image of Henry V that we considered in the first chapter. In theatre stills, performances that originally took place in four dimensions have been foreshortened, radically so in the dimension of time. In the case of Jacob Adler as Shylock in a late-nineteenth-century production in New York, the survival of several different versions of the trial scene suggest how carefully the actors and props have been arranged and rearranged so as to accommodate the camera. (All are available for viewing at http://folger.edu/luna.) Each version functions as a separate cut in what was once, in live performance, a continuous action. Long exposure times demanded these careful arrangements. The viewer of the resulting photographs sees, however, only a single moment, a mere second out of the many seconds it took for the camera to capture the image and the many minutes it took to perform the scene on stage. Digital cameras foreshorten performance even more radically, as live action is converted almost instantaneously into an array of 1 | 0 digital cuts.

The fetishization of photography as a technology that forever changed art forms as well as regimes of seeing has been vigorously attacked by Rebecca Schneider (whose name in German, by the way, means "tailor" or "cutter"). "It may be," Schneider proposes, "that our habit of reading the performed gesture as in-time and therefore 'live' and reading the gesture caught by a camera as out-of-time, and thus somehow no longer live, misses a more complicated leakage of the live (and the remain) across seemingly discrete moments" (Schneider 2011: 141). A major instance of such "leakage," according to Schneider, are the "living stills" that once were major components of theatrical performance. Garrick's four characteristic postures in *Lear*, *Macbeth*, *Richard III*, and *Hamlet* (see Figure 9) are moments of arrested action, focal points in *tableaux vivants* that artists such as Hogarth, Hayman, and McArdell attempted to capture with pencil, brush, and burin. Schneider's observation that statues in Roman theatres and their Renaissance imitations served as "stills" in the very midst of live action prompts the thought that the caryatids that adorned the stage of the 1599 Globe might have functioned in just that way. We know such caryatids existed, because the builder's contract for the Fortune Theatre (1600) calls for "carved proportions called satyrs" to be part of the stage construction (qtd. in Gurr 2009: 169). The division between still and living would have been blurred if the tapestry or painted cloth that covered the stage space "within" contained human figures, as in the curtains at the back of the stage on the title page to Nathaniel Richardson's *Messalina* (1640) (Foakes 1985: no. 34). "Discovery" scenes such as Prospero's revealing Ferdinand and Miranda playing chess in Act 5, Scene 1 of *The Tempest* would have turned these woven or painted figures into the "living stills" that Schneider finds in medieval drama and in royal entries.

We can witness an especially suggestive interplay between still images and living images—between "figure" and "life"—in Figure 19. A theatrical still of an Yoruba-language performance of *The Winter's Tale* by the Renegade Theatre of Lagos, Nigeria, during the 2012 Globe to Globe Festival at Shakespeare's Globe in London captures the momentary contrast between the exuberant dancing of the sheep-shearing festival in Act 4, Scene 4 with the static fixity of elements of the tiring-house wall: a trompe-l'oeil niche with a statue on the upper left, caryatids in the upper center, and human figures on painted cloths hanging below. The immobile figure on the left (probably Polixenes) looks in the photograph to be almost part of the scenery. All of those arrangements change drastically in Act 5, Scene 3, when Hermione's statue comes to life and still becomes living. The elements on the tiring-

Figure 19. *The Winter's Tale* 4.4 as performed in Yoruba by the Renegade Theatre at Shakespeare's Globe, London, 2012. Photograph by Simon Annand. Reproduced by permission of Shakespeare's Globe.

house wall have, in effect, been waiting for this moment. By May 1611, when Simon Forman saw *The Winter's Tale* performed at the Globe, the caryatids had stood witness to performances of at least a dozen new Shakespeare plays in the 1599 Globe, including *Henry V, Julius Caesar*, and *Hamlet*. This time the cut between figure and life was obliterated.

=

In *The Sound of Shakespeare* (2002) Wes Folkerth recounts the story of Henry Irving's first encounter with an Edison recording machine in August 1888. Invited by his friend George E. Gouraud to record a few words into the trumpet of Edison's newly invented device, the usually confident Irving was, witnesses said, "frightened out of his voice" (Folkerth 2002: 2). Ten years later, however, Irving was deeply back into his voice when he recorded the first eleven lines of Richard III's opening speech "Now is the winter of our discontent/ Made glorious summer by this son of York" (*R3* 1.1.1–2) (Folkerth 2000: 5–6). Audio files of that recording are available online and on a two-CD set of *Great Historical Shakespeare Recordings* (Levin and Timson 2000). An alleged

1906 recording of Irving speaking some of Shylock's lines from the trial scene of *Merchant* has not been located (Kilgarriff n.d.), although Ellen Terry's rendition of Portia's "The quality of mercy is not strained" (*Mer.* 4.1.181), recorded in 1911 during one of her tours of "Shakespeare's Heroines," is included in the CD set.

Four kinds of cuts are involved in Irving's recording: a character-cut of the sort we have seen in engravings and photographs (this time aural, not visual), the cut of a famous speech from its context in the original script, the cut of a stylus into a wax cylinder, and a perceptual cut between sound and vision. Of these four, it is the cut of the stylus that is most likely to divert our attention. Recording sound on wax cylinders was a species of engraving: air waves set in motion by the speaker activated a diaphragm not unlike the one in the human ear, which in turn activated a vibrating stylus that cut a distinctive groove into the wax. Playing back the cylinder reversed the process. With each playing, however, more of the groove was destroyed by the vibrating stylus. Early cylinders could be played only a dozen times, later cylinders only a hundred times. For all the cutting involved in this process, the groove in the wax cylinder is continuous. It contains an analogue of the sound. In this respect it differs sharply from the cuts between one electronic signal and another that characterize digital recording.

Once again, let us raise the question of how a new technology for cutting may have dictated new cuts in perception. On the production side, Irving seems to have become more comfortable with sound-recording between his first encounter in 1888 and his confident recitation of "Now is the winter of our discontent" in 1898. That earliest extant recording was made for private use, but commercial cylinders featuring speech-cuts and song-cuts from Shakespeare quickly accustomed listeners to hear Shakespeare in cuts lasting two minutes or less. It is uncanny that Irving's delivery of lines in the theater was already noted for its cutting. As we noted in Chapter 2, Irving was in the habit of inserting pauses in unexpected places, leaving auditors such as Henry James nonplussed. Irving himself, in a lecture delivered three years before his first experience with recording his own voice, describes his aural technique as a matter of carefully timed cuts:

> I can confidently ask you whether a scene in a great play has not been at some time vividly impressed on your minds by the delivery of a single line, or even of one forcible word.... No less an authority than Cicero

points out that pronunciation must vary widely according to the emotions to be expressed; that it may be broken or cut, with a varying or
direct sound, and that it serves for the actor the purpose of color to the
painter, from which to draw his variations (Cole and Chinoy 1976: 358).

As a technology for cutting, sound recording isolates such effects and
trains the ears of actors to deliver them and audiences to hear them. The
results of cutwork with sound can be witnessed on the 2-CD set *Great
Historical Recordings* (Naxos NA220012, n.d., also available as an audiobook).

=

Cuts of a different sort still were introduced by the motion-picture
camera, and the interface between figure and life was rearranged yet
again. We have become so habituated to watching films that the
multiple forms of cutwork involved in films are likely to escape us
entirely. In this particular cutting technology figure seems to disappear
into life. A glance at Figure 11 should correct our vision. "Moving
pictures" may move, but they are made up of stills, and they retain
the two-dimensional flatness of photographs and engravings. Cuts help
to compensate for that flatness and achieve the illusion of depth that has
made cinema such a dominant medium since the1920s. In films based
on Shakespeare's scripts, three kinds of cuts come into play: the excisions and the rearrangements that are already familiar to us from stage
productions, but camera work introduces a powerful new technique—
the camera-cut. Let us consider these three kinds of cuts one by one.

If "the two-hours' traffic of our stage" (*Rom* Pro.12) is, in Shakespeare's case, more like four hours unless lines, speeches, and even
whole scenes are excised, how can Shakespeare's texts possibly be
accommodated within the maximum two-hour format of commercial
films? "Moving pictures" are, after all, *pictures*. It is the visual content
that drives the whole enterprise. A film has a lot more to communicate
than spoken language. That makes Shakespeare a challenge. Charles
Marowitz in a late essay on "Cinematizing Shakespeare" argues that
adapting a novel or a short story into film "is transforming like into
like." Much contemporary prose fiction seems to be constructed, in
fact, with the idea that it can readily be filmed.

When one does the same with stage plays that date from about the
middle of the nineteenth century to the present, one can argue that

they, too, contain "malleable constituents" which can be moved from one medium to the other. But when one goes back only three centuries earlier, one finds works designed for the stage that are inescapably verbal constructs (Marowitz 2013: 72).

The earliest films of Shakespeare plays—the surviving footage of Herbert Beerbohm-Tree in *King John* (dir. William Kennedy and Laurie Dickson, 1899), shorts of *The Tempest* (dir. Percy Snow, 1908), *A Midsummer Night's Dream* (dir. Charles Kent, 1909), *King Lear* (dir. Gerolamo Lo Savio, 1910), *Twelfth Night* (dir. Charles Kent, 1910), *The Merchant of Venice* (starring Ermete Novelli and Francesca Bertini, 1910), and a 22-minute *Richard III* (starring Frank Benson, 1911)— get along without spoken language, indeed without sound at all. (In Benson's case we do have a recording of him, made eleven years earlier, speaking King Harry's speech before the gates of Harfleur, included in the *Great Historical Shakespeare Recordings* set.) Even when sound was added to moving pictures in the late 1920s, the ratio of visual elements to language was entirely different from stage plays— and remains so today.

Shakespeare films that have tried to include the entire text are few and, in the eyes of many critics, seriously compromised. Paul Czinner's *As You Like It* (1935), the first British feature-length film of a Shakespeare script, stays much closer to Shakespeare's text than most later films do, but nonetheless cuts are made to the parts of Jaques and Touchstone, whose cynical wit would otherwise cut the fairy-tale sweetness that Czinner fostered (Rosenthal 2007: 5). George Cukor's *Romeo and Juliet*, released the same year in Hollywood with Norma Sherer (as Juliet) and Leslie Howard (as Romeo), likewise strove for authenticity, including respect for Shakespeare's text, a claim authenticated by Professor William Strunk Jr. of Cornell University (Rosenthal 2007: 207–10). A more recent example is Kenneth Branagh's *Hamlet* (1996), at 243 minutes the longest Shakespeare film ever made (Rosenthal 2007: 45–6). Elaborate camera work in the Branagh film sometimes betrays, to my eye, an anxiety about the relationship of cinematography to spoken language. While Branagh speaks Hamlet's 32-line three-minute soliloquy "To be or not to be," the camera executes a distracting slow pan around a hall of mirrored doors. "How all occasions do inform against me" (4.4, Add. Passages

J.23–57)—often cut in stage productions of *Hamlet* because it is absent from the folio text—is accompanied by a slow, dramatic camera pan-out amid an icy mountain landscape.

Self-contained scene-cuts like "How all occasions do inform against me" illustrate one of Marowitz's shrewd observations about cinema as a medium: it is almost impossible not to indulge in big scenic effects. In modern stage productions, close sequencing of scenes and ever-building momentum are prized by most directors. In films, however, "landscapes, crowd-scenes, lingering close-ups and atmospheric vistas are interspersed throughout the action to augment, illustrate or just beautify the film-product. These often retard the plot-line and indulge in visual effects for their own sake" (Marowitz 2013: 71). The situation is not so different, perhaps, from the spectacular stage pictures that led to wholesale rearrangements in the sequencing of scenes in nineteenth-century stage productions such as Henry Irving's *Merchant* or the "close-ups" provided by *tableaux vivants* in the eighteenth century and the engravings that reproduced them.

=

Trevor Nunn in the revealing notes prefaced to *William Shakespeare's Twelfth Night: A Screenplay* (1996) seizes on the motion-picture camera's capacity to produce quick cuts that in fact heighten the momentum and complicate the action rather than slow it down. He instances in particular how camera-work in his film of *Twelfth Night* turned Viola's soliloquy at the end of 2.1 ("I left no ring with her. What means this lady?" [2.2.17]) into an event that occurred in two times and two places. Viola considered the ring sent from Olivia twice: once in the moment after Malvolio delivered it, and once that night. The lines continued from one scene to the other (with no fewer than twenty-two scenes in between), but camera-cuts caught a mental debate spread out over many hours—and thus enhanced the illusion of life: "Film editing thrives on the energy and momentum of contrast and unlike on stage nobody has to enter or exit; the edit takes you to the next image instantly" (Nunn 1996: unpaginated).

Walter Murch, the Oscar-winning film editor whose remarks we have already visited twice, goes so far as to assert, "We would want to cut even if discontinuity were not of such great practical value." Cutting "is in *and for itself* by the very force of its paradoxical suddenness—a positive influence in the creation of a film" (Murch

2001: 9). For choosing just where a film editor chooses to cut, Murch outlines six criteria and supplies percentages indicating the relative importance of each:

51% emotion
23% story
10% rhythm
7% eye-trace ("concern with the location and movement of the audience's focus of interest within the frame")
5% giving an illusion of depth to the two-dimensional plane of screen
4% attending to the three-dimensionality of the fictional space of action ("where people are in the room and in relation to one another") (Murch 2001: 20).

In his insistence on emotion as the most important factor in cutting, Murch sounds very much like actors and directors in the theatre who justify cutting speeches and abridging scenes in order to keep up momentum and keep the audience engaged.

=

The trial scene in Michael Radford's 2004 film of *The Merchant of Venice*—the first full-length commercial film of the play—can serve as an example of cutwork with the motion-picture camera. The portion of the scene presided over by the Duke (4.1.1–397 in the Oxford text) is realized not only in cuts to the original script but also in camera cuts. Actually, the line cuts (about a hundred by my count, roughly 25 percent of the original text) are quite modest by film standards. Most noticeably absent are the Duke's exchanges with Antonio in the beginning (4.1.1–12), the three asides on wedlock spoken by Portia, Nerissa, and Shylock when Bassanio rates his friendship with Antonio above his love for his wife (4.1.285–92), and many of Graziano's blood-thirsty taunts of Shylock (4.1.129–37, 315, 320, 330, 337–8). Otherwise, most cuts have been made in the interest of shortening speeches and removing difficult allusions.

Camera-cuts are far more important. In the scene's running time of 27 minutes there are, by my reckoning, no fewer than 250 of them. That works out to about 9 per minute, or 1 every 6 seconds. These averages are misleading, however, because rapid cuts are concentrated in moments of high tension. When Portia stops Shylock's hand and tells him he must not shed a drop of blood, the camera quickly gathers reactions from the principals and the crowd. Cuts lasting a minute or more are mostly devoted not to Portia as we might expect, but to Shylock, repeatedly shown in isolation against the courtroom crowd. Many of these longer cuts, to be sure, are enlivened by camera pans. More important still are the close-ups that put Portia and Shylock on intimate terms as the camera cuts, in close up, from one's face to the other's. The intimacy of these cuts allows Portia to speak many of her speeches, including "The quality of mercy," in a quiet almost conversational tone, not at all like a public oration.

The responsibility for these aesthetic decisions is probably Michael Radford's. He is credited not only as director, but also as the author of the screenplay. To what degree should additional credit be given to Benoit Delhomme as director of photography or Lucia Zuccheli as film editor? Camera-cuts and close-ups in Radford's *The Merchant of Venice* certainly illustrate the mimetic power that Murch claims for film alone:

> Film is a dramatic construction in which, for the first time in history, characters can be *seen to think* at even the subtlest level, and these thoughts can then be choreographed. Sometimes these thoughts are almost physically visible, moving across the faces of talented actors like clouds across the sky. This is made possible by two techniques that lie at the foundation of cinema itself: the closeup, which renders such subtlety visible, and the cut—the sudden switch from one image to another— which mimics the acrobatic nature of thought itself (Murch 2001:143).

=

In the transitions from pen-and-ink technology to print to woodcut to engraving to photography to sound recording to film, the white space between cuts becomes smaller. Less and less has to be filled in by the imagination of the reader or viewer or listener. In each successive technology the cutting edge becomes sharper, the figure denser, the medium "warmer." Murch's comments on the replacement of guillotine cutting by digital editing would seem to provide the perfect segue from film to digital technology. Murch outlines an evolution from the beginning of the twentieth century to the end: manual cutting and gluing together of strips of celluloid film in the early years of moving pictures were replaced in the 1920s by splicing and cutting machines, which have now been replaced by computer programs. Digital cutting comes with exponentially greater memory storage, faster speed, the convenience of random access to all the takes, the possibility of creating and comparing multiple versions, and quick duplication of the final cut. The easy duplication of working prints, Murch observes, makes it possible for multiple copies to be worked on by people other than the director, creating a new category, "ghost cuts" (Murch 2001: 116), that the director and the film editor can use in making the final cut. The goal of all this cutting is to make the exhibited cuts look seamless and inevitable.

When we consider the transitions from woodcut to engraving to still photography to film, a master narrative suggests itself: that the cutting edge has got sharper and sharper and the need for imaginative work on the part of perceivers less and less. That grand narrative is disrupted, however, by some nineteenth-century innovations that gave consumers a hand in the cutting. So-called tinsel prints, popular from about 1810 to 1850, anticipate on a small scale the cutwork that digital technology invites users to do for themselves today. Etched portraits of famous actors clothed in elaborate costumes from roles they played on the London stage were intended to be tinted by purchasers with watercolors and adorned with cut-out pieces of fabric, leather, feathers, tinsel, and other scrap materials. By the 1830s it was possible to buy the cut-out pieces ready-made. The example in Figure 20 shows Charles Kean posed as Richard III, with just the suggestion of a scenic context. Large collections of tinsel prints exist in the Victoria and Albert Museum (http://collections.vam.ac.uk) and the Houghton Library at Harvard University (http://oasis.lib.harvard. edu). To judge from the V&A's database, the most popular Shakespeare protagonists in these prints were, in this order, Richard III, Othello, Oberon, Hamlet, Hotspur, Iago, Macbeth, Prince Henry, Claudius, Coriolanus, Cassius, King John, Falconbridge in *King John*, Titania, and Portia.

A related product was produced at the end of the nineteenth century: so-called "scrap sheets" containing chromolithographed Shakespeare characters that had been embossed and die-cut, ready for the purchaser to punch out and paste up on screens, onto greeting cards, or into albums or "scrapbooks." The sheets were sold in packets of twelve and cost one shilling (Hildesheimer 1890). Among the sheets of

Mr. C. KEAN, as
RICHARD III.

Figure 20. Tinsel print of Charles Kean as Richard III, hand-colored engraving with pasted-on additions (mid-nineteenth century) © Victoria and Albert Museum.

Shakespeare scraps preserved in the V&A theater are pairings of Romeo and Juliet, Hamlet and Ophelia, Othello and Desdemona, and Shylock and Jessica. (See http://vam.ac.uk/collections.) The collection in the Folger Shakespeare Library includes almost two hundred Shakespeare-related scrapbooks and scrapbook fragments, dating primarily from the late-nineteenth to mid-twentieth centuries. Websites such as Pinterest cater to the same impulses, although the bulletin-board metaphor in "pin" indicates how much more social scrap-collecting has become compared with albums. A search at https://www.pinterest.com/will turn up hundreds of Shakespeare speech-cuts, character-cuts, scene-cuts, and author-cuts, as well as original cutwork using two or more of these elements.

User-made cutwork using printed images continues in book sculptures (see Figure 24) and in interactive books like *Shakespeare's Globe: An Iinteractive Pop-up Theatre* (2005), designed by Toby Forward and Juan Wijngaard. The book comes equipped with a fold-out model of the Globe and cut-outs of twelve Shakespeare characters that users can move around at will within that cut-out space.

=

Tinsel Shakespeare, scrap Shakespeare, and pop-up Shakespeare all engage the user in cutting and arranging cuts at will, but they are all print projects, and what they offer is primitive compared to the cuts that can be made with computers. Of all the technologies for cutting surveyed in this chapter, the newest—digital technology—has received as much or more critical attention than the others. (On Shakespeare in particular, see the essays collected in Carson and Kirwan [2014] and Fischlin [2014].) Print technology probably runs second, film third, photography fourth, engraving fifth, sound-recording sixth, woodcut seventh, and pen-and-ink eighth. Within the context of this book, the main question concerns the interspace in digital technology between "figure" and "life." Just as surely as the white spaces in print, woodcuts, and engravings, digital technology depends on cuts as openings for experience. In every digital text, in every digital image, in every digital sound file, in every digital video, cuts exist in the form of alternations between 1 and 0, between "on" and "off." (On mp3 files versus analogue recording versus live performance, see Sterne 2012.) Most listeners, vinyl enthusiasts excluded, have learned to ignore the spaces in between. For the purposes of *Shakespeare | Cut*, we must pay attention to those interspaces. Micro-cuts between 1 and 0 facilitate the more obvious cuts that characterize Shakespeare on the web.

The move from the manual to the mechanical to the digital can be witnessed in all the technologies considered in this chapter. In the course of this sequence physical cuts have increasingly become virtual cuts: that is to say, cuts that are imperceptible to eye or ear but that function as cuts nonetheless. That is what "virtual" means: something "that is such in essence, potentiality, or effect, although not in form or actuality" (*OED*, "virtual, *adj.* and *n.*," II.4.a). Traces of the physical do persist in digital technology, at least in how we refer to certain activities. In word-processing, scissors exist in the icon for "cut"; glue-pots, in the icon for "paste." Photoshop provides a "cutting tool" and a "cropping tool." With respect to visual images, we still recognize the cut in the word "woodcut" even if no inked ridges are present for touching. In photography we still shoot, get, or take pictures, even if we now seldom print them. In recorded sound, an artist sill cuts a record, even though no stylus moves in a groove. In cinema, there is no more footage, no workprint, no director's cut or ghost cut, and yet these terms from an obsolete technology are still in use. A huge question concerns the degree to which we continue to *experience* these virtual cuts as physical cuts. We tell ourselves that we are experiencing fluidity, but a virtual blade still cuts the flow.

=

Electronic signals alternating 1 | 0 endow cutwork with possibilities far beyond anything available in earlier technologies. Five factors are at play: (1) ease of execution, (2) impetus toward "short forms," (3) facility to cut from one medium to another, (4) permission to cross boundaries between "high" culture and "low," and (5) control by the user over sequencing, meaning-making, and dissemination of the resulting cutwork. In James J. Gibson's terms, we might think of these five factors as "affordances," as options for action available in a particular environment, given the objects available and the agent's perceptions and goals (Gibson 2015: 119–36; S. O'Neill 2014: 6). The environment in this case is virtual, the objects are digital files, and the agent is creator as well as consumer and disseminator. Let us consider these affordances one by one.

With the right software, anyone can now do cutwork with Shakespeare. For ease of execution, digital technology is faster even than pen and ink and exponentially faster than print, woodcut, engraving, photography, film-making, and sound-recording, all of which require elaborate equipment and, in most cases, skills that take years to acquire. For doing digital cutwork with Shakespeare, apprenticeship in script-writing, acting, directing, composing music, woodcutting, engraving, photography, cinematography, dancing, and singing are not required. Artists who have devoted years to mastering an art or a discipline are sometimes contemptuous of the ease with which digital creations can be made. In the case of Shakespeare, digital cutwork is generally made out of what someone else has already created within a traditional discipline, whether that be film, musical performance, painting, photography, or, in the last analysis, scripts written by a certain professional playwright between 1589 and 1613, even when not a single word is invoked. Whether digital cutwork represents democratization of art or abandonment of art remains an unsettled question. For opposing sides in this controversy see Paul (2015) (pro) and Birkerts (2015) (con). In the meantime, it is worth noting that cutwork with digital technology can be a sophisticated art form in and of itself and coordinated with other media.

The necessity of a new term, "long form," to describe non-fiction writing longer than an article but shorter than a book is testimony to the second affordance of digital technology: brevity. Shakespeare, as Ben Jonson complained, was a "long form" writer if ever there was one. What Jonson couldn't stanch, the internet has. "Short form," a linguistic term for contractions and a handy term for the abbreviations used in social media, is an apt descriptor of how Shakespeare as a long-form author has been turned by digital technology into a short-form author. The major Shakespeare genres on the internet—video clips, sound files, the length of music downloads, still images, blogs— have brevity in common. The shortest Shakespeare on the internet may be the video documenting the world record established in 2009 by Chad Lunders of Kansas City, Kansas, for "'To be or not to be' recited while balancing on a Rola Bola on a picnic table and juggling knives." (See https://recordsetter.com/world-record/recite-to-be-or-not-be-soliloquy-while-balancing-rola-bola-picnic-table-juggling-knives/ 2055.) The record is (or was, when this book was written) 41.21 seconds. Knives figure as the perfect synecdoche for Lunders' achievement.

With video, as with stage and cinema, technology dictates the speed and sets limits on duration. The number of bytes that can conveniently be uploaded and downloaded keeps getting larger, but most YouTube postings run less than fifteen minutes (McKernan

2:1970–2). At the time of this writing, the longest posting on the BardBox and Bardbox 2 channels ran at eleven minutes. Most postings ran at three to five, somewhere in between Irving's "Now is the winter of our discontent" (1 minute 43 seconds, but incomplete) and Percy Snow's 1908 silent film of *The Tempest* (8 minutes). Short-form Shakespeare in fact has a long history, beginning with pen-and-ink transcriptions in commonplace books. The complete Shakespeare texts available online do preserve "long-form" Shakespeare, but many readers use these databases primarily for use in "short forms," such as quotations to be inserted in essays, articles, and book chapters. Vis-à-vis Shakespeare's complete works online, we are likely to use our tablets as Comenius's student uses the book that lies open on his desk in Figure 4: as a source for cuts to be used elsewhere.

As a third affordance, digital technology facilitates cuts across media, making it possible for a user to move, fast or slow, between Shakespeare as stage performance, as film, as opera, as ballet, as visual image, as popular music, as parody. A search for "Merchant of Venice" carried out using Google's search engine on October 7, 2015 turned up 527,000 hits in 0.37 seconds—a modest number of hits by internet standards. Almost nothing in the top thirty-five hits would have given pause to Heminges and Condell, Comenius, or probably Shakespeare himself. After the expected Wikipedia link came several complete texts of the play (with shakespeare.mit.edu first), notes and study guides for students such as SparkNotes and CliffsNotes (commonplacing done for you), reviews and trailers connected with Radford's 2004 film, a link to the Folger edition (in both print and e-book formats) for sale at amazon.com, promotions and reviews connected with various stage productions (including an Original Pronunciation production by Baltimore Shakespeare Factory, directed by David and Ben Crystal, in 2015), quotations at goodreads.com and poets.org (more ready-made commonplaces), and a note at history.com for July 22 recording that on this day in 1598 *The Merchant of Venice* was entered into the Stationers' Register.

The three outliers for me—the three hits demonstrating that cutwork using digital technology is more than updating of earlier technologies—were the website of Venice Merchant, an organic grocery-delivery service in Venice, California (Google clearly knows the location of my computer in Los Angeles), a news posting dated July

8, 2015 on haaretz.com entitled "Argentina's Jews Riled by President Kirchner's 'Merchant of Venice' Comments" (she referred to Shylock in connection with investment funds that have bought up national debt), and a wiki for the videogame "Civilization V" that features a character named "The Merchant of Venice" and a "trivia" heading that tells gamers that "The unit's name is a reference to the William Shakespeare play *The Merchant of Venice*" (http://civilization.wikia.com/wiki/Merchant_of_Venice_%28Civ5%29). We shall pursue Shakespeare-as-meme in Chapter 5.

The fourth affordance, cultural boundary-crashing, is most obviously realized on YouTube. Stephen O'Neill in *Shakespeare and YouTube: New Media Forms of the Bard* (2014) and Luke MacKernan in "Shakespeare and Online Video" (2016) have taken the measure of this breadth. Postings for "Merchant of Venice" range from Radford's film (it ranked number 12 in my Google search) to Jonathan Miller's National Theatre production of 1973 with Laurence Oliver and Joan Plowright to "Shakespeare Summarized" by Overly Sarcastic Productions to cuts of Shylock's "Hath not a Jew eyes" speech delivered (in English, Yiddish, and New York Yiddish-inflected English) by various professional and amateur actors to cuts from the symphonic music of Gilbert and Sullivan's "Merchant of Venice Suite" to cuts from a documentary film about a Maori-language production of *Merchant* (2002) to English-class mash-ups to Andre Tchaikowsky's opera (premiered at the Bregenz Festival in 2013) to a 1910 silent film made in Italy. From earlier technologies we recognize the types of cuts in play here: line-cuts, speech-cuts, character-cuts, scene-cuts. What is different now are the interspaces between them. Parataxis supplies YouTube's syntax, irony its rhetoric. The question is how—and where—we choose to *take* that irony.

Most important of all the digital affordances with cutwork is the opportunity for the user to control sequence, speed, and destination. Phenomenologically, we might consider digital search-and-cut four ways: (1) as moving through a "window," often through a "portal," deeper and deeper into a space beyond; (2) as "surfing" through data, some of it "streamed," using "navigation" devices; (3) as "invention" that moves via rhetorical tropes; and (4) as gaming.

Anne Friedberg has studied how the concept of "window" has evolved from ideas of surface and depth that began in the visual arts of Shakespeare's time. The phrase "surfing the internet" returns us to Tim Tadder's underwater image of Henry V breaching the walls of Harfleur in Figure 1. Amid the flow of information, we are looking for cuts. We seek "hits" that will, momentarily at least, stop the flow. "Navigation" devices lead us to these hits, and the search engine functions as a kind of outboard motor. YouTube helps to direct us through "channels," including several devoted to Shakespeare. The search operation is itself a form of cutting, and the search engine serves as a cutting tool. The click of the "select" command with an index finger executes yet another cut; the click to download, still another. If it is a video that we have selected and downloaded, a horizontal bar at the bottom of the screen allows us to create an instant still and, if we have the right software, to "capture" that still and file it away in an electronic folder.

The rhetoric of internet mobility has been charted by Christy Desmet, who demonstrates how links between YouTube "hits" function as metaphors, linking logically unlike but figuratively alike hits, and as instances of metonymy, linking hits via association (Desmet 2014). To metaphor and metonymy one might add the puns that algorithms are too literal-minded to edit out. "A hit, a very palpable hit": take as a search term Osric's line during the swordfight in *Hamlet* (5.2.231) and you will turn up "hits" in multiple senses—Osric's speech of course, but also miscellaneous fencing references, several YouTube videos that use *Hamlet* 5.2, and Branagh's "hit" film of the play, not to mention all of these links as search "hits" in their own right.

Individual users can put together cuts to suit personal interests, but so can a community of users through the use of tags and comments. Algorithms can make those connections too. In one sense, navigation devices such as keywords, hashtags, and @ handles on Twitter function as paraphs, as markers of discrete cuts: # and @ are the new ¶. If a surfer does not linger at a given hit, the paraphs may also correspond to the "perceptual moments" we studied in Chapter 3: devotions of attention lasting only a few seconds. Slow or fast, however, the paraphs turned up by navigation devices can be used to create sequences. The channels on YouTube can, depending on the user, be arranged and rearranged to create larger wholes. We shall explore these possibilities further in Chapter 5.

=

An immediate measure of the hegemony of digital technology for cutting purposes of all kinds is this very book: most of the research for *Shakespeare | Cut* was carried out on the internet. Virtually all of the pre-nineteenth-century books cited in these pages were accessed via Early English Books Online, Open Source Shakespeare, and other text databases, most of which feature search functions. Still images from all periods were located and in most cases directly downloaded from online databases like those maintained by the Folger Shakespeare Library (http://luna.folger.edu), the Victoria and Albert Museum (http://collections.vam.ac.uk), and the British Museum Department of Prints and Drawings (http://www.britishmuseum. org/research). The camera-cuts in Radford's film of *The Merchant of Venice* could readily be counted using the play/pause/resume functions of the DVD file. Irving's cylinder recording of "Now is the winter of our discontent," once virtually unknown, was available in sound files in several places, including YouTube (https://www.youtube. com/watch?v=7Z4gXiNKR4s) and the website of the Irving Society (http://www.theirvingsociety.org.uk/richard_iii.htm). Best of all, you as the reader of this book can now make your own way to those sites—and from there to places and uses I did not dream of. An ideal version of *Shakespeare | Cut* would not be a printed codex but a digital text with frequent cuts in the form of links, and a blog at the end so I as the writer and other people as readers could find out where you've been and what you've done there.

5

The New Cut

Shuffling Cuts Since 1900

> Here I am Anthony,
> Yet cannot hold this visible shape.…
>
> ……
>
> She, Eros, has
>
> Packed cards with Caesar's, and false played my glory.
>
> —Antony to Eros, *Antony and Cleopatra* 4.15.13–14,
> 18–19 in *Mr. William Shakespeare's Comedies,
> Histories, and Tragedies* (1623), sig. y5v

In his book of satires *Tom Tell-Troth's Message, and his Pen's Complaint* (1600) John Lane lambastes a card game called "new cut." So addicted to this "new invention" are "fine-ruffed ruffians" that they will "cut some other's purse or throat" (sig. C3) to keep playing. "New cut," we learn from John Florio, was a card game known in Italian as *Trinca* (sig. Nn6v). Digital technology is, by now, hardly a new invention, and the cuts it facilitates are commonplace, but some doomsayers still find in it an engine of destruction no less threatening than "new cut" seemed to Lane in 1600. That includes the part about addiction. In this view, 2,700-word plays that were delivered to readers of the First Folio as worthy of being read, and again, and again (Shakespeare 2005: lxxi) now provide the materials for deeply cut stage productions, YouTube mash-ups, or (as Phillip Stubbes would put it) "worse" (sig. L8v). As we have seen many times over by this point in *Shakespeare | Cut*, people have in fact been making cuts in, to, from, and with Shakespeare since the 1590s: line-cuts, speech-cuts, character-cuts, scene-cuts, author-cuts, performance-cuts, and the rest. What seems new is a fascination with the very process of cutting—perhaps indeed an addiction to cutting.

This final chapter of *Shakespeare | Cut* investigates that phenomenon, but locates its origins not in the 1980s or 1990s with the wide availability of digital technology, but at the very beginning of the twentieth century, with the advent of Modernism. Despite our investment in Millennium 21 as a decisive chronological cut and in digital media as an even more decisive technological cut, the evidence invites us to consider the 115 years covered in this chapter as one entity: "the long twentieth century." A chronological survey of modes of cutting up Shakespeare begins with burlesques; turns to Vorticism before the Great War and Dada afterwards; takes up Modernism; lingers on the Post-modern work of Tom Stoppard, The Reduced Shakespeare Company, and Charles Marowitz from the 1960s through the 1990s; and concludes with a consideration of the still more radical cutwork in Shakespeare scissions since the turn of the millennium: a period that I join others in regarding as "Post-post-modern." At each juncture we shall stop and consider not so much *how* cuts were made (that was the subject of Chapter 4) but *why*.

Following John Lane's cue, let us begin with games.

=

"All poetry is a reshuffling of a pack of picture cards," Tzara tells Gwendolyn in Tom Stoppard's *Travesties* (1974),

> and all poets are cheats. I offer you a Shakespeare sonnet, but it is no longer his. It comes from the wellspring where my atoms are uniquely organised, and my signature is written in the hand of chance.

GWEN: Which sonnet—was it?

TZARA: The eighteenth (Stoppard 1974: 53).

Gwen's response, "You tear him for his bad verses?" (54, quoting *Julius Caesar* 3.3.30–1), inaugurates a facetious exchange of lines from eight different Shakespeare plays.

Stoppard's scene is Zurich in 1917, during the Great War. Twenty-seven years earlier William James had chosen the phrase "The pack of cards is on the table" to illustrate his new concept of "stream of consciousness." (See Table 2.) The undulating graph line plots the continuity of the thought across several seconds, but with peaks at "pack," "cards," and "table." It is not clear whether James intends each degree mark ['] to represent a precise number of seconds—the spacing suggests not—but we encounter in the chart something like the "perceptual cuts" that we noted in Chapter 3. The conjunction in James's graph of "stream" and a deck of fifty-two cards, waiting to be cut, returns us yet again to Figure 1 and Tim Tadder's image of Henry V, sword in hand, emerging out of water. Stoppard, in his association of Shakespeare with a pack of cards, is unlikely to be alluding to "The Shakespeare Game," first marketed in 1900, but with Stoppard who knows? (See Figure 21.) The fifty-two cards in "The Shakespeare Game" are each imprinted with a character-cut or a scene-cut and a speech-cut, sorted into four suites: A, B, C, and D. The players take turns reading the quotations on the cards they have been dealt. If another player recognizes a quotation and needs that particular scene to make up a set of four scenes from a single play, he collects the card. The player who wins the game is the one with the most sets and—if chance has been cooperative—with the most knowledge of Shakespeare. Figure 21 shows how the deck incorporates author-cuts (on the cards' backs), scene-cuts (*Hamlet* 1.1.1 and 5 and *Merchant* 4.2), speech-cuts (at the bottoms of each card's face), and character-cuts (Ada Rehan as Katherine in *Shrew*, complete with cutwork costume).

Games as represented in early modern drama, and indeed games as *enacted* in early modern drama, have been suggestively investigated by Gina Bloom in a chapter on "Games" in *Early Modern Theatricality* (2013). Our challenge in *Shakespeare|Cut* is to put ourselves in a position to appreciate the forms of play since 1900. That involves more than learning the rules. Each era employs cutwork to distinctively different ends, and the rules of the game keep changing. James P. Carse's distinction between "finite games" and "infinite games" can help us get our bearings. "A finite game," Carse observes, "is played for the purpose of winning, an infinite game for the purpose of continuing the play" (Carse 1986: 3). Finite games like Lane's "new cut" and Florio's "*Trinca*" have definite rules and take place within definite limits with respect to space, time, and players. In infinite games like Stoppard's and Tzara's the rules are forever changing, just as space, time, and players change. The infinite game of "Shakespeare New Cut" is what this chapter plays.

=

"But/ O O O O that Shakespeherian Rag": the ragtime song that Eliot invokes in *The Waste Land* was relatively new when Eliot

Figure 21. Sample playing cards from "The Shakespeare Game." Cleveland Game Company, 1900. Public Domain.

published his poem in 1922 ("The Shakespearian Rag" had been published ten years earlier), but it was a patchwork of lines from famous speeches intercut with references to contemporary popular culture: the very stuff of nineteenth-century burlesques of Shakespeare and the raw material of Shakespeare remixes on YouTube today:

> "Friends, Romans, Countrymen,
> I come not here to praise,"
> But lend an ear and you will hear
> A rag, yes, a rag that is grand, and
> Bill Shakespeare never knew
> Of ragtime in his days.
> But the high browed rhymes,
> Of his syncopated lines,
> You'll admit, surely fit,
> any song that's now a hit,
> So this rag, I submit (Eliot 2001: 51–4).

To rag a piece of music was to cut it to pieces with syncopated rhythm. And so the lyricists Gene Buck and Herman Ruby rag their Shakespeare. "Lay on MacDuff," "To be or not to be," "My kingdom for a horse," "As you like it" are quoted in the song, while Desdemona, Romeo and Juliet, Brutus, Shylock, and Othello all beg "Bring the rag, right away" (Eliot 2001: 52). It is a nice question which came first: Eliot's "fragments," or "O O O O that Shakespeherian Rag."

Or maybe the first was Thomas Duffett's *The Empress of Morocco* (1673) or Fielding's *Tumble-down Dick* (1736) or John Poole's *Hamlet Travestie* (1811) or W. S. Gilbert's *Rosencrantz and Guildenstern* (1874). All of these Shakespearean burlesques combine line-cuts, scene-cuts, and character-cuts with cuts from contemporary popular culture. The nineteenth century witnessed the apotheosis of the genre (Wells 1978, Schoch 2003, Bradley 2016). Take, for example, the title page of the anonymous *A Thin Slice of Ham let! Cut for fancy fare, in which the original much disputed text is re-arranged, condensed, and amended, also the extremely disgusting denouement ameliorated and consequently rendered more palatable to the fastidious taste of the present refined age* (c.1863). In its devotion to "the original much disputed text," *A Thin Slice of Ham let!* satirizes rearrangements and condensations by the likes of Kean as well as the amendments and annotations of scholarly editors. Amid these cuts, an entity called "Shakespeare" is revered and defended. In that respect *A*

Thin Slice of Ham let! is typical of the genre. Shakespeare's texts may be cut and rearranged, new language may be introduced, characters may turn into caricatures, popular culture may be presented as more down-to-earth, but through it all "Shakespeare" comes through unscathed. In burlesques the object of ridicule is usually not Shakespeare or his plays but what other people have *done* to Shakespeare and his plays. The scenic excesses of the nineteenth-century productions that we noticed in Chapter 2—Charles Kemble's, Charles Kean's, and Henry Irving's in particular—inspired new rounds of burlesques.

=

"The artist of the modern movement is a savage," Wyndham Lewis writes in the first issue of the Vorticist journal *BLAST* (June 1914), "...this enormous, jangling, journalistic, fairy desert of modern life serves him as Nature did more technically primitive man" (Lewis 1914–15: 1:33). The journal's title celebrates artistic violence as a cure for the blandness of modern life—an idea made more shocking by the timing. The Great War broke out within weeks of the first issue's appearance. In Lewis's cause, as in England's, Shakespeare was drafted into service. The first issue opens with lists of "blast" *this* and "bless" *that*. Shakespeare makes the "bless" list "for his bitter Northern Rhetoric of humour" (1:26). Humor, Lewis goes on to explain, "is a phenomenon caused by sudden pouring of culture into Barbary.... It is intelligence electrified by flood of Naivety.... It is Chaos invading Concept and bursting it like nitrogen" (1:38). In Lewis's eyes, Shakespeare possessed—and possesses—that vitalizing power. In the second issue of *BLAST* (July 1915, a year into the Great War) Lewis celebrates Shakespeare as a creator of character-cuts: he was

> a mighty mirror, and his contemporaries [*sic*] mirrors. His figures accumulated by a natural process, and for no reason. They dragged all sorts of burdens of power with them. They were immense outcasts, silhouetted at last in the sunshine of his plays. He whistled Music Hall airs as he worked.... Art is not active; it cuts away and isolates. It takes men as it finds them, a particular material, and works at it. It gets the best out of it, and it is the best that it isolates. The worst is still there too, to keep the man in touch with the World, and freer because of the separation. Perfect art insists on this duality, and develops [*sic*] it (2:70).

Lewis himself was acting on such principles when he designed a lithograph entitled "Timon of Athens" and inserted it as a plate in the first issue of *BLAST*. (See Figure 22.) One can understand why Lewis would be drawn to Timon: an "immense outcast" who "drags burdens of power" into Shakespeare's play and willfully cuts himself off from Athenian culture, blasting the objects, attitudes, and practices he has come to abhor and ending the play in high-minded isolation. Lewis planned, in fact, to publish an edition of *Timon of Athens* in a future issue of *BLAST*, and designed illustrations for the project. (The surviving designs are now divided among several collections. The examples in the Folger Shakespeare Library can be seen at http://luna.folger.edu/luna/.) The artistic route that Lewis has taken toward these designs is implicitly mapped out in articles on Futurism ("The finest Art is not pure Abstraction, nor is it unorganised life" [Lewis 1914–15: 2:134]), German woodcuts ("The quality of the woodcut is rough and brutal, surgery of the senses, cutting and not scratching" [2:136]), and Picasso ("Most of Picasso's latest work...is a sort of machinery" [2:140]).

In the lithograph in Figure 22, contrasts between black shapes and white suggest the brutality of woodcuts, the intersections of lines and circles look like machinery, and the emergence of a human form (its head in the upper left) evinces more than "pure abstraction." The implication of the Timon-figure in the machinery of life—his life, Lewis's life, the viewer's life—presents character-cut in an altogether different guise from anything we witnessed in Chapter 4. Paul Edwards articulates succinctly the aesthetic at work in Lewis's *Timon* designs, some of which include letters:

> The white paper he works on now becomes not a picture-plane but a field around which a limited range of pictorial elements can be distributed at will. Our perception of fragments of figures and lettering out of these blocks, arcs and lines tends to be provisional, as the design takes on different readings with shifts in the viewer's attention (Edwards 1998: 38).

Lewis's cutwork with Shakespeare is not static; the lines, shapes, and contours engage the viewer in dynamic acts of combination and recombination. Picasso's Cubism—already well known in 1914, at least in Lewis's circles provides the fundamental template not only

Timon of Athens.   Wyndham Lewis.

Figure 22. Wyndham Lewis, "Timon of Athens," lithograph from *BLAST* volume one (1914). The Huntington Library.

for Lewis's cutwork with Shakespeare, but also for William Burroughs' in the 1950s and '60s.

For all his talk of primitivism and savagery, of chaos invading concept, Lewis's cutwork with Shakespeare is not destructive. It is, rather, an incentive to create new, more vital forms of art. The difference between destruction and creativity is spelled out in two pages toward the end of the first issue of *BLAST*, in a "word of advice" to Suffragettes:

> WE ADMIRE YOUR ENERGY. YOU AND ARTISTS ARE THE ONLY THINGS (YOU DON'T MIND BEING CALLED THINGS?) LEFT IN ENGLAND WITH A LITTLE LIFE IN THEM.
> IF YOU DESTROY A GREAT WORK OF ART you are destroying a greater soul than if you annihilated a whole district of London.
> LEAVE ART ALONE, BRAVE COMRADES! (1:151–2)

The occasion for Lewis's appeal is Mary Richardson's slashing of the Rokeby Venus earlier in 1914. (See Figure 2.) Lewis did not, of course, "leave Shakespeare alone." Nor did he destroy him. That counterpoise between destruction and reconstitution informs cutwork with Shakespeare through the rest of the twentieth century, and into our own century.

=

If Lewis's cutwork with Shakespeare is violent but serious, Tristan Tzara's is violent but playful. And not a little narcissistic. All three qualities are present in the cutwork that Tzara actually performed at the Galerie de la Cible in Paris in December 1920, when jazz performed by no less than Jean Cocteau, Francis Poulenc, and Georges Auric was interrupted at intervals by Tzara's raising his hands and making pronouncements on love—and on how to write a Dada poem:

> Take a newspaper.
> Take a pair of scissors.
> Choose an article as long as you are planning to make your poem.
> Cut out the article.
> Then carefully cut out each of the words that make up this article and put them in a bag.
> Gently shake.
> Then take out the scraps one after the other.
> Copy these down conscientiously in the order that they were taken out of the bag.
> The poem will resemble you.

And voilà you are a writer infinitely original and endowed with a
sensibility that is charming though beyond the understanding of the
vulgar (quoted in Hentea 2014: 160).

The November issue of the journal *391*, advertising the event, had
included this squib:

> You must read Shakespeare
> He is truly an idiot
>
> …
>
> Read Tristan Tzara
> And you will stop reading (qtd. in Hentea 2014: 159).

Shakespeare also makes appearances in the manifestos of Futurism in
1908 (see http://www.ubu.com/papers/marinetti_futurist-synthetic-
theater.html) and Surrealism in 1924 (see http://www.ubu.com/
historical/breton/Breton-Andre_First-Manifesto-of-Surrealism_1924.
pdf).

In the decades immediately before and after the Great War
(from Wyndham Lewis's Vorticist manifesto in 1914 to Eliot's
The Waste Land in 1922 to André Breton's manifesto of surrealism in
1924), five things converged to encourage cutwork with Shakespeare:
(1) the adversarial but idealistic aesthetic of Futurism and allied
movements such as Vorticism, (2) the playful randomness of Dada,
(3) the cutting-edge technologies of cinema and sound recording,
(4) the ragging of High Culture by popular culture, and, not least,
(5) the four centuries of cutwork with Shakespeare in the form of the
speech-cuts, character-cuts, scene-cuts, and performance-cuts to be
found in books of quotations, single-play editions, visual illustrations,
sound recordings, still photographs, and films. I would argue that
these same impulses are still operative today. Only the dominant
technologies have changed.

=

It is against this earlier history of cutwork that we should consider the
word-cuts, line-cuts, scene-cuts, and character-cuts from Shakespeare
in Eliot's *The Waste Land* (1922). "These fragments I have *spelt into* my
ruins" is Eliot's first draft of the line that became, after cutting and
replacing the original verb and the original preposition, "These

fragments I have *shored against* my ruins" (Eliot 1971: 81, 146 l. 430, emphases added). "Spelled into": in the first draft the cuts from Shakespeare and other classic writers figure as inscriptions, including, implicitly at least, cuts between the letters and the words. "Shored against": in the second version, the cuts figure as broken stone carvings on which the words might be inscribed—carvings salvaged, perhaps, from wrecked libraries and fire-bombed cathedrals of the Great War. When Ezra Pound in his Cantos set out to emulate Eliot's collage technique he recognized Eliot's fragments as cuts from books: "These fragments you have *shelved* (shored)" (Canto 8, l. 1 in Pound 1996: 28). In a 1931 review of *A Draft of XXX Cantos*, Marianne Moore celebrates Pound as a reader of books: "Mr. Pound brings to his reading master-appreciation, and his gratitude takes two forms: he thanks the book and tells where you may see it" (Moore 1955: 64). That includes not only particular editions, but also particular places and times for reading the books he writes about.

Spelled, shored, or shelved, Eliot's "fragments" include more than half a dozen from Shakespeare's plays, three of them explicitly iden-tified in Eliot's footnotes. In their new contexts, these fragments both interrupt the vestigial narratives of Eliot's five-part poem and provide ballast and continuity. "Vestigial" seems the right word for narrative scenarios that have been cut back, sometimes drastically, from the original drafts. The pen that cut these drafts was sometimes wielded by Eliot but more often by Pound, who read the drafts a few months before the poem was published and cut out for his own use Eliot's image of fragments (Eliot 1971: 129, n.1 for p.95). Facsimiles of the drafts are riddled with Pound's linings-through, cross-hatchings, and marginal markings of suggested cuts. The fair copy of the original version of Eliot's quotations from "Full fathom five" (*Tem.* 1.2.399ff), for example, carries in the upper right corner this paraph made with Pound's pen (Eliot 1971: 121):

??
Doubtful

In the event, Eliot followed Pound's advice and cut the seventeen-line "Dirge" in which Shakespeare's line figures, but he reworked images from the poem into Part IV, "Death by Water," and he retained, despite Pound's lining-out (Eliot 1971: 7), another line from Ariel's song, "Those are pearls that were his eyes" (*Tem* 1.2.401), in the midst of Madame Sosostris's cutting of the Tarot deck in Part I, "The Burial of the Dead" (Eliot 1971: 136, l. 48).

Most of Eliot's fragments accentuate cuts between the high culture of the past and the banalities of the present. Thus, Enobarbas's description of Cleopatra, "The barge she sat in, like a burnished throne,/ Burned on the water" (*Ant.* 2.2.198–9), is repurposed by Eliot as a description of a lady at her toilette (Eliot 1971: 137, l. 77). An over-mantle in the lady's dressing room depicts the rape of Philomel, and "withered stumps of time/ Were told upon the walls; staring forms/ Leaned out, leaning, hushing the room enclosed" (ll. 104–6). These "withered stumps of time" recall, from the draft, "the old stumps and bloody ends of time" (Eliot 1971: 11), suggesting a connection with Lavinia's repeatedly noticed "stumps" in *Titus Andronicus* (2.4.4, 3.2.42, 4.1.*29sd*, 4.1.75*sd*, 5.2.181) and with that play's explicitly remarked connections between Lavinia and Philomel.

Ophelia's mad farewell words to the court—"Good night, ladies, good night, sweet ladies, good night, good night" (*Ham* 4.5.71–2)— become the parting words of customers as a pub closes (l. 172). A line remembered from *The Tempest*, Ferdinand's "Weeping again my poor father's wreck" (l. 193), rings ironically in "Musing upon the king my brother's wreck,/ And on the king my father's death before him" (ll. 191–2) as the speaker trudges along a rat-infested canal behind a gas works. In "the king my father's death" I hear also a possible allusion to Hamlet's tragic dilemma. Finally, Ferdinand's reminiscence "This music crept by me on the waters" (*Tem* 1.2.394) is transposed into "The pleasant whining of a mandolin" heard outside a pub in Lower Thames Street (l. 261).

Connectivity among cuts, rather than disruption, figures in Part V, "What the Thunder Said," when a key is heard in a prison lock so that "aetherial rumours/ Revive for a moment a broken Coriolanus" (ll. 415–16). The sound of the key comes fast upon the second, expanding repetition of the "DA/ *Datta/ ...*/DA/ *Dayadhvam*" (ll. 400–1, 410–11) that leads the speaker to the final "DA/ *Damyata*" (ll. 417–18) and to the Sanskrit formula that concludes the entire poem: "*Shantih shantih shantih*" (l. 433). "The Peace which passeth understanding" (footnote to l. 433) has much to do, in my reading, with the consolations of *The Tempest* and the towering heroism of Coriolanus.

=

Ultimately, the Shakespearean fragments in *The Waste Land* serve the
same Modernist agenda that Yeats would later articulate in "Lapis
Lazuli" (1936), a holistic vision that finds meaning by "transfiguring"
cuts. I quote here from Yeats's working manuscript, to show some of
the cutwork that went into the making of this seemingly seamless poem:

> *Yet* men   *their*
> ~~We~~ all perform our tragic plays
> *This*   *that other*
> ~~One~~ man ~~plays~~ Hamlet another Lear,
> *Weep*   *weep*
> <u>Wept</u> Ophelias, wept cordeleas
> But we, should the last scene be there
> The great stage curtain about to drop
> If worthy our prominent part in the play
> Do not break up our lines & weep
>   *are*
> Recall that Hamlet & Lear ~~were~~ gay
> *That*   *ty*   *es*
> ^ Gaiety transfiguring dread (Yeats 2000: 25).

The key word here is "transfiguring." Yeats's refusal to break up
Shakespeare's parts could be read as a manifesto against cuts, a call
to maintain integrity in the face of the cultural disasters of the twentieth
century. Continuity and coherence are secured, in Eliot's case, by the
structuralist premises of Jessie L. Weston's book *From Ritual to Romance*,
cited in Eliot's notes. Cuts from Shakespeare retain secure places in that
edifice; indeed, they help to guarantee it. In Yeats's case, continuity and
coherence are forged in the very act of writing poems that articulate
modern disruptions, and exorcise them in the act of composition.

=

As Carse points out, finite games can take place within infinite games
(14). The rules change for the moment, space and time are reconfig-
ured, and the new game is played to its end, but the infinite game goes
on, around it and beyond it. Such is the case with William
S. Burroughs' "cut-ups" with Shakespeare. Burroughs' cutwork with
Shakespeare began in Paris in 1959, when his friend Brion Gysin
pointed out how painters for the past fifty years had been using cut

techniques to viscerally powerful effect. It was time for writers to catch up. At Gysin's suggestion, the pair proceeded to experiment with cutting apart "only the best, only the high-charged material," including the Song of Songs in the King James Bible, Eliot's translation of St. John Perse's *Anabase*, "Shakespeare's sugar'd sonnets," and "a few lines from *The Doors of Perception* by Aldous Huxley about his mescaline experiences" (Gysin and Wilson 2012). According to Burroughs, they started with words on paper and then later experimented with spoken words that could be cut and spliced using magnetic tape. Burroughs' explanation, and an example of their tape-recorder cuts, was available at the time of this writing on YouTube: https://www.youtube.com/watch?v=Rc2yU7OUMcI. In an interview with Jean-Jacques Lebel in 1982, Gysin and Burroughs stress the physical violence of their actions:

> B.G.: I used words as raw material, in the same way that a painter spreads paint over the surface of a canvas. You grasp words like physical objects which you can then manipulate and rearrange. You grab hold of words and cut off their dirty little heads with scissors, if you like. Why not? Words aren't sacred.

> W.B.: Some writers—Jack Kerouac, for example—said: "These cut-ups, I do them in my head as I write." It's not true. When you write with a pen or a typewriter, you're not actually cutting into the substance of words. With cut-ups, you *physically* slice up the words with a pair of scissors or a knife and reorganize the pieces (Lebel 2013 [in Heil and MacFayden]: 145).

The goal here may at first seem to be the creation of randomness, but Gysin and Burroughs had more serious ends in view. Particularly fruitful, they discovered, were cuttings that juxtaposed fragments of Shakespeare sonnets with fragments of poems by Arthur Rimbaud. The results demonstrated, Burroughs claims, that "Shakespeare Rimbaud live in their words," not in the organized visual images of their words that readers usually encounter: "Cut the word lines and you will hear their voices" (Burroughs and Guysin 1978: 31–2). You will also find yourself occupying a new mental space: "No two minds ever come together without, thereby, creating a third, invisible, intangible force which may be likened to a third mind…. The third mind is there when two minds collaborate" (Burroughs 1978: 25). In an interview with the

Paris Review in 1966, seven years after the experiments began, Burroughs acknowledged T. S. Eliot's example: "Of course, when you think of it, 'The Waste Land' was the first great cut-up collage" (Burroughs 1978: 6).

None of Burroughs' and Gysin's cut-ups of Shakespeare seem to have made the final cut in Burroughs' "Cut-up Trilogy" *The Soft Machine* (1961), *The Ticket That Exploded* (1962), and *Nova Express* (1964), and none figure in the visual collages, now in the Los Angeles County Museum of Art, that Gysin and Burroughs assembled for their unpublished book *The Third Mind* (scheduled by Grove Press for 1970). (Texts from the abandoned project were eventually published by Viking as *The Third Mind* in 1978, but without the visual collages.) Examples of Burroughs' and Gysin's cut-ups with Shakespeare do survive, however, in the Burroughs archive now in the Berg Collection of the New York Public Library.

The Shakespeare cut-ups in the Berg Collection exist in two forms. The majority are $8\frac{1}{2} \times 11$-inch sheets on which Burroughs has typed out, in all caps, cuts from Shakespeare that have been spliced together with cuts from other writers, including passages that Burroughs himself has written. More fun to confront are boxes containing paper fragments that have *not* already been spliced together: quadrants from typescript sheets cut with scissors or knife just as Burroughs advises in the interview with Lebel, newspaper clippings, Scientology pamphlets, cut-up letters from Burroughs' publishers and from his brother in St. Louis, and miscellaneous other texts. With the typescript sheets Burroughs has already done the job of cutting and splicing and has typed up the results. With the boxes of fragments the reader gets to do the arranging and the splicing. The effect is very much like a game, "The Third Mind Game" perhaps.

As an example of one of the full typescript sheets consider this one, complete with a small burned-out hole, apparently from cigarette ash:

CUT FROM OUR EVER LIVING POET WILLIAM SHAKESPEARE

ON THIS GREEN LAND ADVENT YOU NOT TOO LATE.LOUD TOPPED

TOWERS THE GREAT GLOBE ISTSELF YEA ALL ARE RACKED AND

LIKE THIS INSUBSTANTIAL LAND ANSWER YOUR SUMMONS.AND

ARE MELTED INTO AIR STAGE.DREAMS MADE IN SETTING FORTH

(Burroughs Archive, Box 26, folder 8).

Remarkable in this particular cut-up is the use Burroughs has made of Thomas Thorpe's dedication page to the 1609 quarto of *SHAKE-SPEARES SONNETS*. In addition to the all-cap typography that imitates Thorpe's dedication—typography that is generally reproduced in modern editions—Burroughs recognizes the pun in "setting forth" as (1) starting out on a journey and (2) publishing (as in putting the words "out there"). Intercut with fragments from the 1609 quarto of the sonnets and from *The Tempest* are fragments that Burroughs returns to obsessively in these typescripts: the current state of America in "this green land" and "this insubstantial land" and the curious "cut" phrase "stage—full stop—dreams," in which "stage" figures as both a noun and verb.

An example of unspliced Shakespeare cut-ups is this one from a box of fragments made in preparation for *The Soft Machine*:

> AS AN IMPERFECT ACTOR ON THE
> WHEN I DO COUNT THE CLOCK TH
> ETERNITIE PROMISED. AND SEE
> NIGHT.BY OUT EVER LIVING POET
> PAST PRIME. WISHETH THE WELL
> WHEN THOU DOST STAY. ADVENTU
> (Burroughs Archive, Box 42, Folder 2, sleeve 15)

The sleeves of fragments in these boxes, and the fragments within each sleeve, are ordered just as they were received from Burroughs, who provided a catalog of the archive himself. Just before "As an unperfect actor…" is this fragment:

> LICHEN OF THE SUN AND AZUR
> ——THE YELLOW DAWN OF P——
> ——UNKNOWN SAPS. GLACIERS SILV
> ——SERPENTS EATEN BY LICE TRES
> ——THE TEMPEST HAS BLESSED MY
> ——I DANCED ON THE WAVES SWEET

Just after comes a sheet from a pamphlet on "Modern Scientology at Work" (Burroughs Archive, Box 42, Folder 2, sleeve 15). The larger context into which these cuts are inserted are typed sheets describing male homosexual acts that would have been deemed obscene in Britain and the United States in 1960–1, when Burroughs was working on these particular cuts. The restored text (2014) of *The Soft Machine* gives ample opportunities for experiencing, albeit without Shakespeare, the third-mind effect that Gysin and Burroughs wished for their viewers and readers. In the last analysis, Gysin's and Burroughs' Shakespeare cut-ups is a thoroughly Modernist project, with Modernist expectations about finding, or imposing, order in the midst of chaos.

=

In Tom Stoppard's work the finite game changes once again. Or is it, in Stoppard's case, an infinite game? In *Travesties* Stoppard stages a hat-trick that shows the persistence of Dada in the very different cultural circumstances of 1974, in an era that many culture historians would identify as the beginning of Post-modernism, with a sense of irony far more high-minded than Tzara's. In the scene from *Travesties* cited at the outset of this chapter, James Joyce, Lenin, and Tzara are assembled in a library in Zurich. At separate tables and chairs, they are writing what turn out to be some of the seminal texts of the twentieth century. Joyce is dictating his text to an assistant named Gwendolyn, and Lenin is writing quietly, but Tzara is pursuing a different writing technique:

> *On his table are a hat and a large pair of scissors.* TZARA *finishes writing, then takes up the scissors and cuts the paper, word by word, into his hat. When all the words are in the hat he shakes the hat and empties it on the table. He rapidly separates the bits of paper into random lines, turning a few over, etc., and then reads the results in a loud voice* (Stoppard 1975: 17–18).

The collage of words that Tzara pronounces seem of a piece with the phrases from *Ulysses*-in-the-making that Joyce now dictates to Gwendolyn. Joyce, we later discover, keeps his phrases on scraps of paper in his pockets. Tzara takes his own cut-up words, puts them back into the hat, and pulls out the pieces for a new poem. The Russian words that Lenin speaks to his assistant Nadya sound, in this context, as much like nonsense as Tzara's random words and Joyce's impenetrable phrases.

In his lecture "Is It True What They Say about Shakespeare?," delivered before the Deutsche Shakespeare Gesellschaft in the early

1980s, Tom Stoppard declares his admiration for Shakespeare's quick exchanges of speeches, particularly in *Hamlet*:

> The parts which most bear repeating for me now are not the great speeches or the set pieces. What I find repeatedly thrilling and timeless are the rapid, sharp exchanges which drive the action on: I always deeply regretted being unable to fit into my play about Rosencrantz and Guildenstern the passage where Hamlet asks Guildenstern "Will you play upon this pipe"—"My Lord, I cannot!"—"I pray you"—"Believe me, I cannot"—"I do beseech you"—"I know no touch of it, my Lord"—"It is as easy as lying!" Is it not passages like these which keep Shakespeare vibrant in the modern theatre even more than the great, introspective speeches which halt the action? (Stoppard 1982: 10–11).

We have in Stoppard's quoted lines of stichomythia an instance of cutwork that, as we observed in Chapter 3, is already present in Shakespeare's scripts.

=

These effects of cutting apart, speeding up, and positioning odd bits side by side are played out brilliantly in Stoppard's *Rosencrantz and Guildenstern Are Dead* (1966–7), *Dogg's Hamlet, Cahoot's Macbeth* (1979), and the film of *Rosencrantz and Guildenstern Are Dead* (1990). Stoppard's ways with cut-up Shakespeare are not Lewis's or Eliot's or even Tzara's. The violence of Lewis has been erased. Tzara's playfulness has been heightened. Eliot's High Culture seriousness has been maintained, but with a distinctively ironic edge. Burroughs' third mind has been made available to audiences and readers who prefer to be amused, not shocked.

Jill L. Levinson has observed three distinct "strategies" at play in *R&GAD*: (1) Shakespeare's *Hamlet*, (2) Beckett's *Waiting for Godot*, and (3) Wittgenstein's *Philosophical Investigations*. In *R&GAD* these strategies are "superimposed" or set at play within a force-field; in *D'sHam, C'sMac* they are "juxtaposed" (163). Levinson quotes Stoppard on "a Beckett joke": "It appears in various forms but it consists of confident statement followed by immediate refutation by the same voice" (qtd. in Levinson 2001: 160). As Levinson demonstrates, such sequiturs are often interrupted syllogisms. Non sequiturs—or, rather, *seeming* non sequiturs—are Stoppard's stock in trade. When, for example, Guil goes through a variety of explanations for why the coins they are flipping always turn up heads, Ros says,

> I've never known anything like it!
> GUIL: And a syllogism. One, he has never known anything like it. Two, he has never known anything to write home about. Three it is nothing to write home about.... Home...What's the first thing you remember?
> ROS: Oh, let's see... (16).

In the linguistically impoverished world inhabited by Guil and Ros, logic goes nowhere. It keeps getting interrupted, with (for us) delightful results.

Cuts in *D'sHam, C'sMac* are even sharper. The comma between the two titles insinuates a cut in the very midst of the performance. We have in this diptych of two plays not just three "strategies" but three *languages*: (1) a primitive language called "Dogg" (derived from Wittgenstein, the language of performance for a fifteen-minute *Hamlet* in *D'sHam*, and for the final segment of *Macbeth* in *C'sMac*), (2) fragments and longer stretches of Shakespeare's early modern English, and (3) colloquial modern English (spoken by a lorry driver in *D'sHam* and by a political censor called The Inspector in *C'sMac*). In *D'sHam* the dominant idiom is Dogg; in *C'sMac*, Shakespeare's English. The final effect of the linguistic cuts in *R&GAD* and *D'sHam, C'sMac* is, as Levinson argues, quite different. In *R&GAD* the flipped coins that begin the play create a series of cuts in the action—cuts that defy logic because the coin always lands heads-up. That happenstance is prophetic, since the letter that Claudius later sends with Ros and Guil specifically asks the king of England to cut off their heads. More immediately, the flipped coins set up the action of the play, which cuts back and forth among three distinct *ethoi*: (1) Ros and Guil in their Beckettian existential void, (2) the protagonists of Shakespeare's *Hamlet* in their linguistically rich plot-driven world, and (3) the traveling players who do indeed travel as mediators between the world of Ros and Guil on the one hand and the play of *Hamlet* on the other.

The three *ethoi* coincide in the final sequence when Hamlet returns from England just in time to witness the carnage of Shakespeare's Act 5, Scene 2, and Guil becomes so fed up with the tragedians' slights of word and hand that he grabs The Player's dagger and holds the point at The Player's throat while exclaiming that death, *real* death, is not just a bit of dramatic artifice:

> I'm talking about death—and you've never experienced that. And you cannot *act* it. You die a thousand casual deaths—with none of that intensity which squeezes out life…and no blood runs cold anywhere. Because even as you die you know that you will come back in a different hat (*R&GAD* 5.2.123).

Guil finishes the speech by pushing the dagger's blade into The Player's neck right up to the hilt. The Player dies a magnificent death—then leaps up to receive applause. It was a trick knife: the blade slides into the handle.

In the final moments of the play Tzara's hat gets passed, and the person who receives it is Shakespeare. He gets the last word. *R&GAD* closes with Horatio and the ambassador from England delivering *Hamlet* 5.2.320–40. In this action Stoppard, in my view at least, delivers the audience to an ending altogether more affirmative than Beckett ever manages, an ending that celebrates Shakespeare's genius and Stoppard's own wit in the same breath. We find ourselves in a position not so far from Eliot's fragments and Burroughs' third mind. Are Rosencrantz and Guildenstern really dead? Within the fiction of Shakespeare's *Hamlet*, yes. Within the fiction of Stoppard's *R&GAD*, no more dead than The Player who leaps back to life, puts on a different hat, and begins a new play, perhaps even a reiteration of *this* play.

The ending of *D'sHam, C'sMac* is a more complicated affair philosophically and politically. The language we hear—and *see*—at the end of *C'sMac* is Dogg, a variety of the cut-down primitive language Wittgenstein invents in *Philosophical Investigations*. Cut short by The Inspector's modern English, the actors are able to complete their performance of *Macbeth* within the Inspector's hearing only by speaking in Dogg as they construct a platform—a political platform, perhaps, as well as a theatrical platform—by moving about the five basic words in the Wittgenstein language that inspired Stoppard's Dogg: "plank," "slab," "block," "brick," and "cube." All five building blocks, let us note, are cut objects. Stoppard's *D'sHam, C'sMac* returns us to the parlous place of Shakespeare in Vorticism and Cubism at the beginning of the twentieth century: an of-a-piece artistic whole, two of them actually, blasted into fragments that can be rearranged to powerful but dislocating effect. Compared to the mind games played in Stoppard's plays, the film of *R&GAD* (1990) is rummy, in more ways than one. It operates within the finite rules of the Hollywood film game even while trying to stretch those rules if not break them. In an interview quoted by Levinson, Stoppard said that cinema allowed him to "change the frame" of *R&GAD* (Levinson 2001: 167). The "frame" here is controlled by the camera. Stoppard's changes involved cutting half the play's lines and, typically for film, shifting the emphasis from words to actions. Only about 250 lines of Shakespeare's *Hamlet* make the cut (Rosenthal 2007: 44). Whatever has been lost in the way of Beckett's verbal play is made up by foregrounding Beckett's slapstick.

=

In the 1960s, Peter Brook, whose performatively inventive but textually uncut production of *A Midsummer Night's Dream* (1970–3) remains a landmark in Shakespeare theater history, told Charles Marowitz that it would be fascinating to see *Hamlet* played as a series of discontinuous scenes, "reshuffled like a deck of familiar cards" (Cole and Chinoy 1976: 432). Marowitz's *Collage Hamlet* (aka *The Marowitz Hamlet*, 1964) was the result. In a later interview Brook elaborated his idea of play production as card play. "Shakespeare's plays are like a pack of cards," he explained to Ralph Berry.

> Shakespeare can be understood as a vast human deck of cards that has total identity, card for card, total concentration, but yet can be shuffled and redealt in endless permutation in each place, in each context, in each period of history. This understood, then one is approaching something of the nature of Shakespeare's works.

In sum: "there is no deck like Shakespeare's" (Berry 1977: 10–11).

Marowitz took Brook's advice, but could never make up his mind which game he wanted to play with the deck. *The Marowitz Hamlet*, as it came to be known, was adjudged at the time to be a more radical experiment than Stoppard's, not least by Marowitz himself. In Berlin in 1964 Marowitz saw a 25-minute excerpt of what later became Stoppard's *R&GAD* and concluded: "It struck me, and most everyone else, as a lot of academic twaddle" (qtd. in Levinson 2001: 158).

Marowitz's own experiment, first performed in Berlin a few months later, not only cuts out vast quantities of Shakespeare's text; it reassigns speeches from one character to another, transfers lines from scene to scene, moves abruptly between scenes (*"Cut into a new scene"* is the repeated stage direction [Marowitz 1978: 30]), speeds things up by having characters speak famous lines (not necessarily to each other) in "the rapid, sharp exchanges" that intrigued Stoppard, and even directs characters to speak simultaneously. The first version, according to Marowitz, "was essentially a clever exercise in Burroughs-like cut-ups. In the later, expanded, 85-minute version, which played in Germany, Italy and later London, the style was better assimilated, the play had more intellectual content and was at the service of a clear-cut interpretation" (Marowitz 1991: 32–3). "Clear-*cut.*" Noted.

A stretch near the beginning of the fuller version illustrates the effect of these sharp cuts and startling relocations. Shakespeare's prolix speeches become jabs of stichomythia:

HAMLET.   (*To* GHOST) Speak, I am bound to hear.
OPHELIA.   (*Entering*) You are keen, my Lord, you are keen.
QUEEN.   I prithee stay with us, go not to Wittenberg.
GHOST.   The serpent that did sting thy father's life…

(Marowitz 1978: 30–1).

The cuts and the jabs become even sharper when the King and the Ghost are scripted to speak simultaneously—something that happens in Shakespeare only in crowd scenes:

(The next two speeches are counterpointed with the KING's in prominence, and the GHOST's as a dulled accompaniment)

KING	GHOST
'Tis sweet and commendable in your nature, Hamlet,	With juice of a cursed hebenon in a vial
To give these mourning duties to your father.	…swift as quicksilver it courses through
But you must know, your father lost a father	The natural gates and alleys of the body;
That father lost, lost his, and the survivor bound	And with a sudden vigour it doth posset
In filial obligation for some term	And curd, like eager droppings into milk,

To do obsequious sorrow.   The thin and wholesome
                                                      blood...

HAMLET.   (*To himself*) Hold my heart:
      And you my sinews grow not instant old:
      But bear me stiffly up (30–1).

For all the bravura of these effects, Marowitz's ultimate purpose in
cutting up *Hamlet* was partly conservative. "Why cut it up in the first
place?" Marowitz asks in his Introduction to *The Marowitz Shakespeare*
published in 1978, four years after Stoppard's staging of Tzara's hat-
technique in *Travesties*.

> In my view, radical theatrical experiments need to be justified, if at
> all, only when they fail. The *Hamlet* collage was, on the whole,
> successful, and earned a certain credibility of its own. But if one
> were hard-pressed for justification, I would say that the re-structuring
> of a work, the characters and situations of which are widely known, is
> an indirect way of making contact with that work's essence (Marowitz
> 1978: 12).

Tzara, Wyndham Lewis, and Burroughs, if not Stoppard, would have
found such a pronouncement retrograde. Marowitz in his Introduction takes pride in the fact that on two occasions his *Hamlet* was staged
in conjunction with productions of Shakespeare's original. "Whatever
my misgivings about each production," he reports, "what became
abundantly clear was that every notion which seemed so far-fetched
in the context of the collage, was viable in terms of the original work
and could be conveyed through conventional interpretation"
(Marowitz 1978: 12). By cutting up Shakespeare, one gets at the
essential Shakespeare. Unclear is how this statement squares with
Marowitz's presentation of Hamlet as an object of ridicule, "the
supreme prototype of the conscience-stricken but paralyzed liberal:
one of the most lethal and obnoxious characters in modern times"
(13). Further cut-up experiments by Marowitz followed in *A Macbeth*
(1969, note the indefinite article), *The Shrew* (1973, note the definite
article), *Measure for Measure* (1975), *Variations on The Merchant of Venice*
(1977), and *Julius Caesar* (printed 1991).

We can observe in Marowitz's statements about his cutwork with
Shakespeare two conflicting impulses. One the one hand, he can

sound pugilistic like Tzara and Lewis. In setting up "clanging incompatibles," Marowitz declares that his work is "nothing more nor less than a head-on confrontation with the intellectual substructure of the plays, an attempt to test or challenge, revoke or destroy the intellectual foundation which makes a classic the formidable thing it has become" (Marowitz 1978: 24). On the other hand, his statements on *Hamlet* and *Julius Caesar* espouse poetic principles that even Eliot would have approved. Marowitz's essay "On Collage" (which follows an essay on "How to Rape Shakespeare") proclaims an ultimately conservative agenda. The speed, discontinuity, and dramatic juxtapositions of "theatrical collage" serve to deliver information quickly, Marowitz explains, permitting the play to express "interior meanings" more powerfully than "the more plodding movements of unfolding psychology" and to "provide more dramatic information than is possible through sequential development." In sum: "the effect of this swift, fragmentary method is to generate a surreal style that communicates experience from a subjective standpoint, thereby shifting the focus of events from an exterior to an interior reality" (Marowitz 1991: 32). One thinks of Eliot's "unreal city" (*The Waste Land* l. 207) and the "fragments… shored against my ruins" (l. 430). In the last analysis, Marowitz pivots between the pugilistic and the poetic. One of the high aims of Modernism was holding opposites in a state of tension. In their distinctive ways, Eliot and Yeats pursued that goal in their invocations of Shakespeare. Marowitz's cutwork veers between Modernism's state of tension and the more radical goals of deconstruction in the later twentieth century. Marowitz attempted to play two games—two finite games—at once.

=

During the 1980s and '90s theater-goers in London could choose between the real RSC at the Barbican or "the other RSC" at the Jeanette Cochrane Theatre in Southampton Row and later, for nine straight years, at the Criterion Theatre in Piccadilly Circus. Boasting that they enacted all thirty-seven of Shakespeare's plays in just ninety-seven minutes, the Reduced Shakespeare Company in *The Complete Works of William Shakespeare (Abridged)* cut all but the most famous lines but also added inter-cuttings between Shakespeare's texts and contemporary popular culture, all delivered at dizzying speed and with high-energy physical gusto. The inspiration for the other RSC's abridged *Complete Works*, as Peter Holland points out in "Shakespeare Abbreviated," was Tom Stoppard's *Fifteen-Minute Hamlet* (1976), later expanded as *Dogg's Hamlet* and finally combined as a double bill with *Cahoot's Macbeth* (1979) (Holland 2007: 42–3). "Abbreviated Shakespeare," Holland observes,

> makes widely varying assumptions about what its audiences know of/ about Shakespeare and what they assume 'Shakespeare' to be, turning lengthy verse-drama into highlights and famous quotations, narrowed narratives and sentimentalized action, often recreating a memory of the agonies of the schoolroom and even more frequently acting as an emphatic sign of the audience's alienation from forms of high-cultural social approval (Holland 2007: 28).

As so often with cuts, what gets left out can turn out to be just as important—maybe more important—than what gets retained. You can't appreciate Stoppard's witty way with the shears without knowing the cut-out bits. The work of the Reduced Shakespeare Company certainly depended on audiences knowing that huge stretches of text had been cut in the interests of speed, and to recognize the incongruity of cross-cutting contemporary popular culture with Shakespeare's august words, but the philosophical dimension of Stoppard's work and the political commitments of Marowitz's were lacking. The other RSC's cutwork was "reduced" Shakespeare in more ways than one. On YouTube it has been reduced even more, in the form of clips lasting three minutes or less.

＝

If we need to make a cut separating Modernist and Post-modernist cutwork with Shakespeare, on the one hand, from Post-post-modernist cutwork on the other, 2005 might be the year. As it happens, YouTube was launched on April 23, 2005, Shakespeare's four hundred forty-first birthday (McKernan 2016: 2:1971). It was in March 2005, one month before YouTube's premiere, that the Wooster Group started rehearsals for its landmark production of *Hamlet*, in which live performance was coordinated with video projections of film cuts from Richard Burton's stage performance in 1964. (For a full description see Cartelli 2008.) The concatenation in the Wooster Group's *Hamlet* of stage performance (Burton's in 1964) → film (1964) → video (2005) ↔ stage performance (2005–13) is widely regarded as the origin of multimedia performances of Shakespeare today. The events of 2005 invite us to consider that year as the cut between older forms of cutwork with Shakespeare and the fetish of the cut that we witness today. We shall investigate these new forms of cutwork in three media: live performance, liquid-crystal-display screens (LCDs) and organic-light-emitting-diode screens (OLEDs), and altered books. The distinctions here are, as we shall see, more than somewhat arbitrary, since each of the three media is now intercut with the others.

=

Slide and film projections in dialogue with live performance have been traced by Greg Giesekam and Thomas Cartelli back to the 1920s and the work of V. E. Meyerhold in Russia and Erwin Piscator in Germany (Giesekam 2007, Cartelli 2016a). If Judith Buchanan is correct, it may have started as early as 1905, when Herbert Beerbohm-Tree perhaps used a two-minute silent film (now lost) of the opening storm scene in *The Tempest* in his contemporaneous production of the play, especially when the production was on tour to theaters lacking elaborate scenery (Buchanan 2011: 25–6). Multiple media in all these twentieth-century instances were deployed to reinforce one another; in the Wooster Group's twenty-first-century *Hamlet*, directed by Elizabeth LeCompte, something more complicated was going on.

Cuts between media were played up as cuts, and digital technology enhanced the effect. The film of Burton's performance was digitally altered, so spectators could get the impression that Scott Shepherd performing Hamlet was not only responding to Burton's performance, but was also manipulating it. Final Cut software had been used to achieve this effect. Shepherd describes the process:

> If there was a pause where I didn't like it I would just cut it out with the video attached and move it somewhere where I thought there needed to be a pause. So now we use that video which has all these jumps in it which gives us a physicality that is a little bit strange and removed. The same happens with the vocal performances because the tendency to pause in order to make some sort of emotional leap from one state to another so that when you take that pause out you get a jump that is sort of startling. And inserting a pause where there wasn't one also creates interesting effects (qtd. in Pellegrini 2012: 248).

In copying the cut-up film, the actors had to inhabit the jumps and skips, so that cuts in the film were realized as cuts onstage. "Keeping up with these technical disruptions through physical and vocal tics," David Pellegrini reports, "engendered a distinctive visceral kinetics that shaped the performances considerably" (Pellegrini 2012: 248).

Before the Wooster Group's *Hamlet* there had already been some radical experiments with disjunctive media in productions of Shakespeare. Two examples are Robert Wilson's 1986 production of Heiner Müller's already cut and compressed *Hamletmachine* (1977–9) in a production at New York University (Cartelli 2016a: 2:1470) and Peter Sellars' 1994 production of *The Merchant of Venice Beach* for the Goodman Theater, Chicago, and the Barbican Theatre, London. In Sellars' production Shakespeare's text was spoken in front of a bank of video monitors showing scenes from Los Angeles, including the Rodney King race riots. Shylock's "Hath not a Jew eyes" speech was delivered with the actor's back to the audience; the audience saw his face on the monitors, thanks to a supernumerary with a hand-held video camera who shot the speech as Shylock spoke it (Richards 1994). The effect of the multiple images on the monitors was to put speech-cuts and scene-cuts at odds, to cut the play's visual and aural elements into pieces and make audiences experience chronological and techno-logical disjunctions between Shakespeare's play and contemporary events but also thematic confluences.

To judge by the ubiquity of video projections in Shakespeare productions today, the Wooster Group succeeded in domesticating multimedia cutwork from the wilds of Wilson and Sellars. In terms of social media, the Wooster Group created a meme that now extends even to amateur productions. The company went on to develop cutwork between stage performance and video in *Cry, Trojans!*, a version of *Troilus and Cressida* (2012).

=

Ivo van Hove's production of Shakespeare's *Roman Tragedies* (2007–10, revivals 2012, 2014) with the Toneelgroep Amsterdam extended cuts between stage performance and digital media even further. Van Hove cut all the scenes having to do crowds and battles, a decision that served to shift emphasis entirely on the power ploys of the politicos (Ball 2013, Cartelli 2016b). The retained text was adhered to closely, and each of the three plays was granted its textual integrity. In effect, audiences became the excised crowds, as large screens provided the constant barrage of information that characterizes contemporary life. In this saturated electronic environment, audiences during the six-hour performance were free to move about, chat, buy food and drink, even check their email and post Tweets. But Shakespeare's words—many of them, at any rate—were carried through, in order, from beginning to end. The important cuts in Van Hove's *Roman Tragedies* were dislocations in space and time, not in the three dramatized fictions in which audiences were caught up for six straight hours.

Similar cuts in space and time characterize the Toneelgroep's *Kings of War* (premiered 2015), in which speech-cuts, scene-cuts, and character-cuts from *Henry V*, the three parts of *Henry VI*, and *Richard III* are played out in multiple dimensions. As with the *Roman Plays*, lines, speeches, scenes, and entire characters are cut from Shakespeare's scripts, even as the narrative sequence is preserved. Ultimately, these textual cuts are much less important than the cuts that audiences actually witness. Figure 23 shows Henry V at a news conference before the Battle of Agincourt. A map of France is visible behind him. Henry is in fact "conferring" with no one. The military decisions have been made somewhere inside the disappearing

Figure 23. Production still from *War of Kings*, directed by Ivo van Hove, Toneelgroep Amsterdam (2015). Photograph by Jan Versweyveld. Reproduced by permission of Toneelgroep Amsterdam.

corridors of the brightly lit white box at the back of the acting space. The audience's only access to those corridors of power comes via cameras and video projections. At a rehearsal for *Kings of War* Van Hove is reported to have compared the white box's visually hidden spaces to "corridors in a big palace, or in the White House, or wherever people are negotiating and making decisions. What happens in the corridors is something you shouldn't say in the public world, in open life" (Mead 2015: 56).

At the same time, audiences *do* get access to those proceedings, via 1 | 0 cuts and camera-cuts. The result is a kind of double cut between figure and life. In Henry's news conference audiences can cut their attention from Henry speaking live to Henry figured on the screen. Some members of the audience probably choose to watch Henry's speech on the video screen, just as they would watch a sports event or a concert in a large arena. Speaking "Hath not a Jew eyes," the Shylock in Peter Sellars' 1994 production of *The Merchant of Venice Beach* spoke with his back to the audience; only video projections allowed the audience to see him frontally. The effect, by all reports, was alienating. In Figure 23, by contrast, Van Hove's Henry speaks at a ninety-degree angle to the audience, giving them a choice—a phenomenological choice as well as a political choice. A comparison of Figure 3 with Figure 23 will show how far we are here from the "breach" in Charles Kean's production of *Henry V* in 1859. The troops in their dozens in Kean's production are a ghostly absence in Van Hove's. The fixed perspective in Grieve's design for the siege of Harfleur has been cut into multiple perspectives. Audiences are free to move into, between, and beyond those cuts.

=

The moving is physical in Punchdrunk's *Sleep No More* (2009–continuing at the time of this writing). In the New York version of this mash-up of installation/performance-art/theater, audiences move from room to room in a large warehouse as they experience cuts from *Macbeth*. The moment of their entry into this fluid space is determined at the start by a card-draw—providing further evidence of the accuracy of Stoppard's observation, via Tzara, that all poetry is a reshuffling of a pack of cards. For spectator-listeners of Annie Dorsen's *A Piece of Work* (performed 2009–13), the cutting of Shakespeare's deck was done by a computer. The "piece" in the title presents the "work"

as a cut or cuts from a larger whole. Co-produced by theater organizations in Bergen, Oslo, Vienna, Paris, Seattle, and New York, each
performance of *Hamlet* in Dorsen's "algorithmic theatre" was different, thanks to computer algorithms that generated entirely new combinations of words, visuals, lighting, and music over the course of five
"parts" corresponding to Shakespeare's five acts. The algorithm
shifted from one part to the next, and from one evening's performance
to the next. The resulting cuts—including speech prefixes and stage
directions—were projected on a large screen. Only in part four/Act 4
did a live actor come up from the audience to speak a soliloquy
that was being created then and there by the computer's algorithm-
of-the-moment and transmitted to the actor "in real time," as they say,
via ear-buds (Cartelli 2015).

In the performances at the Brooklyn Academy of Music in December 2013 the only prop, other than the screen, was a platform with a
hole in the middle, perhaps an allusion to the platform in the original
production of *Hamlet* at the Globe and to the trap door that served as
Ophelia's grave. Smoke billowed up through the hole from time to
time, an emanation perhaps of "the ghost in the machine." (An
alternate title for *A Piece of Work* was *A Machine-Made Hamlet*: "The
ghost in the machine" is Gilbert Ryles's coinage for Descartes' dualism
between body and soul.) "A scrambled series of minimalist word
sculptures" is how Charles Isherwood described the effect in his
review for the *New York Times*: "In the process we in the audience are
amusingly (or uncomfortably) restored to the state of excited disorien-
tation we probably first felt when encountering the exotic syntax and
language of Shakespeare" (Isherwood 2013).

In Dorsen's *A Piece of Work*—Shakespeare without a human author,
Shakespeare without a human actor (except briefly)—spectator-
listeners perforce become makers of meaning for themselves. "The
program is the performer," as Dorsen explains in a statement "On
Algorithmic Theater".

> One might even call it the protagonist, with the audience tracking its
> choices and changes, instead of those of a human actor.... Audience
> members may feel an energetic transfer or they may get swept up and
> absorbed—or they may not. But *if* they do, they have to acknowledge that
> it's a feeling of their own making, a trick of their own brains, and there is no
> objective reality to the impression of community or contact (Dorsen 2016).

Like Van Hove, Dorsen deploys cuts as ways of engaging, or not, each audience member's own subjectivity.

=

On the LCD screens of computers and the OLED screens of smartphones, as in live performances, all the cuts made with earlier forms of technology can be present: line-cuts, speech-cuts, character-cuts, scene-cuts, camera-cuts, even author-cuts. To these older forms, digital technology has added a new kind of cut: the "you-cut." What have changed are two things: (1) how cuts are arrayed, and (2) the affordances cuts give to users and perceivers.

As of this writing, Shakespeare on YouTube has already received sharp critical attention in Stephen O'Neill's book *Shakespeare and YouTube* (2014), Christy Desmet's article on "YouTube Shakespeare, Appropriation, and Rhetorics of Invention" in the anthology *Outerspeares: Shakespeare, Intermedia, and the Limits of Adaptation* (Fischlin 2014), and Luke McKernan's chapter on "Shakespeare and Online Video" in *The Cambridge Guide to the Worlds of Shakespeare* (McKernan 2016). For the purposes of *Shakespeare | Cut* the question is not how the cuts are made in YouTube (we considered the affordances of digital media in Chapter 4) or what the YouTube genres are with respect to Shakespeare (O'Neill, Desmet, and McKernan have supplied those), but how the cuts are fitted together, and to what ends. Does cutwork with Shakespeare on YouTube constitute a brash eruption of popular culture into a traditionally high-culture preserve? Do YouTube cuts in, to, from, and with Shakespeare coalesce in a deep structure ("Shakespeare as Genius" perhaps) or a third mind? Does YouTube Shakespeare figure as frenetic disruptions that replicate the digital distractions of everyday life? The answer is patent: all of the above, depending on who is doing the cutting. The website is, after all, called *You*Tube, not *He*Tube or *They*Tube.

In charting YouTube cuts between figure and life, we might distinguish two dimensions in which cuts are made: horizontal and vertical. I take these dimensions from the up-and-down and left- and-right arrows on conventional keyboards and from the swipe functions on Windows 10 Pro and other operating systems (When I swipe the screen I do so with my index finger: an electronic equivalent of the manicule in early annotations made with pen and ink.) The horizontal dimension shows up in the large number of clips from classic and recent films. As we observed in Chapter 4 with respect to *The Merchant of Venice*, archived "footage" figures prominently in the top YouTube hits. While it is possible to watch an entire Shakespeare film on YouTube (Michael Radford's 2004 film of *Merchant*, for example, with Al Pacino as Shylock or the 1974 film based on the National Theatre's production with Laurence Olivier as Shylock), most users will click on cuts from these films. Olivier's version of "Hath not a Jew eyes?" can readily be juxtaposed with Pacino's version. When it comes to even more famous speeches, such as Hamlet's "To be or not to be," the possibilities of comparison are exponentially greater. The horizontal effect comes into play when these character-cuts and speech-cuts are viewed in sequence. No earlier technology has offered this particular affordance.

Deeper into the YouTube window, after passing through the hits with the greatest number of viewers, one encounters amateur cutwork that also operates in a horizontal dimension. A particularly interesting example is (or at least was at the time of this writing) Leia Len's "Hamlet Gone Viral," a sequence of Google search screens, email messages, Facebook postings, GPS images, and video cuts from the 2009 film with David Tennant, made in response to an English-class assignment "Create a Modern Interpretation of Shakespeare's *Hamlet*" (https://www.youtube.com/watch?v=5gp4TP9kpP4). The relatively small number of viewings of this rather ingenious and sometimes moving project since the posting in 2012 stands in contrast to the thousands of viewings of out-and-out parodies. Eighteenth- and nineteenth-century Shakespeare burlesques are alive and well on YouTube. Beyond the first few windows, parody quickly becomes the dominant YouTube genre. Typically, these parodies intercut clips from Shakespeare films with scenes from contemporary popular culture.

Michel Foucault gives us guidance in understanding parodies as the dominant Shakespeare genre on YouTube. "Knowledge is not made for understanding; it is made for cutting": with respect to cutting-as-dividing, Foucault's aperçu in "Nietzsche, Genealogy, History" would seem to be spot-on with respect to Burroughs' Shakespeare cut-ups, Stoppard's *Rosencrantz and Guildenstern Are Dead*, and Dorsen's logarithm-driven *A Piece of Work*. But ultimately Foucault has something more reductive in mind. At our present pass in history, Foucault argues at the end of his treatise, "veneration of monuments becomes parody; the respect for ancient continuities becomes systematic dissociation; the critique of the injustices of the past by a truth held by men in the present becomes the destruction of the man who maintains knowledge by the injustice proper to the will to knowledge" (Foucault 1984: 97). A consummation devoutly to be wished, by some. Not all contemporary instances of cutting-as-dividing substantiate Foucault's claim. As Schoch, Wells, Holland, McKernan, O'Neill, Bradley, and others have all pointed out, burlesques and parodies actually serve to shore up "Shakespeare" as a cultural monument in the very act of seeming to cut him down.

Cuts in the vertical dimension can also be deployed to parodic effect. In these instances character-cuts and scene-cuts from classic films are overlaid with contemporary popular music or trailers from popular films such as Disney's *The Lion King*, which is widely supposed to incorporate plot elements from *Hamlet*. (See https://www.youtube.com/watch?v=Vv5GMfHMVg8 for an example.) Cutting in the vertical dimension, stacking layers from different cultural levels and/or different media, offers more serious possibilities as well. A memorable example is "Hamlet on the Street," curated by McKernan on the BardBox channel (https://bardbox.wordpress.com). In this posting an eighteen-year-old Black American teenager, Craig Bazan, speaks Hamlet's soliloquy "O what a rogue and peasant slave am I" (2.2.552ff) while standing amid a destroyed streetscape in Camden, New Jersey, a poor suburb of Philadelphia (https://www.youtube.com/watch?v=Oa-cfEncd6Y). In this case the cut between the visual and the verbal cuts multiple ways. Time, space, race, and hierarchies of "high culture" and "low culture" all have to be adjusted by the viewer/listener. In McKernan's words, "There is a powerful sense that this is where Shakespeare belongs, not on a stage but to be spoken wherever we might find ourselves" (McKernan 2016).

Another example of cutwork along a vertical axis is "Ophelia Drowns," posted by Amy L. in 2011 (https://www.youtube.com/watch?v=mmq3ylfVJ3Q). With harmonious results, three elements are intercut along a vertical axis: Beethoven's "Moonlight" piano sonata, a voice-over of Gertrude's description of Ophelia's death at *Hamlet* 4.7.138–55 ("There is a willow grows aslant a brook…"), and a video, shot by a creek near the creator's home. Dressed in a flowing gown that recalls the figure in John Everett Millais's famous painting in Tate Britain, the Ophelia in Amy L.'s video is tracked by the camera as she wanders to the stream, contemplates her fate, and slips into the water to her death.

The Shakespeare channels that users have set up on YouTube raise a question that has polarized commentators on the arts as well as artists themselves: to what degree is such cutwork an appropriation of other people's creative work and to what degree is it a creative act in itself? The term "curating" has provided the focal point for this controversy. It is easy enough to accept Luke McKernan as the original curator of BardBox (he was, at the time, Lead Curator of News and the Moving Image at the British Library) and to consider the YouTube channels sponsored by the Royal Shakespeare Company, Shakespeare's Globe, and the Folger Shakespeare Library (see https://www.youtube.com/user/TheShakespeareNinja) as "legitimate." Paul O'Neill in *The Culture of Curating and the Curating of Culture(s)* (2012) and Hans Ulrich Obrist in *Ways of Curating* (2015) offer distinctly different takes on "curating" as the new "collecting." As we noted in Chapter 4, "scrap" Shakespeare goes back to the mid-nineteenth century. What have changed are not just technologies of cutting but the purposes of cutting. Cuts on the Royal Shakespeare Company's YouTube channel may seem very different from Shakespeare cuts on Pinterest, but the very availability of multiple channels and sites assures us that Shakespeare 2.0 is a Post-post-modern phenomenon: an array of multiple media, unexpected juxtapositions, non-sequiturs, no through plotline, and mathematically infinite varieties of play. Curatorship, in my view, is a creative response to that plenitude. Curators, amateur or professional, cut through chaos.

=

On LCD screens, YouTube Shakespeare has commanded the most attention, but videogame Shakespeare shows Post-modern cutwork in yet another guise. Digital search-and-cut is itself a form of game-playing. That effect is most obvious in videogames, several of which purport to be inspired by "Shakespeare." Since the first digital computer game made its appearance in 1961, there has been plenty of time for an artification of that technology/genre/practice, just as there has been for other forms of popular culture like phonography, film, radio, television, YouTube, and social networks. In *Works of*

Game: On the Aesthetics of Games and Art (2015) John Sharp surveys convergences of videogames and artistic practices in three forms: "game art" (in which designers, flouting the rules of videogames, transfer game tropes into artistic forms), "artgames" (in which designers, operating within the rules of videogames, turn games into expressive art forms), and "artist's games" (in which designers do both) (Sharp 2015: 8–16). With respect to Shakespeare, I would judge that none of these artistic possibilities has been exploited, with the possible exception of "Kill Shakespeare."

In Chapter 4 we noted "The Merchant of Venice" as a character-cut in "Civilization V." The videogame "Mabinogi" (released in Korea 2004, in the United States 2008) is more complex—but no less tangentially connected to Shakespeare's play. As a game with sequential storylines, "Mabinogi" has gone through multiple generations, requiring greater levels of skill and investments of time on the part of players: *Hamlet* (Generation 13), *Romeo and Juliet* (Generation 14), *The Merchant of Venice* (Generation 15), and *Macbeth* (Generation 16). (See the wiki at http://wiki.mabinogiworld.com/view/Shakespeare.)

"Shakespeare" (aka "The Tragic Bard") is the mastermind of an invented world called Erinn. He has the power to see into the future and attempt to change it through his powers as a playwright. An author-cut thus presides over the game. The promotional wiki for Generation 15, *The Merchant of Venice*, uses a character-cut to establish a subject position for the game-player: "the merchant," whose backstory takes him from his rural village to Venice and thence to "Belvast," where he amasses "ducats" (game-points) by buying goods in one town and selling them in another, all the while battling bandits on the road (https://www.youtube.com/watch?v=PCpCLZWIKjs). When the game was launched, the first person to reach the highest level of trading was awarded a new computer, $500 in cash, and three nights in a hotel in (where else?) Venice Beach, California.

If "Mabinogi" is a play (in more ways than one), the promotional wiki serves as a Chorus. The more usual way of communicating the story in videogames is through "cut-scenes," cinema-like sequences that interrupt the game and carry the story forward. In general, it is more accurate to think of Shakespeare in videogames in terms not of storylines but of memes, such as Yorick, skull in hand. Yorick appears in this guise in what videogame-players call "Easter eggs," hidden details that delight the astute finder. As the first two Shakespeare generations in "Mobanogi" would lead us to expect, *Hamlet* and *Romeo and Juliet* supply the most frequent memes. Meme-Shakespeare is quintessentially cut-Shakespeare.

Videogames, comics, staged readings, scholarly editions, and board games converge in "Kill Shakespeare." Designed by Conor McCreery and Anthony Del Col, "Kill Shakespeare" was originally conceived as a videogame (https://en.wikipedia.org/wiki/Kill_Shakespeare, accessed October 12, 2015). In the event, it was published as a series of comic books—Volume One ("A Sea of Troubles," six issues, 2010), Volume Two ("The Blast of War," six issues, 2011), and Volume Three ("The Tide of War," five issues, 2013)—before Volumes One and Two were collected as a substantial hardbound book with a leather-look binding—*Kill Shakespeare: The Backstage Edition* (2015)—complete with annotations by Shakespeare scholars. In 2011 the first twelve issues were adapted for a staged reading in Toronto (Douglas Lanier, personal communication).

As with "Mabinogi," the universe of "Kill Shakespeare" is Manichean: good guys are on a quest to find a reclusive wizard (who else but William Shakespeare?), and they must battle at every turn with bad guys. The good guys are character-cuts from Shakespeare: Hamlet, Juliet, Othello, Falstaff, Romeo, and Puck. And so are the bad guys: Richard III, Lady Macbeth, and Iago. In the course of their adventures all of these character-cuts are given speech-cuts from Shakespeare's plays, cuts that in turn give the scholar-annotators to the "backstage edition" *their* cue. Before the annotators got busy, the character-cuts and speech-cuts functioned as memes, as "Easter eggs" for clever "players" of what appears to be a static comic book but functions as an allusion-driven game not unlike the 1900 "Shakespeare Game." In 2014 "Kill Shakespeare" did indeed become a board game, complete with quests determined by drawing cards.

Most deaths in "Kill Shakespeare," as in Shakespeare's plays, are effected with daggers and swords. In this respect, too, "Kill Shakespeare" stays true to its videogame inspiration. Richard Bartle has divided into four types the people who play MUDs, or games in "multi-user domains" where players encounter one another electronically: "explorers" (who enjoy the virtual world of the game), "achievers" (who seek to perfect and demonstrate their skills), "socializers" (who use the game to commune with fellow players, who need not be physically present), and "killers" (who seek to "hack and slash" their way to winning). "Kill Shakespeare", especially in its board game version, accommodates all four types of players. So does the academic Shakespeare world. At the time of this writing, a more high-minded use of Shakespeare cuts was being developed by Gina Bloom and her collaborators in the ModLab at the University of California Davis in a videogame called "Play the Knave." The game allows players to project themselves into Shakespeare scenes through immersive 3-D technology. Gamers can choose the character they would like to play, the scene, the type of theater, even the music and the lighting, and proceed to perform the scene karaoke-style, using their full bodies to animate the avatar-actors on the screen. A prototype of the game was tried out successfully at the Stratford, Ontario, Shakespeare Festival in summer 2015. In "Mabinogi" and most other videogames based on Shakespeare, game and story are cut apart; "Play the Knave" promises to integrate game and story.

As tablets, smartphones, and watches replace laptops as electronic devices of choice, smaller but higher-resolution OLED screens are joining LCD screens as displays for cutwork Shakespeare. At the time of this writing, "App Shakespeare" was just beginning, but the affordances seem promising—more promising, perhaps, than Shakespeare on the World Wide Web. Two examples are Shakespeare Pro, developed by PlayShakespeare.com, which delivers the complete works in a form that is handy in more ways than one, complete with searchable concordance (https://www.playshakespeare.com/). With the Folger Luminary Shakespeare Apps, developed by Luminary Media and the Folger Shakespeare Library, the possibilities for intercuts are even greater. Users can cut back and forth from fully edited texts from the Folger Shakespeare editions to video cuts from productions to still images to pithy comments from academics like me (http://www.folger.edu/folger-luminary-shakespeare-apps). (I provided the scholarly commentary to the Luminary app for *A Midsummer Night's Dream*.)

In 2011–12 Katherine Rowe and I, working with grants from the Office for Digital Humanities of the National Endowment for the Humanities, developed and tested an app that could be used by directors and actors in preparing Shakespeare plays for production. "MyShx," developed for use on iPad, offered an editing environment that made every element of the text freely adjustable. Cuts could be stored and reinstated; rearrangements and additions could be executed and later undone. An export tool allowed the director to share changes with actors and designers in real time and to archive each version of the script. An annotation tray included editorial notes and glosses, private note-taking, and shareable comments for director's notes and line notes. When the app was tried out with actors of the American Shakespeare Center in Staunton, Virginia—an "original practices" company—the actors proved to be, in the lingo of software development, "medium agnostic." Younger members of the company adopted the app enthusiastically; older members preferred to stick with a printed text and a pen—in effect, the same technology that the Smock Alley company used in the 1660s, '70s, and '80s. (See Figure 6.).

The small size of tablets, smartphones, and watches—their easy fit with the hand that cuts—raises a fundamental question: do these apps serve to miniaturize "Shakespeare" and thus heighten the cut between Shakespeare's works and the ambient life of the twenty-first century? Or do they lessen the cut, by making it easier for users to cut between "the life" (the user's life, that is) and "the works"? One affordance that seems genuinely new is the user's ability to perform cutwork on the spot by recording sounds, taking pictures, and intercutting them, in the user's imagination if not also on social networks. One wonders what Ben Jonson might have thought about the interface between "figure" and "life" if he could behold tourists taking selfies with their smartphones outside Shakespeare's birthplace or, surreptitiously, making their own scene-cuts and character-cuts during performances by the Royal Shakespeare Company.

＝

Considering the increasing importance of Digital Humanities as an academic discipline and the proliferation of books and articles celebrating digital media, some readers may find it frivolous, if not perverse, to end this survey of cutwork from the long twentieth century with physical books. But these are *cut* books. "Book sculptures," "altered books," or "repurposed books," as they are called, are the subject of an entire book by Garrett Stewart: *Bookwork: Medium to Object to Concept to Art* (2010). In the book sculpture shown in Figure 24, Anita Francis, an artist working in Beaufort, North Carolina, has

Figure 24. Anita Francis, "The Collected Works of Shakespeare," book sculpture (2014). Photograph reproduced by permission of the artist.

taken the pages of a nineteenth-century edition of Shakespeare's complete plays and folded them tightly to create curtain-like partitions—scene-cuts of a sort—out of which character-cuts stride into the viewer's twenty-first-century space. Francis offers in her sculpture an intermedial version of "The Complete Works of Shake-speare," something in between codex, engraving, and sculpture. Perhaps it is the increasingly unread status of books that explains the phenomenon of turning books into materials for sculpture.

Book sculptures invite a perceiver to marvel at the handiwork of the cutting tool and, with the thought that it might be fun to try one's hand at producing such an object, perhaps feel traces of that handiwork in the muscles of hand and arm. The resulting sculpture might present itself as an object to be viewed, but the sculpted material is a book, which asks to be touched in the act of viewing. Not only that, it asks to be *read*—and not just "read" in the way art history would advise. In *Bookwork* Stewart regards repurposed books as "demediated" (Stewart 2011: xiv–xv). My own sense of such objects—in the case of Shakespeare, at least—is "intermediated." It is not just any old book that has been cut up in Francis's "Complete Works of Shakespeare"; it is a book containing texts by *Shakespeare*, and those texts have a life of their own beyond the materiality of any specific codex. In Francis's "Complete Works" the texts have been cut into sculpture, but the resulting art object—"bookwork," in Stewart's coinage—exists somewhere in between text and sculpture. Francis invites us to read Shakespeare in a new way: in four dimensions.

In altered books Shakespearean texts may provide the physical material for new creations, but the part of "Shakespeare" in the enterprise is viscerally physical. Book-lovers may feel a certain horror at the violence that book sculpture visits on old copies of Shakespeare. What invites such a response? After all, we do not feel the violence done to stone by the sculptor's chisels. Is it reverence for the words that provokes a more visceral reaction? A sense of violation of our own imaginative experience with those words? The brute reminder that old books have become expendable objects that need "repurposing"? For whatever reason, we cannot escape the cut—and, I believe, the vestigial violence of the cut. The ease of bladeless cutting in digital technology has enhanced, if not caused, that ubiquity.

=

Why so much cutwork with Shakespeare? Why now? One cause, surely, is the ease of making cuts with digital technology, a phenomenon we noticed in Chapter 4. Another explanation might be fragmentation in contemporary culture—fragmentation that may itself be a function of digital technology. Long before that technology made cutwork ubiquitous, however, we can identify a cutting impulse in Dada, Vorticism, and Eliot's Modernist version of ragtime. Unlike Eliot, Yeats, and Burroughs in the early- to mid-twentieth century, many writers, performers, and visual artists in the twenty-first seem to have given up the project of finding order, even the order that inspires the playful irony of Post-modernism in Stoppard's work. Has "chaos," as Wyndham Lewis hoped in 1914, finally invaded "concept"? Has chaos finally *conquered* concept? Unlikely, given the current hegemony of conceptual art in all its manifestations since the 1960s. Dorsen's *A Piece of Work* has struck several commentators (Isherwood 2013, Cartelli 2016b) as being as much a concept as a performance: something more interesting to *think* about than to *experience* in the theater.

Another explanation may be the speeding up of contemporary life, the "clip culture" that O'Neill has described on YouTube, the product not only of download times but, according to observers such as Nicholas G. Carr, ever-shorter attention spans. The two hours' traffic of the stage now needs to be no longer than fifteen minutes—or so it would seem from YouTube. As we noted in Chapter 3, however, attention spans vary widely from object to object, from individual to individual, from occasion to occasion. Attention spans have not necessarily been shrinking since Shakespeare's time. The longest piece of composed music from the late sixteenth and early seventeenth centuries in England, for example, takes no longer than fifteen minutes to perform (Richard Wistreich, personal communication)—a far cry from the 95 minutes that it takes the Philadelphia Orchestra under Charles Dutoit to perform Hector Berlioz's "symphonie dramatique" *Roméo et Juliette* (a performance available for download at the time of this writing on Amazon music downloads, as selected movements or the entire piece), or the 120 minutes required to watch Peter Greenaway's film *Prospero's Books*, or the whopping 243 minutes needed to take in Branagh's film of *Hamlet* in its entirety, or the 360 minutes' running time of Van Hove's *Roman Tragedies*, cut up though it be. To judge from the audience disruptions catalogued by Andrew Gurr, we can assume that Shakespeare's original audiences did not sit quietly for the two hours' traffic in which they had paid to participate (Gurr 2009: 275–82).

More disturbing is the thought that the violence of contemporary cutwork—its radicalism, its defiance of tradition, its psychological fascination—is connected with violence in the culture at large. If so, the situation now may not be so very different from the situation in Shakespeare's lifetime. As R. A. Foakes has demonstrated, violence is a major feature of early modern popular theater (Foakes 2003). With their scenes of multiple cuttings—in the senses that Shakespeare and his contemporaries knew best—plays such as Shakespeare's *Hamlet* (1599–1600), *King Lear* (1605), and *Macbeth* (1606, revived 1616 likely with cuts as well as additions by Thomas Middleton), *The Revenger's Tragedy* (1606), John Webster's *The White Devil* (1612), and Middleton's *Women Beware Women* (1621) evince a culture in which representations of cuts were just as sensational as they are now. As we discovered in

Chapter 2, the cutwork that went into making those representations was no less remarkable. At a deep level there seem to be connections, in early modern culture and in contemporary culture, between cuts as bodily violence and cuts as violent ways of making art.

Ease of cutting things up with digital technology, fragmentation, acceleration, fascination with the violence of cuts: beyond these cultural variables two factors persist across all historical periods: the "gappy" nature of perception, as Dennett (1992) calls it, and the fundamental function of cuts in all forms of creativity. We should recall from Chapter 3 that even the most complicated event is apprehended in a series of "perceptual moments" lasting from a fraction of a second to an outer limit of about three seconds. It may simply be the case that digital Shakespeare deals in shorter, more frequent perceptual moments than stage plays and films do. Perceptual moments may vary according to how focused perceivers are on what is before them, but duration of perceptual moments is also a factor of psycho-physiology, and the range of those durations has probably not changed appreciably since 1600. What Sarah Kember and Joanna Zylinska have to say in *Life After New Media* (2012) applies equally to life *before* new media:

> The process of cutting is one of the most fundamental and originary processes through which we emerge as "selves" as we engage with matter and attempt to give it (and ourselves) form. Cutting reality into small pieces—with our eyes, our bodily and cognitive apparatus, our language, our memory, and our technologies—we enact separation and relationality as the two dominant aspects of material locatedness in time (Kember and Zylinska 2012: 75).

Kember and Zylinska return us to the premises with which I began this book: to the cut as a phenomenon fundamental not only to perception, but also to artistic creation.

=

Taking the long view of cutwork with Shakespeare across four centuries, we discover that the choice in each period has been not between cut and uncut, but between different kinds of cut. We delude ourselves if we think there is any such thing as an uncut original. Contemporary cutwork with Shakespeare is not a latter-day example of Mary Richardson taking a cleaver to the Rokeby Venus. (See

Figure 2.) Ultimately, "cut" versus "uncut" is a false dichotomy. Cutwork is, and always has been, part and parcel of artistic creation. As we noted in Chapter 2, jointly authored scripts in Shakespeare's time—he participated in at least four such ventures—were parceled out not character by character, but scene by scene. Even scripts authored by Shakespeare alone incorporate all sorts of internally cued cuts: speaking turns, asides, flourishes and drum rolls, explicitly announced changes in fictional location and in time, plays-within-the-play, "discoveries." "Uncut" at the point of origin is a convenient fiction, something that we want to imagine. *Love's Labor's Won*, as I quipped in Chapter 4, is Shakespeare's only uncut play.

We will come closest to understanding cutwork if we forget about uncut originals and set up a continuum that stretches from smoothly seamed creations at one end to the display of disruptive cuts at the other end. (See Table 4.) The ordinate in Table 4 is the degree to which cuts call attention to themselves as cuts. I take the term "seamed" from Margaret Cavendish's metaphor for play construction in *Plays Written by the Thrice Noble, Illustrious and Excellent Princess, the Lady Marchioness of Newcastle* (1662), as quoted and analyzed in Chapter 2. The term "tattered" I take from Simon Forman's memory of Autolychus in *The Winter's Tale* coming in "all tattered like Coll Pixie," cited in Chapter 3. In structural terms, we might label the left-hand end of the continuum "holistic"; the right-hand end, "cut-up" or perhaps "deconstructed." It is important to note, however, that the continuum does *not* extend from "uncut" to "cut." Rather, some degree of cutting is recognized all along.

There are some surprising chronological discoveries when we consider "Shakespeare|Cut" this way. Taking stock of where we stand

Table 4. Continuum of Cuts.

"seamed"						"tattered"
←						→
Yeats	Stoppard	anthologies	burlesques	YouTube originals	card games	Dorsen
Eliot	Van Hove	declamations	the "other" RSC		video games	Wilson
Burroughs	Wooster Group	recitals				
		YouTube clips				

now, we can appreciate the wit and the aptness of Richard Burt's and Julian Yates's coinage "Bardoclash" to describe the state of indeterminacy that contemporary cuts across media can work on Shakespeare's texts:

> Bardoclash signals the intervening function of the media that mediates, which permits the Shaky translation, and raises a question therefore as to its functions. It is political in the strict sense that it requires us to decide on its status, but it communicates also the madness of decision, the way in which deciding relies, as its Latin root recalls, on an irreversible cutting (Burt and Yates 2013: 50).

The "before" and "now" implications of this pronouncement do, however, need to be qualified. On the continuum I am proposing the deconstructed end is indeed occupied by Shakespeare parodies on YouTube and recent stage productions such as Dorsen's, but the holistic end is occupied, in my view at least, not by Shakespeare's original scripts but by works of High Modernism. In between we find creations that stretch from Shakespeare's career into our own cultural moment. In effect, the possibilities range from "Bardoclash" to "Bardolatry." Shakespeare's own position on the continuum, in my judgment, is somewhere toward the middle, as Chapter 2 attempts to demonstrate.

David Garrick is not the only Shakespearean with an "atti-tude"—in his case, with several attitudes. (See Figure 9.) Most of what has been written about cutting up Shakespeare in the long twentieth century has taken one of two stances toward Shake-speare's ghost: the belligerence of Garrick's Macbeth, knives in hand, or the astonishment of Garrick's Hamlet, hands raised in wonder. What attitude *should* we bring to the fetishized cutwork that has been done with Shakespeare in the long twentieth century? Ultimately, that depends on who is looking, what they are looking for, and how they do the looking. One possibility—concentrating on cutting-as-creating rather than on cutting-as-trashing—invites a mobile position that takes note of cuts, investigates how they are made, and finds delight in the changing interspaces between "fig-ure" and "life." I would describe such a position—the one played out in this book—as "appreciative irony." In Carse's terms, such a position is necessary to keep the game going, So far at least, the

Shakespeare game has proved to be an infinite game within which finite games come and go. "Surprise in infinite play is the triumph of the future over the past," Carse proposes. "Since infinite players do not regard the past as having an outcome, they have no way of knowing what has been begun there. With each surprise, the past reveals a new beginning in itself" (Carse 1986: 18). Cut to the future. Only then will we come to know what was begun in 1590, when William Shakespeare started the game.

Sources Cited

Aarseth, Espen 2012. "Playing Research: Methodological Approaches to Game Analysis." In *Travels in Intermedia[lity]: Reblurring the Boundaries*. Ed., Bernd Herzogenrath. Hanover, NH: Dartmouth College Press. 175–91.

Allott, Robert, comp. 1600. *England's Parnassus, Or the Choicest Flowers of our Modern Poets*. London: N. Ling, C. Burby, and T. Hayes.

Anderson, Judith 1996. *Words That Matter: Linguistic Perception in Renaissance English*. Stanford, CA: Stanford University Press.

[Anonymous] c. 1830. "Richard III." Tinsel print, Victoria and Albert Museum, S.736-1981, description. http://collections.vam.ac.uk/item/O1155930/tinsel-print-unknown/, accessed October 31, 2015.

Baldwin, T. W. 1947. *Shakspere's Five-Act Structure: Shakspere's Early Plays on the Background of Renaissance Theories of Five-act Structure from 1470*. Urbana: University of Illinois Press.

Ball, J. R. 2013. "Staging the Twitter War: Toneelgroep Amsterdam's Roman Tragedies." *TDR: The Drama Review* 57.4: 163–70.

Bartle, Richard 1996. "Hearts, Clubs, Diamonds, Spaces: Players who suit MUDS." http://mud.co.uk/richard/hcds.htm, accessed November 14, 2013.

Baugh, Christopher 2005. *Theatre, Performance, and Technology: The Development of Scenography in the Twentieth Century*. Basingstoke: Palgrave.

Baugh, Christopher 2016. "Scenery." *The Cambridge Guide to the Worlds of Shakespeare*. Gen. ed., Bruce R. Smith. 2 vols. Cambridge: Cambridge University Press. 2:1449–56.

Beale, Peter 1980–93. *Index of English Literary Manuscripts* 1450–1700. 4 vols. London: Mansell.

Berry, Ralph 1977. *On Directing Shakespeare: Interviews with Contemporary Directors*. London: Croom Helm.

Birkerts, Sven 2015. *Changing the Subject: Art and Attention in the Internet Age*. Minneapolis: Graywolf.

Blake, Erin 2016. "Book Illustrations." *The Cambridge Guide to the Worlds of Shakespeare*. Gen. ed., Bruce R. Smith. 2 vols. Cambridge: Cambridge University Press. 2:1873–9.

Blayney, Peter W. M. 1991. *The First Folio of Shakespeare*. Exhibition catalogue. Washington: Folger Shakespeare Library.

Bloom, Gina 2013. "Games." *Early Modern Theatricality*. Ed., Henry S. Turner. Oxford: Oxford University Press. 189–211.

Booth, Michael R. 1986. "Pictorial Acting and Ellen Terry." *Shakespeare and the Victorian Stage*. Ed. Richard Foulkes, Cambridge: Cambridge University Press. 78–86.

Bradley, Lynne 2015. "Parody, Burlesque, Satire." *The Cambridge Guide to the Worlds of Shakespeare.* Gen. ed. Bruce R. Smith. 2 vols. Cambridge: Cambridge University Press.

Brinsley, John 1622. *Ludus Literarius: Or, the Grammar School.* London: Thomas Man.

The British Spouter; or, Stage Assistant: Containing the Most Celebrated Prologues and Epilogues, that have been Lately Spoken, in the Different Theatres, at the Acting of the most Eminent Plays. The Whole Being Intended to make Young Persons Acquainted with the Art of Speaking, and to Impress upon their Minds Sentiments of Morality. 1773. London: J. Roson for J. Shepherd, and T. Lewis.

Brown, John Russell, comp. 2000. *Shakescenes: Shakespeare for Two.* New York: Applause.

Buchanan, Judith 2011. *Shakespeare on Silent Film: An Excellent Dumb Discourse.* Reissue ed. Cambridge: Cambridge University Press.

Bulman, James C. 1991. *The Merchant of Venice.* Shakespeare in Performance series. Manchester: Manchester University Press.

Burnim, K. A. 1961. *David Garrick, Director.* Pittsburgh: University of Pittsburgh Press.

Burroughs, William S., and Biron Guysin 1978. *The Third Mind.* New York: Viking.

Burt, Richard, and Julian Yates 2013. *What's the Worst Thing You Can Do to Shakespeare?* New York: Palgrave Macmillan.

Caines, Michael 2013. *Shakespeare and the Eighteenth Century.* Oxford: Oxford University Press.

Carnicke, Sharon Marie 2016. "Acting Techniques." *Cambridge Guide to the Worlds of Shakespeare.* Gen. ed., Bruce R. Smith. 2 vols. Cambridge: Cambridge University Press. 2:1430–43.

Carr, Nicholas G. 2010. *The Shallows: What the Internet is Doing to Our Brains.* New York: Norton.

Carse, James P. 1986. *Finite and Infinite Games: A Vision of Life as Play and Possibility.* New York: Free Press.

Carson, Christie, and Peter Kirwan, eds. 2014. *Shakespeare and the Digital World: Redefining Scholarship and Practice.* Cambridge: Cambridge University Press.

Cartelli, Thomas 2008. "Channeling the Ghosts: The Wooster Group's remediation of the 1964 electronovision *Hamlet.*" *Shakespeare Survey* 61 (2008): 147–60.

Cartelli, Thomas 2015. "Playing the Cut: Shakespeare staged three ways in Dmitry Krymov's *Midsummer Night's Dream,* Matias Piñeiro's *Viola,* and Annie Dorsen's *A Piece of Work.*" Paper delivered at the annual meeting of the Shakespeare Association of America, Vancouver, April 2015. Unpublished manuscript.

Cartelli, Thomas 2016a. "Visual Projections." *The Cambridge Guide to the Worlds of Shakespeare.* Ed., Bruce R. Smith. 2 vols. Cambridge: Cambridge University Press 2:1467–74.

Cartelli, Thomas 2016b. "High Tech Shakespeare in a Mediatized Globe: Ivo van Hove's *Roman Tragedies* and the Problem of Spectatorship." *The Oxford Companion to Shakespeare and Performance*. Ed., James Bulman. Oxford: Oxford University Press.

Cavendish, Margaret 1662. *Plays Written by the Thrice Noble, Illustrious and Excellent Princess, the Lady Marchioness of Newcastle*. London: A. Warren for John Martyn, James Allestry, and Thomas Dicas.

Chafe, Wallace 1994. *Discourse, Consciousness, and Time: The Flow and Displacement of Conscious Experience in Speaking and Writing*. Chicago: University of Chicago Press.

Cole, Toby, and Helen Krich Chinoy, eds. 1976. *Actors on Acting*. New York: Crown.

Comenius, Johannes Amos 1659. *Orbis Sensualium Pictus...Visible world, or, A picture and Nomenclature of all the Chief Things that are in the World, and of Men's Employments Therein*. Trans., Charles Hoole. London: J. Kirton.

Crary, Jonathan 1991. *Suspensions of Perception: Attention, Spectacle, and Modern Culture*. Cambridge, MA: MIT Press.

Cressy, David 1980. *Literacy and the Social Order: Reading and Writing in Tudor and Stuart England*. Cambridge: Cambridge University Press.

Daw, Kurt, and Julia Matthews 1998. *A Guide to Scenes and Monologues from Shakespeare's Stage*. Portsmouth, NH: Heinemann.

Dawson, Anthony B. 1995. *Hamlet*. Shakespeare in Performance series. Manchester: Manchester University Press.

de Beau-Chesne, Jehan, and John Baildon 1602. *A Book Containing Diverse Sorts of Hands*. London: Richard Feld.

de Grazia, Margreta 1991a. *Shakespeare Verbatim: The Reproduction of Authenticity and the 1790 Apparatus*. Oxford: Clarendon Press.

de Grazia, Margreta 1991b. "Shakespeare in Quotation Marks." *The Appropriation of Shakespeare: Post-Renaissance Constructions of the Work and the Myth*. Ed., Jean I. Marsden. New York: Harvester Wheatsheaf.

Delabastita, Dirk 2016. "Shakespeare without Sweat: Updating and Simplifying Shakespeare's English." *Cambridge Guide to the Worlds of Shakespeare*. Gen. ed., Bruce R. Smith. 2 vols. Cambridge: Cambridge University Press. 2:1410–15.

Deleuze, Gilles 1994. *Difference and Repetition*. Trans., Paul Patton. New York: Columbia University Press.

Deleuze, Gilles, and Félix Guattari 1987. *A Thousand Plateaus*. Trans., Brian Massumi. Minneapolis: University of Minnesota Press.

Dennett, Daniel C. 1992. *Consciousness Explained*. Boston: Back Bay Books.

Derrida, Jacques 1981. *Dissemination*. Trans., Barbara Johnson. Chicago, IL: University of Chicago Press.

Desmet, Christy 2014. "YouTube Shakespeare, Appropriation, and the Rhetorics of Invention." *OuterSpeares: Shakespeare, Intermedia, and the Limits of Adaptation*. Ed., Daniel Fischlin. Toronto: University of Toronto Press. 53–74.

Dessen, Alan C. 2002. *Rescripting Shakespeare: The Text, the Director, and Modern Productions*. Cambridge: Cambridge University Press.

Dessen, Alan C., and Leslie Thomson. 1999. *A Dictionary of Stage Directions in English Drama, 1580–1642*. Cambridge: Cambridge University Press.

Dorsen, Annie 2016. ANNIE DORSEN CONTACT. http://www.anniedorsen.com/, accessed February 4, 2016.

Downes, John 1708. *Roscius Anglicanus, or An Historical Review of the Stage*. London: H. Playford.

Early English Books Online, Text Creation Partnership. Online: http://www.textcreationpartnership.org/tcp-eebo/.

Edwards, Paul. 1998. "Wyndham Lewis's "Timon of Athens" Portfolio: The Emergence of Vorticist Abstraction," *Apollo* 148, no. 440: 34–40.

Eliot, T. S. 1971. *The Waste Land: A Facsimile and Transcript of the Original Drafts Including the Annotations of Ezra Pound*. Ed., Valerie Eliot. New York: Harcourt Brace Jovanovich.

Eliot, T. S. 2001. *The Waste Land*. Ed., Michael North. Norton Critical Edition. New York: Norton.

Elliott, Ward E. Y. 2016. "Language: Key to Authorship." *The Cambridge Guide to the Worlds of Shakespeare*. Gen. ed., Bruce R. Smith. 2 vols. Cambridge: Cambridge University Press. 2:231–40.

Erne, Lukas 2013. *Shakespeare as Literary Dramatist*. 2nd ed. Cambridge: Cambridge University Press.

Evans, G. Blakemore 1960–96. *Shakespearean Prompt-books of the Seventeenth Century*. 8 Vols. Charlottesville: University of Virginia Press. http://bsuva.org/bsuva/promptbook/.

Evans, Vyvyan 2005. *The Structure of Time: Language, Meaning, and Temporal Cognition*. Amsterdam: John Benjamins.

Fielding, Henry 1736a. *Pasquin. A Dramatic Satire of the Times*. London: J. Watts.

Fielding, Henry 1736b. *Tumble-down Dick: or, Phaeton in the Suds*. London: J. Watts.

Fielding, Henry 1750. *The Author's Farce; with a Puppet-show called The Leisures of the Town*. 3rd ed. London: J. Watts.

Fischlin, Daniel, ed. 2014. *OuterSpeares: Shakespeare, Intermedia, and the Limits of Adaptation*. Toronto: University of Toronto Press.

Florio, John 1598. *A World of Words, or Most Copious, and Exact Dictionary in Italian and English*. London: Edward Blount, 1598.

Foakes, R. A. 1985. *Illustrations of the English Stage 1580–1642*. Stanford: Stanford University Press.

Foakes, R. A. 2003. *Shakespeare and Violence*. Cambridge: Cambridge University Press.

Folkerth, Wes 2002. *The Sound of Shakespeare*. London: Routledge.

Forward, Toby, and Juan Wijngaard 2005. *Shakespeare's Globe: An Interactive Pop-up Theatre*. Somerville, MA: Candlewick Press.

Foucault, Michel 1984. "Nietzsche, Genealogy, History." *The Foucault Reader*. Ed., Paul Rabinow. New York: Pantheon.

Foulkes, Richard 2002. *Performing Shakespeare in the Age of Empire*. Cambridge: Cambridge University Press.

Friedberg, Anne 2009. *The Virtual Window: From Alberti to Microsoft*. Cambridge, MA: MIT Press.

Gibson, James J. 2015. *The Ecological Approach to Visual Perception*. Classic ed. New York: Psychology Press.

Giesekam, Greg 2007. *Staging the Screen: The Use of Film and Video in Theatre*. Basingstoke, UK & New York: Palgrave Macmillan.

Grant, Stephen H. 2014. *Collecting Shakespeare: The Story of Henry and Emily Folger*. Baltimore, MD: Johns Hopkins University Press.

Granville, George 1698. *Heroic Love a Tragedy: As it is Acted at the Theatre in Little Lincolns-Inn-Fields*. London: F. Saunders, H. Playford, and B. Tooke.

Greenaway, Peter, dir.1991. *Prospero's Books*. Miramax Films. DVD edition. Potsdam-Babelsberg, Germany: FilmConnect Home Entertainment. Video.

Gregory, Richard L. 1997. *Eye and Brain: The Psychology of Seeing*. Princeton: Princeton University Press.

Gurr, Andrew 1999. "Maximal and Minimal Texts: Shakespeare v. the Globe." *Shakespeare Survey* 52:147–65.

Gurr, Andrew 2009. *The Shakespearean Stage 1574–1642*. 4th ed. Cambridge: Cambridge University Press.

Gurr, Andrew 2016. "*Henry V*: Victorian Stagings." *Cambridge Guide to the Worlds of Shakespeare*. Gen. ed., Bruce R. Smith. 2 vols. Cambridge: Cambridge University Press. 2:1571–5.

Gysin, Brion, and Terry Wilson 2012. *Here to Go: Interviews and Texts*. Ubuweb Papers. http://www.ubu.com, accessed February 12, 2016.

Hall, Peter 1984. *Peter Hall's Diaries: The Story of a Dramatic Battle*. Ed., John Goodwin. New York: Harper & Row.

Hall, Peter 2003. *Shakespeare's Advice to the Players*. New York: Theatre Communications Group.

hamlet-shakespeare.com. http://www.hamlet-shakespeare.com/actors/charles_kean.html, accessed October 22, 2015.

Haynes, Claire 2016. "Graphic Satire." *The Cambridge Guide to the Worlds of Shakespeare*. Gen. ed., Bruce R. Smith. 2 vols. Cambridge: Cambridge University Press. 2:1879–84.

Hayward, Maria 2015. "Textiles and Clothing Construction." *The Cambridge Guide to the Worlds of Shakespeare*. Gen. ed., Bruce R. Smith. 2 vols. Cambridge: Cambridge University Press. 1:288–93.

Hellwarth, Will 2014. "Close Your." http://www.closeyour.com/#about, accessed February 10, 2016.

Henslowe, Philip, and Edward Alleyn 1590–1600. The Henslowe-Alleyn Digitalization Project. http://www.henslowe-alleyn.org.uk, accessed October 18, 2015.

Hentea, Marius 2014. *The Real Life and Celestial Adventures of Tristan Tzara*. Cambridge: MIT Press.

Heywood, Thomas 1633. *The English Traveler. As it hath been Publicly Acted at the Cock Pit in Drury Lane by Her Majesty's Servants.* London: Robert Raworth.

Hildesheimer, Sigmund 1890. [Scrap with Shakespeare characters.] Victoria and Albert Museum, S.1:3-2008, description. http://collections.vam.ac.uk/item/O1110940/print-collection-scrap-siegmund-hildesheimer-co/, accessed October 31, 2015.

Hirsh, James E. 1981. *The Structure of Shakespearean Scenes.* New Haven: Yale University Press.

Holland, Peter 2000. "Film Editing." *Shakespeare Performed.* Ed., Grace Ioppolo. Newark: University of Delaware Press. 173–298.

Holland, Peter, ed. 2006. *Shakespeare, Memory, and Performance.* Cambridge: Cambridge University Press.

Holland, Peter 2007. "Shakespeare Abbreviated." *The Cambridge Companion to Shakespeare and Popular Culture.* Ed., Robert Shaughnessy. Cambridge: Cambridge University Press. 26–45.

Holt, Robin J. 1988. *Scenes from Shakespeare: A Workbook for Actors.* Jefferson, NC: McFarland.

Horowitz, Seth S. 2012. *The Universal Sense: How Hearing Shapes the Mind.* New York: Bloomsbury.

Ingelby, C. M., L. Toulmin Smith, and F. J. Furnivall 1909. *The Shakspere Allusion-Book: A Collection of Allusions to Shakspere from 1591 to 1700.* Rev., John Munro. 2 vols. London: Chatto & Windus.

Ioppolo, Grace 2015. "Manuscripts Containing Texts by Shakespeare." *The Cambridge Guide to the Worlds of Shakespeare.* Gen. ed., Bruce R. Smith. 2 vols. Cambridge: Cambridge University Press. 1:986–95.

Isherwood, Charles 2013. "There Be Madness in This Method" (review). *The New York Times,* December 19, 2013. www.nytimes.com/2013/12/20/theater/reviews/a-piece-of-work, accessed December 20, 2013.

Jackson, Russell 2012. "Shakespeare Their Contemporary." *Shakespeare in the Nineteenth Century.* Ed., Gail Marshall. Cambridge: Cambridge University Press. 76–95.

James I and VI 1585. *The Essays of an Apprentice in the Divine Art of Poesy.* Edinburgh: Thomas Vautroullier.

James, Henry 1948. "The London Theatres 1880." *The Scenic Art: Notes on Acting and the Drama: 1872–1901.* Ed., Allan Wade. New Brunswick, NJ: Rutgers University Press.

James, William 1890. *The Principles of Psychology.* Boston: Henry Holt.

Johnston, Mark 2011. *Beard Fetish in Early Modern England: Sex, Gender, and Registers of Value.* New ed. London: Routledge.

Jones, Emrys 1971. *Scenic Form in Shakespeare.* Oxford: Clarendon Press.

Jonson, Ben 2012. *The Cambridge Edition of the Works of Ben Jonson.* Ed., David M. Bevington, Martin Butler, and Ian Donaldson. 7 vols. Cambridge: Cambridge University Press.

Kathman, David 2004. "Reconsidering *The Seven Deadly Sins.*" *Early Theatre* 7.1: 13–44.

Kember, Sarah, and Joanna Zylinska 2012. *Life after New Media: Mediation as a Vital Process*. Cambridge, MA: MIT Press.

Kilgarriff, Michael nd. "Henry Irving and the Phonograph." The Irving Society. http://www.theirvingsociety.org.uk/, accessed September 13, 2014.

Knight, Jeffrey Todd 2013. *Bound to Read: Compilations, Collections, and the Making of Renaissance Literature*. Philadelphia: University of Pennsylvania Press.

Knight, Jeffrey Todd 2016. "Collecting and Reading Shakespeare's Quartos." In *Cambridge Guide to the Worlds of Shakespeare*. Gen. ed., Bruce R. Smith. 2 vols. Cambridge: Cambridge University Press. 2:1684–8.

Lacy, John 1672. *The Dumb Lady, or, The Farrier made Physician as it was Acted at the Theatre-Royal*. London: Thomas Dring.

Lane, John 1600. *Tom Tell-Troth's Message, and his Pen's Complaint*. London: R. Howell.

Lebel, Jean-Jacques 2013. "Cut In–Cut Out" (interview). *William S. Burroughs/Cut*. Ed., Axel Heil and Ian MacFadyen. Series The Future of the Past, Vol. 2. Köln: Walther König.

Lesser, Zachary, and Peter Stallybrass 2008. "The First Literary *Hamlet* and the Commonplacing of Professional Plays." *Shakespeare Quarterly* 59:371–420.

Levin, Eliot (selection) and David Timson (liner notes) 2000. *Great Historical Shakespeare Recordings*. London: Naxos. Audio and print.

Levinson, Jill L. 2001. "Stoppard's Shakespeare: Textual revisions." *The Cambridge Companion to Tom Stoppard*. Ed., Katherine E. Kelly. Cambridge: Cambridge University Press. 154–68.

Lewis, Wyndham 1914–15. *BLAST: Review of the Great English Vortex*. 2 vols. London: John Lane.

Lieberman, Philip, and Sheila E. Blumstein 1988. *Speech, Physiology, Speech Perception, and Acoustic Phonetics*. Cambridge: Cambridge University Press.

Macready, William Charles 1912. *The Diaries of William Charles Macready, 1833–1851*. Ed., William Toynbee. 2 vols. New York: G. P. Putnam's Sons.

Magalhães, Ernâni, and L. Nathan Oaklander, eds. 2010. *Presentism: Essential Readings*. Lanham, MD: Rowman and Littlefield.

Markowitsch, Hans J. 2005. "Neuroanatomy of Memory." *The Oxford Handbook of Memory*. Ed., Endel Tuving and Fergus I. M. Craik. Oxford: Oxford University Press. 465–84.

Márkus, Zoltán 2016. "Shakespeare in Quotation Marks." *The Cambridge Guide to the Worlds of Shakespeare*. Gen. ed., Bruce R. Smith. 2 vols. Cambridge: Cambridge University Press. 2:1694–6.

Marlowe, Christopher 1993. *Doctor Faustus: A- and B-Texts*. Ed., David Bevington and Eric Rasmussen. The Revels Plays. Manchester: Manchester University Press.

Marowitz, Charles 1978. *The Marowitz Shakespeare*. New York: Drama Book Publishers.

Marowitz, Charles 1991. *Recycling Shakespeare*. New York: Applause Theatre Book Publishers.

Marowitz, Charles 2013. "Cinematizing Shakespeare." *Reinventing the Renaissance: Shakespeare and his Contemporaries in Adaptation and Performance*. Ed., Sarah Annes Brown, Robert I. Lublin, and Dynsey McCulloch. Basingstoke, UK: Palgrave Macmillan.

Marsh, Christopher 2016. "Woodcuts and their Wanderings in Early Modern England." *Huntington Library Quarterly* 79.2.

Masten, Jeffrey 1997. *Textual Intercourse: Collaboration, Authorship, and Sexualities in Renaissance Drama*. Cambridge: Cambridge University Press.

McCloud, Scott 1993. *Understanding Comics: The Invisible Art*. New York: Kitchen Sink.

McCreery, Conor and Anthony Del Col 2015. *Kill Shakespeare: The Backstage Edition*. Vol. 1. San Diego, CA: IDW Publishing.

McDonald, Russ 2001. *Shakespeare and the Arts of Language*. Oxford: Oxford University Press.

McKernan, Luke 2016. "Shakespeare and Online Video." *The Cambridge Guide to the Worlds of Shakespeare*. Gen. ed., Bruce R. Smith. 2 vols. Cambridge: Cambridge University Press. 2:1970–4.

McKernan, Luke, curator. "BardBox." YouTube channel. http://www.youtube.com/playlist?list=PL33FA48C492A976F3, accessed August 3, 2014.

McKernan, Luke, curator. "BardBox 2." YouTube channel. http://www.youtube.com/playlist?list=PL302E6A0BBA3EF29E, accessed August 3, 2014.

McLuhan, Marshall 1964. *Understanding Media: The Extensions of Man*. Reprint ed. Cambridge, MA: MIT Press.

McMillin, Scott 1973. "'The Dead Man's Fortune' and '2 Seven Deadly Sins': Inferences for Theatre Historians." *Studies in Bibliography* 26: 235–43.

Mead, Rebecca 2015. "Theatre Laid Bare: Ivo van Hove's New Productions Bring out the Elemental Drama of Classic Works." *The New Yorker*, October 26, 2015: 54–63.

Merchant, W. Moelwyn 1986. "Artists and Stage Designers." *Shakespeare and the Victorian Stage*. Ed., Richard Foulkes. Cambridge: Cambridge University Press. 14–22.

Middleton, Thomas 2007. *The Collected Works*. Ed., Gary Taylor and John Lavagnino. Oxford: Clarendon Press.

Moore, Marianne 1955. "The Cantos" (1931). Rpt. in *Predilections*. New York: Viking.

Moss, Ann 1996. *Printed Commonplace-Books and the Structuring of Renaissance Thought*. Oxford: Clarendon Press.

Movable Book Society. www.movablebooksociety.org, accessed September 22, 2014.

Moxon, Joseph 1958. *Mechanick Exercises on the Whole Art of Printing*. Ed., Herbert Davis and Harry Carter. Oxford: Oxford University Press.

Murch, Walter 2001. *In the Blink of an Eye: A Perspective on Film Editing.* 2nd ed. Los Angeles: Silman-James Press.

Muybridge, Eadweard 1887. *Animal Locomotion. An Electro-photographic Investigation of Consecutive Phases of Animal Movement.* Vol. 1. Philadelphia: University of Pennsylvania Press.

Myklebost, Sven-Arve 2016. "Comic Books and Manga." *The Cambridge Guide to the Worlds of Shakespeare.* Gen. ed., Bruce R. Smith. 2 vols. Cambridge: Cambridge University Press. 2:1899–905.

Nakano, Tamani, et al. 2013. "Blink-related Momentary Activation of the Default Mode Network while Viewing Videos." *Proceedings of the National Academy of Sciences* 110.2 (8 January 2013): 702–6. http://www.ncbi.nlm.nih.gov/pmc/articles/PMC3545766/?report=reader.

Nunn, Trevor 1996. *William Shakespeare's Twelfth Night: A Screenplay.* London: Methuen.

Nyhus, Erika, and David Bardre 2015. "Memory Retrieval and the Functional Organization of the Cortex." *The Wiley Handbook on the Cognitive Neuroscience of Memory.* Ed., Donna Rose Addis, Morgan Barense, and Audry Duarte. Oxford: Wiley-Blackwell. 131–49.

O'Neill, Paul 2012. *The Culture of Curating and the Curating of Culture(s).* Cambridge, MA: MIT Press.

O'Neill, Stephen 2014. *Shakespeare and YouTube: New Media Forms of the Bard.* The Arden Shakespeare. London: Bloomsbury.

Obrist, Hans Ulrich 2015. *Ways of Curating.* New York: Penguin.

Oregon Shakespeare Festival 2015. "Play on! FAQ." OSF website. https://www.osfashland.org/experience-osf/upcoming/play-on/play-on-faq.aspx, accessed October 21, 2015.

Oxford English Dictionary Online. Oxford: Oxford University Press. Online: http://www.oed.com, accessed October 17, 2015.

Palfrey, Simon, and Tiffany Stern 2011. *Shakespeare in Parts.* Oxford: Oxford University Press.

Park, Katharine 1988. "The Organic Soul." *The Cambridge History of Renaissance Philosophy.* Ed., Charles B. Schmitt. Cambridge: Cambridge University Press. 464–84.

Parkes, M. B. 1993. *Pause and Effect: An Introduction to the History of Punctuation in the West.* Berkeley: University of California Press.

Partridge, A. C. 1969. *Tudor to Augustan English: A Study in Syntax and Style from Caxton to Johnson.* London: Deutsch.

Paul, Christiane 2015. *Digital Art.* 3rd ed. New York: Thames and Hudson.

Pellegrini, David 2012. "Kate Valk." *The Routledge Companion to Actors' Shakespeare.* Ed., John Russell Brown. London: Routledge. 240–53.

Pollack-Pelzner, Daniel 2015. "Why We (Mostly) Stopped Messing with Shakespeare's Language." *The New Yorker*, October 20, 2015.

Potter, Lois 2002. *Othello.* Shakespeare in Performance series. Cambridge: Cambridge University Press.

Pound, Ezra 1996. *The Cantos of Ezra Pound.* New York: New Directions.

Puttenham, George 2002. *The Art of English Poesy: A Critical Edition*. Ed., Frank Whigham and Wayne A. Rebhorn. Ithaca, NY: Cornell University Press.

Rasmussen, Eric 1997. "The Revision of Scripts." *A New History of English Drama*. Eds., John Cox and David Kastan. New York: Columbia University Press. 441–60.

Richards, David 1994. "Sellars' Merchant of Venice Beach," *New York Times*, October 18, 1994, http://www.nytimes.com/1994/10/18/arts/theater-review-sellars-s-merchant-of-venice-beach.html.

Roach, Joseph 1985. *The Player's Passion: Studies in the Science of Acting*. Newark, DE: University of Delaware Press.

Roach, Joseph 2016. "Production History." *The Cambridge Guide to the Worlds of Shakespeare*. Gen. ed., Bruce R. Smith. 2 vols. Cambridge: Cambridge University Press. 2:1545–57.

Rosenthal, Daniel 2007. *100 Shakespeare Films*. London: British Film Institute.

Rowe, Katherine 1997. "'God's Handy Worke.'" *The Body in Parts: Fantasies of Corporeality in Early Modern Europe*. Ed., Carla Mazzio and David Hillman. London: Routledge. 285–312.

Rumbold, Kate 2016. "Anthology Shakespeare." *The Cambridge Guide to the Worlds of Shakespeare*. Gen. ed., Bruce R. Smith. 2 vols. Cambridge: Cambridge University Press. 2:1688–94.

Salgādo, Gāmini 1975. *Eyewitnesses of Shakespeare: First Hand Accounts of Performances 1590–1890*. Brighton: Sussex University Press.

Saussure, Ferdinand de 1959. *General Course in Linguistics*. Ed., Charles Bally and Albert Sechehaye. Trans., Wade Baskin. New York: Philosophical Library, 1959.

Savage, Richard, ed. 1887. *Shakespearean Extracts from "Edward Pudsey's Booke."* Stratford-upon-Avon: John Smith.

Schlueter, June 1999. "Rereading the Peacham Drawing." *Shakespeare Quarterly* 50.2: 171–84.

Schneider, Rebecca 2011. *Performing Remains: Art and War in Times of Theatrical Reenactment*. London: Routledge.

Schoch, Richard W. 1998. *Shakespeare's Victorian Stage: Performing History in the Theatre of Charles Kean*. Cambridge: Cambridge University Press.

Schoch, Richard W. 2003. *Not Shakespeare: Bardolatry and Burlesque in the Nineteenth Century*. Cambridge: Cambridge University Press.

Scott, William 2013. *The Model of Poesy*. Ed., Gavin Alexander. Cambridge: Cambridge University Press.

Selden, Samuel, and William-Alan Landes 1993. *Short Scenes from Shakespeare: Nineteen Cuttings for the Classroom*. Studio City, CA: Players Press.

Senelick, Laurence 1982. *Gordon Craig's Moscow* Hamlet. Westport, CT: Greenwood Press.

Senelick, Laurence 2014. *Stanislavsky: A Life in Letters*. London: Routledge.

The Sentimental Spouter: or, Young Actor's Companion: Containing I. A Treatise on Oratory in General, and Theatrical Acquirements in Particular. ... II. A Collection of the Most Celebrated Scenes, Speeches, and Soliloquies, Selected from the most Admired

Tragedies and Comedies… The Whole Comprising the Essence of Theatrical Delivery. And the Beauties of Dramatic Poetry. 1774. London: J. Wheble and T. Axtell.

Serres, Michel 1997. *The Troubadour of Knowledge*. Trans., Sheila Faria Glaser. Ann Arbor: University of Michigan Press.

Shakespeare, William 1676. *The Tragedy of Hamlet, Prince of Denmark as it is now Acted at His Highness the Duke of York's Theatre*. London: Andrew Clark for J. Martyn and H. Herringman.

Shakespeare, William 1709. *The Works of Mr. William Shakespear…Adorned with Cuts*. Ed., Nicholas Rowe. 6 vols. London: Jacob Tonson.

Shakespeare, William 1725. *The Works of William Shakespear*. Ed., Alexander Pope. 6 vols. London: Jacob Tonson.

Shakespeare, William 1774. *Bell's Edition of Shakespeare's Plays, As they are now Performed at the Theatres Royal in London; Regulated from the Prompt Books*. 2nd ed. 5 vols. London: John Bell.

Shakespeare, William 1784. *The Beauties of Shakspeare; Selected from his Works. To Which are Added the Principal Scenes in the Same Author*. London: G. Kearsley.

Shakespeare, William 1859. *Shakespeare's Tragedy of Hamlet, Prince of Denmark / Arranged for Representation at the Royal Princess's Theatre, with Explanatory Notes, by Charles Kean, F.S.A. As Performed on Monday, January 10, 1859*. London: Bradbury and Evans.

Shakespeare, William 1993. *The Merchant of Venice*. Ed., Jay Halio. The Oxford Shakespeare. Oxford: Clarendon Press.

Shakespeare, William 1999. *Hamlet Prince of Denmark*. Ed., Robert Hapgood. Shakespeare in Production series. Cambridge: Cambridge University Press.

Shakespeare, William 2002. *The Merchant of Venice*. Ed., Charles Edelman. Shakespeare in Production series. Cambridge: Cambridge University Press.

Shakespeare, William 2005. *The Complete Works*. 2nd ed. Ed., Stanley Wells and Gary Taylor. Oxford: Clarendon Press.

Shakespeare, William 2008. *Hamlet*. Ed., Jonathan Bate and Eric Rasmussen. The RSC Shakespeare. New York: Modern Library.

Shakespeare, William 2009. *King Lear*. Ed., Jonathan Bate and Eric Rasmussen. The RSC Shakespeare. New York: Modern Library.

Shakespeare, William, and John Fletcher 1634. *The Two Noble Kinsmen*. London: Thomas Cotes for John Waterson.

Sharp, John 2015. *Works of Game: On the Aesthetics of Games and Art*. Cambridge, MA: MIT Press.

Shattuck, Charles H. 1965. *The Shakespeare Prompt Books: A Descriptive Catalogue*. Urbana, IL: University of Illinois Press.

Sherman, William H. 2008. *Used Books: Marking Readers in Renaissance England*. Philadelphia: University of Pennsylvania Press.

Sidney, Philip 1973. *A Defence of Poetry. Miscellaneous Prose*. Ed., Katherine Duncan-Jones and Jan van Dorsten. Oxford: Clarendon Press.

"Silent Shakespeare" 2000. Harrington Park, NJ: Milestone Films. DVD.

Sillars, Stuart 2013. *Shakespeare and the Victorians*. Oxford: Oxford University Press.

Sillars, Stuart 2016a. "Shakespeare and the Visual Arts." *The Cambridge Guide to the Worlds of Shakespeare*. Gen. ed., Bruce R. Smith. 2 vols. Cambridge: Cambridge University Press. 2:1861–73.

Sillars, Stuart 2016b. "Photography." *The Cambridge Guide to the Worlds of Shakespeare*. Gen. ed., Bruce R. Smith. 2 vols. Cambridge: Cambridge University Press. 2:1884–9.

Smith, Bruce R. 1988. *Ancient Scripts and Modern Experience on the English Stage 1500-1700*. Princeton: Princeton University Press.

Smith, Bruce R. 2006. "Shakespeare's Residuals." *Shakespeare and Elizabethan Popular Culture*. Ed., Stuart Gillespie and Neil Rhodes.

Smith, Bruce R. 2013. "Scene." *Early Modern Theatricality*. Ed., Henry S. Turner. Oxford: Oxford University Press. 93–112.

Southern, Richard 1952. *Changeable Scenery, Its Origin and Development in British Theatre*. London: Faber & Faber.

Sterne, Jonathan 2012. *MP3: The Meaning of a Format*. Durham, NC: Duke University Press.

Stewart, Garrett 2011. *Bookwork: Medium to Object to Concept to Art*. Chicago: University of Chicago Press.

Stone, George Winchester Jr 1934. "Garrick's Long Lost Alteration of *Hamlet*." *PMLA* 49: 890–920.

Stoppard, Tom 1967. *Rosencrantz and Guildenstern are Dead*. New York: Grove Press.

Stoppard, Tom 1975. *Travesties*. New York: Grove Press.

Stoppard, Tom 1982. "Is It True What They Say About Shakespeare?" International Shakespeare Association Occasional Paper No. 2. Stratford-upon-Avon: International Shakespeare Association.

"Ten Famous Works of Art that Are Forever Damaged by Carelessness, Negligence, Anger or Pure Insanity" 2011. artdaily.org: http://artdaily.com/index.asp?int_sec=11&int_new=47248#.ViLqVkbwy9Y, accessed October 17, 2015.

Stubbes, Phillip 1583. *The Anatomy of Abuses...in a Very Famous Island Called Ailgna*. London: Richard Jones.

Turner, Henry S. 2006. *The English Renaissance Stage: Geometry, Poetics, and the Practical Spatial Arts 1580–1630*. Oxford: Oxford University Press.

Urkowitz, Steven 2012. "Did Shakespeare's Company Cut Long Plays Down to Two Hours Playing Time?" *Shakespeare Bulletin* 30.3:239–62.

van Hove, Ivo 2015. Toneelgroep Amsterdam website. http://tga.nl/en/productions/kings-of-war, accessed October 27, 2015.

Vickers, Brian 1981. "The Emergence of Character Criticism, 1774-1800." *Shakespeare Survey* 34: 11–21.

Wells, Stanley, ed. 1978. *Nineteenth-Century Shakespeare Burlesques*. 5 vols. London: Diploma.

Whitfield, Peter 2013. *Illustrating Shakespeare*. London: The British Library.

Wilson, Michael 1993. *Scenes from Shakespeare: Fifteen Cuttings for the Classroom.* Englewood, CO: Meriwether Publishing.

Wilson, Michael 1999. *More Scenes from Shakespeare: Twenty Cuttings for Acting and Directing Practice.* Englewood, CO: Meriwether Publishing.

Wordsworth, William 1800. Preface to *Lyrical Ballads.* Harvard Classics ed. http://www.bartleby.com/39/36.html.

Worthen, William 1984. *The Idea of the Actor: Drama and the Ethics of Performance.* Princeton: Princeton University Press.

Yeats, William Butler 2000. New Poems: *Manuscript Materials.* Ed., J. C. C. Mays and Stephen Parrish. The Cornell Yeats. Ithaca: Cornell University Press.

Index